Applying the Assessment Center Method

PGPS - 71

PERGAMON GENERAL PSYCHOLOGY SERIES

Editors: Arnold P. Goldstein, *Syracuse University*
Leonard Krasner, *SUNY, Stony Brook*

TITLES IN THE PERGAMON GENERAL PSYCHOLOGY SERIES
(Added Titles in Back of Volume)

APPLYING THE ASSESSMENT CENTER METHOD

Joseph L. Moses
and
William C. Byham
Editors

PERGAMON PRESS
New York / Toronto / Oxford / Sydney / Frankfurt / Paris

Pergamon Press Offices:

U.S.A.	Pergamon Press, Inc., Maxwell House, Fairview Park, Elmsford, New York 10523, U.S.A.
U.K.	Pergamon Press Ltd., Headington Hill Hall, Oxford OX3, OBW, England
CANADA	Pergamon of Canada, Ltd., 75 The East Mall, Toronto, Ontario M8Z 5WR Canada
AUSTRALIA	Pergamon Press (Aust) Pty. Ltd., 19a Boundary Street, Rushcutters Bay, N.S.W. 2011, Australia
FRANCE	Pergamon Press SARL, 24 rue des Ecoles, 75240 Paris, Cedex 05, France
WEST GERMANY	Pergamon Press GmbH, 6242 Kronberg/Taunus, Frankfurt-am-Main, West Germany

---

Library of Congress Cataloging in Publication Data
Main entry under title:

Applying the assessment center method.

    (Pergamon general psychology series ; 71)
    1. Executives, Rating of-- --Addresses,
lectures. 2. Executives, Training of-- --Addresses,
essays, lectures. I. Moses, Joseph L. II. Byham,
William C.
HF5549.5.R3A65   1976   658.4'07'112   76-30476
ISBN 0-08-019581-4
ISBN 0-08-019580-6 pbk.

Printed in the United States of America

CONTENTS

CONTRIBUTORS

Mr. Albert Alon
Director of Personnel
Miracle Food Mart
75 Rexdale Boulevard
Rexdale, Ontario, Canada

Dr. Alan Boche
Consultant
New York, New York

Dr. Virginia R. Boehm
Project Manager—Research
American Telephone & Telegraph Company
295 North Maple Avenue, Room 6135G3
Basking Ridge, New Jersey 07920

Dr. Douglas W. Bray
Director—Basic Research
American Telephone & Telegraph Company
295 North Maple Avenue, Room 6114H2
Basking Ridge, New Jersey 07920

Mr. Robert P. Bourgeois
Chief of Managerial Assessment & Research Division
Personnel Psychology Center
Public Service Commission
West Tower, L'Esplanade Laurier
300 Laurier Avenue
Ottawa, Ontario, Canada

Dr. William C. Byham, President
Development Dimensions, Inc.
250 Mt. Lebanon Boulevard, Suite 419
Pittsburgh, Pennsylvania 15234

Mrs. Lois A. Crooks
Research Psychologist
Educational Testing Service
Princeton, New Jersey 08540

Dr. W. E. Dodd
IBM Corporation
Parson's Pond Drive
Franklin Lakes, New Jersey 07417

Dr. Douglas Holmes, Chief
ARI Unit—USAREUR
Department of the Army
U.S. Army Research Institute for the Behavioral and Social Sciences
APO, New York 09403

Mr. David F. Hoyle
Manager, Selection & Assessment
American Telephone & Telegraph Company
295 North Maple Avenue, Room 6136H2
Basking Ridge, New Jersey 07920

Dr. James R. Huck
Wickes Corporation
515 North Washington
Saginaw, Michigan 48607

Dr. Thomas A. Jeswald
R. R. Donnelley & Sons Inc.
2223 Martin Luther King Drive
Chicago, Illinois

Dr. Donald W. MacKinnon
Professor of Psychology
University of California
2240 Piedmont Avenue
Berkeley, California 94720

Dr. Joseph L. Moses
Personnel Manager—Research
American Telephone & Telegraph Company
295 North Maple Avenue, Room 6133H3
Basking Ridge, New Jersey 07920

Dr. L. W. Slivinski
Director—Personnel Psychology Center
Public Service Commission
West Tower, L'Esplanade
Laurier Building
300 Laurier West, 11th Floor
Ottawa, Ontario, K1AOM7, Canada

Dr. Thomas E. Standing
Manager—Psychological Service
The Standard Oil Company (Ohio)
1521 Midland Building
Cleveland, Ohio 44115

PREFACE

This book represents the culmination of a project which began over eight years ago. In late 1967 and early 1968, many organizations were first learning about the use of the assessment center method. Assessment centers had, at that time, been successfully applied in several large organizations such as AT&T, Standard Oil (Ohio), General Electric, and IBM. For the most part, knowledge concerning the application of this method was shared among psychologists and managers in these specific organizations.

To meet the growing demand for information and experiences related to this process, a special conference was held in May 1969. This conference was jointly sponsored by the New York State Psychological Association and the Metropolitan New York Association for Applied Psychology. Representatives from over 80 organizations attended this conference, testifying to the growing awareness of interest in this area. At about the same time, a group of researchers involved in implementing assessment operations in their respective organizations began to meet informally to share their experience and findings. Informal meetings led to the development of a more formal organization, which became known as the Assessment Center Research Group.

The group is composed of psychologists and managers who are directly involved in developing, establishing, or maintaining assessment center programs in their organizations. The group consists of representatives from 16 different organizations ranging from manufacturing and retailing organizations to government and nonprofit foundations. The goal of the group is to foster research findings, applications, strategies, and knowledge concerning the assessment center method itself. In our early meetings, much of the activity was related to describing the mechanics and operations of individual assessment centers as they applied in each of the members' organizations. This quickly changed to a focus on newer methods and approaches to assessment, specific research findings, and a variety of successful implementation strategies. It became apparent that a vast body of knowledge existed among the membership of this group concerning the assessment center method. Putting this knowledge together in one place made this book possible. With a few exceptions, each chapter has been written by a member of the Assessment Center Research Group. The wide scope of the chapter content is attributable to the diversity of interest and applications developed by members of the group in dealing with problems faced by their organizations.

This book has several audiences. It is written for the business community interested in learning about the assessment center method itself. It is particularly appropriate for those managers who are responsible for developing and interpreting corporate human resource personnel strategies. It is also written for those managers directly involved in implementing the process. This book can provide a useful guide for new assessors as well as experienced assessors. The book is also written for behavioral scientists as well as students of the management literature. Its focus is to summarize what is known about applying assessment center methods as well as to provide an insight into perspective research and implementation strategies.

PLAN OF THE BOOK

The book is divided into three parts. Part One, *Method*, describes the process, its history, and its current status. Chapter 1 defines the method, Chapter 2 describes its early history, and Chapter 3 reviews its current use. Chapter 4 is particularly valuable for those organizations that are planning to initiate an assessment center. Part Two, *Implementation*, deals with installing this method. The early chapters in this section describe the exercises, how assessors are trained, attitudes toward the program, and the evaluation and feedback process. The final three chapters in Part Two describe three distinct applications of assessment: selection, management development, and organizational development. Part Three, *Evaluation and Beyond*, stresses the research base of assessment. Chapters 13 and 14 are parallel chapters dealing with both nonresearch and research-related issues arising from assessment. The final chapter, "Current Trends and Future Possibilities," puts the assessment center method into a perspective of both additional applications as well as its integration into a meaningful human resource identification, development, and utilization system.

Any discipline needs a set of guidelines and practices. These are presented in the *Appendix*. The "Standards and Ethical Considerations" have been developed by professionals in the field and are approved by the Assessment Center Research Group and the International Congress of Assessment Center Administrators.

With two exceptions (Chapters 13 and 14), all of the contributions were prepared specifically for this book. As such, they represent a wide range of training, experience, and practice. The editors have encouraged the contributors to describe their points of view. Brief editorial remarks at the beginning of each chapter help to put the chapter in perspective.

The editors particularly would like to thank Marilyn Mc Ilhone for her assistance and efforts in typing the manuscript, as well as the individual chapter contributors for their prompt response to our varied requests.

JLM
WCB

PART ONE

METHOD

THE ASSESSMENT CENTER METHOD

Joseph L. Moses

INTRODUCTION

The assessment center method as a means of formally identifying potential has been used for nearly 20 years. In this chapter, Dr. Joseph L. Moses of AT&T describes the fundamental process and some of its assumptions.

He notes that there are specific components which make an assessment center what it is. These are: a series of characteristics to be measured, a means of measurement which incorporates the use of simulations, and an especially trained staff to administer and interpret the behaviors observed.

Each of these components is reviewed in detail in subsequent chapters. In Chapter 1, an overview is presented of how data are integrated and used. The reader may want to refer to "Standards and Ethical Considerations for Assessment Center Operations" found in the Appendix for additional detail on what is (as well as what is not) meant by the term "assessment center."

* * *

By now you have probably heard the term "assessment center" used in a variety of ways. It is generally associated with a system used for identifying individual strengths and weaknesses for some specified purpose such as promotion, upgrade, development, or placement. The term "assessment" usually refers to a comprehensive, multifaceted view of the individual in which information from a variety of measurement techniques is brought together.

In the psychologist's jargon, assessment refers to information provided from a variety of techniques such as an interview, paper-and-pencil tests, individualized intelligence tests, and personality measures, which are often used for individualized diagnostic screening as well as for therapeutic guidance. The essence of assessment is that it brings together information from a variety of sources and judgmentally arrives at a summary recommendation and/or description of the individual being evaluated. In this respect, assessment requires the evaluators to weigh various input sources. They may pay attention to some data, ignore others, and contrast similarities and/or differences in results.

The assessment center method integrates this kind of information in a formal setting. In this context, an assessment center can be thought of as both a place and a process. It is a place where individuals participate in a variety of measurement techniques. It is also a process designed to provide standardized and objective conditions of evaluation.

The strength of the assessment center method is two-fold. First, it uses techniques designed to simulate critical behaviors related to success on the job. It then facilitates the integration of this information by pooling data from a variety of assessment sources.

A typical assessment center usually brings a group of six to 12 individuals together. These individuals participate in a variety of exercises and techniques designed to measure predetermined qualities or abilities. These techniques include group exercises, business games, in-basket exercises, pencil-and-paper tests, and interviews. They may also include specifically designed role-playing problems, phone calls, or simulated interviews.

Reports are prepared describing the assessment outcome. Depending on the intent of the center, these reports can contain diagnostic information concerning a participant's strengths and weaknesses, or simply a statement predicting the participant's potential for success in a more demanding position.

Performance by participants in the assessment center process is observed by a trained team of evaluators. These individuals usually are representatives of the organization who are knowledgeable about the kinds of behavior that are found to be effective. These evaluators, or assessors, receive special training and participate as members of the assessment team.

Each assessor has several key functions to perform. He or she must conduct the assessment exercises and observe participant performance during this part of the process. The assessor must also report on what behaviors were observed to other members of the evaluation team and then judge, along with other members of the assessment team, the effectiveness of the behaviors noted. While the length of training varies from center to center, all assessors receive special instructions concerning these aspects of the process.

An assessment center can also be defined as a sophisticated rating process which is designed to minimize as many forms of potential rater bias as possible.

Each participant is given the same opportunity to demonstrate his or her abilities in standardized situations.

There are sufficient assessors available so that each participant is observed by more than one judge. The process requires that independent judgments of behaviors and effectiveness be made. Multiple observers, multiple sources of information, and specifically defined objective dimensions of performance all add to the objectivity of the process.

One other characteristic of the assessment center method is its flexibility in adapting to local organizational needs. There are wide variations in assessment center approaches. For example, some centers operate the year round. Many others, particularly those in smaller organizations, are assembled for a week or two as needed. Some centers are conducted in specially built facilities, others are conducted at a nearby company location or motel. The training of assessors can run from several hours to several weeks, depending on the organization of the center and the degree of expectation of assessor performance. The kinds of techniques vary considerably. The role of the assessor also varies. Some organizations use specially trained individuals to role play typically faced problems. These simulations are usually observed by an independent assessor. In some organizations, little information is provided to the participant during the assessment process. In others, feedback of a highly developmental nature characterizes the process itself. These differences are all a function not so much of the methodology of assessment but of the intent of the program. This intent can range from selection to placement, to individualized counseling and development. These are not mutually exclusive outcomes, and frequently a center will address itself to a variety of purposes.

THE COMPONENTS OF AN ASSESSMENT CENTER

Regardless of the intent of the assessment center itself, the following aspects are present in each assessment center. These components consist first of a list of qualities or dimensions related to the characteristics sought in the position or job level in question. A second component consists of a series of techniques designed to provide information useful in evaluating these qualities or dimensions. The final component is a staff to administer the assessment process as well as to interpret the behaviors observed.

The Dimensions to be Assessed

Obviously, the dimensions or qualities to be evaluated are critical factors. These vary, depending upon the purpose of the assessment center, the kinds of skills and abilities evaluated, and the level within the organization of the participant and assessor. For example, in an assessment center designed to evaluate potential for further advancement, the qualities or dimensions typically evaluated are heavily weighed toward management abilities such as leadership, communication skills, and decision-making administrative-type skills. On the other hand, assessment centers designed for individual development strategies focus on areas that can be amenable to change and may include such aspects as personal career-planning strategies and increased self-awareness based on feedback associated with the assessment. In all cases, however, determining the kinds of qualities or dimensions to be evaluated is a critical factor in establishing an assessment center. Generally, these dimensions should be ones that are stable and do not change rapidly over time, are observable using assessment center techniques, can be definable and meaningfully interpreted, and make sense to the organization.

There are a variety of methods used for defining the dimensions to be assessed. A job analysis, designed to determine critical behaviors in the position in question is often needed. Observation and experience of management representatives are more often used. Dimensions found to be particularly successful in other assessment center programs are also often drawn upon. Often there is a great deal of similarity in management functions across organizations; consequently, we can expect to see some overlap in dimensions assessed in different organizations. We will examine how to determine which dimensions are most appropriate to a given organization in Chapter 4, "Issues in Establishing an Assessment Center."

For the most part, however, a typical center evaluates from eight to 25 different dimensions. These may include such diverse skill areas as interpersonal, administrative, and communications effectiveness. Commonly used dimensions include leadership, persuasiveness, perception, flexibility, decisiveness, organizing and planning skills, problem-solving skills, and oral and written communications skills.

Assessment Techniques

The techniques used to measure these qualities also vary. As a general rule, no single technique is designed to provide information on all of the dimensions typically evaluated in an assessment center. Considerable research has indicated that certain techniques provide information that is highly relevant to specific dimensions. For example, measuring an individual's intellectual abilities is best done using standardized mental ability tests. Trying to evaluate this dimension based on prior scholastic accomplishments or current writing skills is generally much less accurate. Similarly, the most effective way of evaluating interpersonal kinds of behaviors requires a live, interpersonal interaction with others. Asking the individual to respond, for example, to the kinds of leadership approaches he or she may prefer in a given setting is not as realistic as simulating an actual situation which requires leadership capabilities. Consequently, various group exercises and games have been developed to measure these kinds of abilities. Administrative skills, such as organizing, planning, and decision making, are best evaluated through a special individual exercise known as an in-basket. These techniques, as well as others currently in use are discussed in Chapter 5, "The Selection and Development of Assessment Center Techniques."

The Assessment Staff

The final component of an assessment center is the staff itself. In many respects, this is one of the most critical components of the process. Since assessment is a judgmental process, the quality of the judge is of great importance. The assessor must be able to assimilate a great deal of information rapidly, must be relatively free of personal biases, and must be perceived by his or her organization as an effective individual. This last factor is of great importance in terms of how the results of the program are used. If the organization perceives the assessment staff as marginal, then it will tend to ignore the results of the process. On the other hand, if assessors represent the best that the organization has to offer, the results of the process take on greater significance.

Many centers use special selection techniques for assessors. It is also not uncommon to see assessors drawn from prior successful assessment participants.

As noted earlier, there are wide variations in terms of the staffing approaches used by different organizations. The background of the assessor, training of the assessor, and the judgmental strategies employed by the assessor are discussed in two separate chapters—Chapter 6, "Assessor Selection and Training," and Chapter 7, "How and Why Assessment Works."

Perhaps an example at this point would be appropriate to show the intent of the assessment center process. Suppose, for a moment, that you were asked to identify an individual whose major responsibility will be speaking to audiences on a variety of topics. Obviously, one of the dimensions to be observed for this position is the extent to which the individual can make an effective oral presentation. This is but one dimension of many which may be relevant, but, for our example, it is the one considered.

There are several ways of determining whether or not a candidate is suitable for this assignment. One common method is simply to ask the applicant for a self-report. For example, you might determine whether the individual does have prior speaking experience. The applicant might be asked whether he or she is comfortable in addressing large groups, whether he or she has had prior public speaking training, and so forth. While this might be relevant and useful background information, it does not help in determining the skills of the candidate in question. As an alternative approach, you could obtain reference/

appraisal-type data about the speaking skills of the applicant. For example, you could solicit the opinion of a manager who may have heard the individual make an oral presentation. This kind of data gathering is quite common for many management selection decisions. Obviously, it suffers from considerable bias based on the original opportunities presented to the candidate as well as the frame of reference of the evaluator.

A third method would combine some of the information from the first two approaches with observations made during the interview of the individual. Again, this is a common and easily administered procedure. This method is useful in predicting *only* those behaviors that are present *both* in an interview setting and in addressing a large group. For example, knowing that a candidate is poised in a face-to-face interview setting does not guarantee that he or she will behave similarly in front of a large audience.

While all of the above approaches are widely used, none of these approaches really addresses the question at hand. Realistically, the best way of evaluating whether an individual can make an effective oral presentation is simply to put him or her in the situation under standardized conditions and observe how effectively the individual made the actual presentation. In this setting, specific attention could be given to the method and manner of presentation, the content of ideas, audience attentiveness, and a host of other related evaluative behaviors. This, in the long run, will be a much more accurate prediction of effectiveness than any of the preceding methods.

In a similar manner, other kinds of skills are evaluated in an assessment center. Exercises are designed to simulate critical behaviors that are related to job success. A variety of techniques are used, leading to a wealth of data that can then be used for evaluative purposes.

THE HISTORY OF THE ASSESSMENT CENTER METHOD

While assessment centers have been successfully used by many organizations for the past 15 years, the origin of this approach goes back well before this. Some early references to an assessment center concept can be seen in the work of German psychologists in the early 1900s. The most commonly accepted date for the development of a historical frame of reference for this process goes back to the 1940s and the work of the Office of Strategic Services (OSS).

During World War II, considerable concern was directed toward identifying operatives who successfully could undertake hazardous intelligence-gathering missions. A group of psychologists, under the general direction of Dr. Henry Murray of the Harvard Psychological Clinic, developed the first widely used assessment center approach. At about the same time, assessment centers were developed by the British War Office Selection Board and the British Civil Service

Selection Board for military and civil service officer selection. In many respects, these early assessment center approaches have a great deal of relevance to the process as it is used today. In retrospect, it seems quite apparent that the procedures used for identifying a successful spy by the OSS, for example, bear a close relationship to the kinds of procedures used to identify a successful manager. While the actual techniques and exercises obviously vary, the process and method used are essentially the same. This, as noted earlier, first requires an evaluation of the kind of behaviors related to successful performance (be it spy or manager), a series of techniques to evaluate these behaviors, and, finally, a staff to interpret and evaluate these behaviors.

The story of the OSS assessment center has been recorded in *The Assessment of Men*. This book, originally published in 1948, has recently been republished and provides some very interesting reading. Over 5,000 recruits were assessed. Participants in the OSS procedure underwent comprehensive types of data gathering and measurement sources. Some of these were traditional psychological measures of ability and personality, some were designed for the mission at hand, and some were designed to tap specific behaviors such as map-reading skills. The details of this procedure and the history of the original OSS centers are spelled out in Chapter 2 of this volume.

After World War II, the OSS type of assessment center was essentially abandoned in the United States except for some internal use in intelligence-gathering operations by the CIA. Some of our allies continued using the assessment process—the British Civil Service Selection Board, for example. Also, the Australians identified participants for selection to their military college, based on the War Officer Selection Board Assessment Center, and the South Africans used the technique to identify supervisors in gold mines.

There were a few scattered attempts to use assessment centers for predicting success in specific academic and clinical psychology training programs but these centers had very mixed results. Generally, successful assessment centers had assessors who were quite familiar with the job or duties they were assessing, used simulations rather than relying heavily on pencil-and-paper techniques, and made predictions in terms of specific outcomes rather than in terms of personality traits or individual characteristics. The less successful programs relied heavily on tests rather than simulations and made descriptions of personality traits rather than predictions of specific behaviors.

Assessment centers specifically applied for industrial usage can be traced back to the early 1950s and the pioneering work of Robert K. Greenleaf and Douglas W. Bray of the American Telephone & Telegraph Company. In the middle 1950s, an ambitious longitudinal research project, known as the Management Progress Study, was initiated at AT&T. The purpose of this study was to follow a large sample of young business managers, tracing their growth, development, and progress, over a career in the telephone business. In order to determine the initial effectiveness of the sample, a special research assessment center was developed. This consisted of a three and one-half day process in which groups of the young managers in the study were evaluated by a team of psychologists and specially trained executives and managers.

The subjects participated in a variety of techniques including both leaderless group exercises, business games, a specially developed in-basket, and intensive in-depth interviews, as well as a host of psychological and personality measures. Twenty-five management qualities were evaluated, including such ability areas as leadership, decision making, organizing and planning skills, as well as motivational characteristics such as advancement motivation, social objectivity, and value orientation.

Each participant was rated on the 25 dimensions and an overall judgment of the likelihood each would have in reaching middle management in the next 10 years was made. The assessment data were not made available to either the participant or his organization.

Follow-up data have been collected from both participants and their companies. A series of yearly interviews with each participant as well as data from his bosses have been continuously collected. The study is presently in its 20th year, and the data from interview sources alone consist of over 20,000 single-spaced typewritten pages.

In addition to the follow-up interviews, each participant still with the company eight years after his original assessment, was reassessed. The results of this reassessment, as well as the development of the college graduate managers in the study, are presented in *Formative Years in Business*, a book by Bray, Campbell, and Grant, published in 1974.

The results of the Management Progress Study Assessment Center did much to establish the validity of the assessment process. Strong relationships existed between the predictions made at the assessment center and subsequent career progress. The stability of performance between assessment and reassessment provided rich data on the reliability and consistency of the abilities evaluated. Finally, the contribution of the various assessment techniques evaluating specific ability areas was also established.

Managers of one of the first telephone companies in the Management Progress Study were quite impressed with the process and asked that a program be developed to select first-level foremen. This program, the first operational assessment program for line use, was developed in 1958. It consisted of a modification of the techniques used in the assessment center of the Management Progress Study, with a heavy emphasis on behavioral rather than test data. Gradually, the scope of assessment activities considerably expanded within the Bell System to the point that over 150,000 men and women have participated in an assessment center program. Programs were developed for higher level management assessment as well as for the early identification of potential in very recent employees. Special assessment procedures were developed for such diverse occupational groups as salesmen and engineers.

Other organizations began adapting the AT&T assessment center method. Standard Oil (Ohio), IBM, General Electric, Sears, and Caterpillar Tractor were among the first organizations to use assessment in the United States. Internationally, early programs were developed at IBM World Trade, Shell (Brazil), and by the Canadian Government, as well as the English and Australian derivatives of the OSS application. Gradually, assessment center approaches began to take hold in a variety of settings. Chapter 3, "Application of the Assessment Center Method," brings us up to date on current applications of this method. As we shall see, the uses and varieties of assessment continue to grow and multiply.

Assessment centers have been used for many purposes. Originally developed for selection of management personnel, the process has been used for individualized counseling, management development, and organizational development. Once installed only in large organizations with great manpower needs, the method has been used successfully in civilian and military agencies, universities, and in many smaller organizations. The success of assessment implementation rests heavily on a well-documented and well-reported research base. It relies on a very successful blend of research, organizational needs, and practice.

CHAPTER 2

FROM SELECTING SPIES TO SELECTING MANAGERS — THE OSS ASSESSMENT PROGRAM

Donald W. MacKinnon

INTRODUCTION

In any discipline there is a need for a historical frame of reference. Assessment centers have been founded on a well-documented research base and have a rich history despite their relative youth.

Dr. MacKinnon is an able historian. As Director of the original Office of Strategic Services Assessment Center at Station S, he has been closely associated with the process of assessment for over 30 years, and was one of the contributors to the book *Assessment of Men*, which documented the OSS experience.

This chapter provides both personal and in depth insights of the "original" assessment process. While many of today's centers use greatly different exercises and techniques, the parallel to selecting a spy and a manager is quite clear. The linking pin is prediction of behavior, based on critical examination of behavior.

Because of its unique place in history, this chapter appears early in the book—it serves to remind us that empirical documentation and evaluation are the cornerstones of scientific knowledge. Of particular note are the recommendations presented at the close of the chapter, statements that are as accurate today as they were almost 30 years ago.

* * *

Five months before Pearl Harbor, President Roosevelt created yet another of his alphabetical bureaucracies. This time it was the COI, the Office of the

Coordinator of Information, and at its head he placed General William Joseph Donovan, a World War I hero and holder of the United States' three highest military decorations. Known since his youth as "Wild Bill," Donovan was an Irish Catholic, a Hoover Republican, and a millionaire Wall Street lawyer; but, above all, he was a man of enormous energy and imagination.

His task would be to lead the "New Deal's" excursion into espionage, sabotage, "black" propaganda, guerrilla warfare, and other "un-American subversive practices" (Smith, 1972, p. 1). Donovan was an understandable choice to head the COI, since it was he who had convinced Roosevelt of the need for such an agency. Having observed the successes of the fascist fifth column in Europe, he urged the development of an international secret service for the United States to meet the Nazi challenge. His forceful advocacy of American involvement in the European conflict as well as his prediction that England would not collapse under the pounding of the Luftwaffe had impressed Roosevelt. Because of this and his personal audacity and imagination, he was Roosevelt's choice for this new, bold venture.

One division of the COI was the propaganda wing, headed by the playwright Robert E. Sherwood, and staffed by such writers as Thornton Wilder and Stephen Vincent Benet. From the beginning, there was friction between Donovan, the men of action he recruited—lawyers, bankers, PR men—and the sensitive writers.

Six months after Pearl Harbor (May 1942), the propaganda wing was split from the COI to become the OWI—the Office of War Information—leaving the other activities to be directed by Donovan in a new agency, the Office of Strategic Services (OSS), with an ambiguous mandate "to plan and operate special services as may be directed by the United States Joint Chiefs of Staff" (Smith, 1972, p. 2).

The variety of activities in which the OSS engaged is suggested by the titles of its various branches: SI, Secret Intelligence; R&A, Research and Analysis; SO, Special Operations—destructive operations behind enemy lines working with resistance groups; MO, Morale Operations—black propaganda in contrast to the white propaganda of the OWI; Counter-Intelligence; a Schools and Training Branch, where recruits would learn the tricks of OSS trades; and others.

During the first year of its operation, there were three channels of entry into the OSS: recruitment of military personnel by the Personnel Procurement Branch, recruitment of civilians by the Civilian Personnel Branch, and recruitment of both military and civilian personnel through the initiative of individual OSS members—all of this without benefit of any professional or uniform screening process. Nobody knew who would make a good spy or an effective guerrilla fighter. Consequently, large numbers of misfits were recruited from the very beginning, and this might have continued had it not been for several disastrous operations such as one in Italy for which, on the assumption that it takes dirty men to do dirty works, some OSS men had been recruited directly from the ranks of Murder, Inc. and the Philadelphia Purple Gang. The need for professional assistance in selection was obvious, but was resisted by many in the organization.

In October 1943 an OSS official back from London suggested that a program of psychological-psychiatric assessment similar to that in the English WOSBs (War Office Selection Boards) be set up in the OSS. This idea was picked up and pushed by Robert C. Tryon, a psychologist on leave from the University of California, who was Deputy Chief, Planning Staff, OSS. He recommended that an assessment center be set up in the Schools and Training Branch in collaboration with three other California PhDs, James A. Hamilton, John W. Gardner, and Joseph Gengerelli, and he began planning the first assessment center in the United States.

By November, a physical facility had been acquired: the Willard Estate, the spacious residence and grounds of the owners of the Hotel Willard in Washington, which was to become Station S (for Schools and Training, though most preferred to think the S stood for Secret) in Fairfax, Virginia, some 18 miles from Washington.

The first planning conference for the program of Station S was held in early December with Henry A. Murray (Harvard) and Donald Adams (Duke) joining the California psychologists. Shortly thereafter, the director of the OSS authorized the establishment of an assessment unit, and 15 days later the first assessment was held with a skeleton staff!

Although the push for an assessment program in the OSS came from the California psychologists, the ultimate form and nature of the program was most significantly shaped by Henry A. Murray.

In addition to the speed with which it was initiated, the assessment program suffered from other handicaps. Although backed by General Donovan and some of the bureau chiefs, it was opposed by others (especially by the military). We lacked knowledge about the assignments, most of them novel, to which our assessees would be sent. Without job analyses, we did not know specifically for what we were assessing. We needed experts to write job descriptions, but there were none in the field. At best, job assignments were described by single terms: language expert, cartographer, news analyst. Had we known what specific skills would be required, there would have been so many of them as to preclude a testing of them all.

Later we would learn more about what was required for successful execution of OSS assignments from branch chiefs who had by then received more specific job descriptions, from reports of returnees, from assessors who had received training in OSS schools, and from assessors who had traveled abroad for firsthand observations.

In the beginning it was the lack of specific knowledge that led us to conclude that our assessments could not be of the specific skills of a given candidate for a specific job but rather in each case an assessment of the "man as a whole," the general structure of his being, and his strengths and weaknesses for rather generally described environments and situations. As it turned out, there were some advantages to our having taken this stance toward assessment, for we soon discovered that very often assessees were never assigned to the job for which they were recruited. Typically, two to eight months elapsed between assessment and job assignment overseas. The candidate had first to be trained; by the time that had been accomplished, the war had moved on and the job for which he had been recruited no longer needed to be done.

Only those destined for overseas assignment were assessed; those who remained in the States were exempt. At first, our assessment reports were only for the information of bureau chiefs. They were free to accept or reject our recommendations as they saw fit. After two months, all that changed. By order of General Donovan, only those who received a positive recommendation from Station S could be sent overseas. This was personally flattering, but very frustrating to our scientific egos since it meant that pure validity studies of our assessment operation could not be made. This order meant that Station S with its three and one-half day program would not be able to assess all those destined for overseas duty. Thus, in late winter of 1944, a one-day assessment center, Station W, was set up in Washington, to assess a large number of candidates, many of whom were to be assigned to headquarters and rear bases overseas rather than to operations in the field. Two months later, a center to assess candidates recruited on the West Coast was established at Laguna Beach, California. This was Station WS. Later, assessment stations to screen native agents were set up in Ceylon, Kunming (Yunan Province), Calcutta, and Hsian. During the period of their operation, Stations S and W assessed 5,391 recruits.

The program for Station S, set up hurriedly and with little knowledge of what OSS assignments would entail, was bound to undergo many changes. There were seven periods in the history of Station S, but there were no radical changes in the program during the last six periods (June 1944 to V-J Day, September 1945) during which time I served as Director of Station S. This is the program I shall describe.

I have spoken of some handicaps under which the assessment program had to operate. Let me mention two others. From its inception, the OSS had to guard against infiltrations by foreign agents, and, of course, if its operations were to succeed they had to be kept secret. But these concerns hardly justified the extreme secrecy which was maintained and which merely added to the atmosphere of cloak-and-dagger mystery that enshrouded the organization. This was nowhere more obvious than in the recruitment of OSS personnel. Barred from mentioning the OSS by name but free to talk about mysterious, exciting overseas assignments with a government agency, the pitch made by OSS recruiters was especially attractive to the bored, to the pathologically adventure-some, to those neurotically attracted to danger, and to psychopaths in general. Thus, we had more than our share of misfits to weed out, and of course it is psychopaths who have a special talent to make a good impression over brief periods of time. Under the given circumstances, the branch representatives who briefed candidates for their visit to Station S were wary about telling them much about the work for which they had been recruited. Many, when seen in assessment, had no idea of what their assignment would be, and some even thought they were in the State Department!

The other handicap we faced, or so it seemed at first, was that we would not know whom we were assessing. That is, they were now allowed to reveal their true names to us or to the other members of their assessment class. In December 1943, when Station S was established, many of the recruits into OSS were refugees from Europe, often with families and relatives in occupied territory. If their true identity were to become known to others in the organization who had infiltrated it, they might become subject to blackmail through threats to relatives abroad.

Not knowing who our assessees were was not, however, entirely disadvantageous. Quite innocently, we could be a check on the misuse of nepotism, turning down even a Roosevelt or a Donovan if his performance at Station S left something to be desired. In any case, since we had to live with the anonymity of our assessees, we turned it into an assessment exercise!

Assessment at Station S ran in two-week cycles, during which three groups of 18 candidates would be assessed: the first group would arrive on a Sunday afternoon and would leave the following Thursday morning; that afternoon a second group would arrive and, assessed over the weekend, would leave Monday morning; that afternoon a third group would arrive and would leave Friday morning. That weekend the staff would draw its breath and prepare for the next two-week cycle, which would begin again on Sunday afternoon.

Each recruit for OSS, upon arrival in Washington, would report to the Branch representative who would supervise him throughout training and who had authority then and there to reject the candidate if he was obviously unsuitable. Otherwise and usually, the recruit would be told something, but not much, about the type of work for which he had volunteered, and he would fill out a Student Information Sheet.

He was then informed that he would spend the next three and one-half days at an assessment school in the country, where he would be asked many questions and given many tests by a group of psychologists and psychiatrists. He was told there was no reason to feel apprehensive, that most who had gone through the school had enjoyed it. He was urged to do his best. He was also told that he would go incognito for his own protection. And, finally, he chose a name by which he would be known during assessment.

During that day in Washington, he was given a medical examination and that afternoon he would report to Schools and Training Headquarters, an old brick schoolhouse that stood where Watergate now stands! He would report at 3:30 if he was an enlisted man, at 4:00 if a civilian, and at 4:30 if an officer. Reporting was staggered in this fashion so that each might know the status of some of the men in his own group, the fewer the better, but not the others (e.g., no officer would know who were enlisted men and who were civilians, etc.).

Upon arrival at Headquarters, the candidate would be taken to a room, stripped of his clothing and anything else that might identify him, issued army fatigues and boots, and ushered into a waiting area. At 5:00, the group would be put in a completely closed army van and driven over the 18 winding miles to Station S.

After a brief welcome and orientation to the program, the candidates were told that during their stay at S each would have to build up and maintain as completely as possible a cover story for himself, claiming to have been born where he wasn't, to have been educated in institutions other than those he had attended, to have been engaged in work or profession not his own, and to live now in a place that was not his true residence. The cover story was to be maintained with staff and students alike at all times except under X conditions, at which time candidates could reveal anything about themselves except their name and true identity. X conditions prevailed when filling out a Personal History Form, in a Life History Interview, when a staff member established X conditions, and when in case of need a student asked for X conditions and a staff member granted them.

Thus, Station S was one grand simulation, each candidate having the task of consistently simulating a person he was not. Since many of the candidates would eventually be living abroad under cover, the relevancy of the cover story task seemed clear enough.

The variables rated on the Station S report for each candidate offer a rationale for the assessment exercises which were developed for the program. The rated dimensions were: motivation, practical intelligence, emotional stability, social relations, leadership, physical ability, observation and reporting, propaganda skills, and maintaining cover. Each variable was rated on a 6-point scale: very inferior, inferior, low average, high average, superior, very superior. Note that to force a spread of ratings, using more of the whole scale, no rating of "average" was given. If the dimension was not measured, that fact was indicated in the final report.

Components of each of the dimensions were printed on the face sheet in the following manner:

Motivation: energy, zest, effort, initiative, war morale, interest in assignment.

Practical intelligence: speed and accuracy of judgment, resourcefulness in solving problems.

Emotional stability: emotional control and maturity, absence of neurotic symptoms.

Social relations: social awareness, goodwill, teamwork, tact, absence of annoying traits.

Leadership: social initiative, organizing ability, ability to evoke cooperation.

Physical ability: agility, daring, ruggedness, stamina.

Observation and reporting: ability to search, question, observe and recall, infer, report.

Propaganda skills: ability to affect others through acts, words, or displays.

Maintaining cover: caution, ability to remain inconspicuous, bluff, mislead, keep a secret.

If one of the components of a variable (let us say, tact) was especially high, it would be underlined; if especially low, it would be crossed out.

The core of the assessment program was a rather detailed life-history psychiatric *Interview* conducted by a senior staff member. In preparation for the interview, the interviewer read a *Personal History Form* which the candidate had filled out as well as a *Projective Questionnaire*, a *Sentence Completion Test*, a *Health Questionnaire*, and a *Work Conditions Survey* which described 43 conditions that the candidate rated on a 6-point scale, ranging from (1) "highly desirable" to (6) "would make job impossible." In the light of all this material, the interviewer had some impression of the candidate and knew the areas in which he would want to get more information in the interview.

Two conventional measures of intellectual ability were administered—the *Otis Self-Administering Test of Ability* and a *Vocabulary Test*—plus two tests of special aptitudes—the *Bennett Mechanical Comprehension Test* and the *Signal Corps Aptitude Test*—but we were less interested in our candidates' scores on intelligence tests than in the effectiveness with which they used whatever intelligence they had. And this as well as most of the dimensions of behavior which we rated was more clearly to be seen in the most novel aspect of the OSS program—the situational tests which we developed, tests which today would be more often referred to as simulations or simulation exercises. Our objective was to observe as much of our candidates' behavior in situations which simulated as realistically as feasible the kinds of situations they would be likely to encounter in OSS assignments.

For those destined to work in Secret Intelligence, the abilities to search, to question, to observe and recall, to infer, and to report would be of crucial importance and a variety of tests (some situational) to tap the dimension we called "Observation and Reporting" were devised. Examples of such tests (in which, of course, other variables could also be observed and rated) were:

Belongings Test. In this test the candidate would be taken to a bedroom in which 26 items—such as articles of clothing, written materials, a time table, newspaper clippings, a ticket receipt, etc.—were placed openly on the bed, chairs, and tables. His task was to examine them, to size up the man who left them, to learn all he could about the person, what he was like, etc. Objects could be picked up and examined, but had to be replaced. After four minutes, the candidate was taken to another room to answer a 36-item questionnaire, a test of the candidate's ability to observe and draw correct inferences.

Map Memory Test. Here the candidate was to assume that he was an agent operating in the field and that he had just made a secret rendezvous with a courier who had a map of the territory that the agent would be covering. After a few minutes, the courier had to leave with the map and, since it would be dangerous for the agent to have it, he had to memorize it. After eight minutes to examine the map, it was taken away and the candidate answered a set of multiple-choice statements about the terrain of the map.

Interrogation Test. In this situational test a junior staff member played the role (a standardized one) of an escaped prisoner of war who would be interrogated by the candidate. Background material for the interrogation was supplied in the form of a map and some general information about the imprisonment and escape of the prisoner who had served as a tailgunner of a B-29 before its crash landing. Another staff member would sit by and rate the candidate's skill in developing rapport, asking productive questions, following up leads and hints by the "prisoner," etc.

For those destined to work in Morale Operations (MO), the ability to affect others through acts, words, or displays would be crucial, and special tests were devised in which these skills might be displayed, thus providing the assessors with some estimate of the "Propaganda Skills" of candidates. Two examples of this type of test of propaganda skills would be the *OWI Test* and the *Manchuria Test.* In the former, a test of one's sensitivity to cultural differences, the candidate was to assume that he was working for OWI in Korea and knew nothing about the country. He had 20 minutes to indicate the kind of information he would want to have in order to work up a propaganda program designed to win Koreans to our side. In the *Manchuria Test*, the candidate, given some background facts, was, over a day and a half, to prepare two pieces of propaganda to lower the morale of Japanese railway workers and guards on the South Manchurian Railway. In this task, candidates were urged to use whatever graphic skills they had.

One of the better known of our situational tests was the *Brook Test* (a leaderless group situation) in which a group of six candidates would be taken to a shallow, quiet stream whose banks were eight feet apart. On one bank was a heavy rock, on the other a log. There were trees on both sides and scattered on the side where the group stood were a number of boards (none long enough to reach from bank to bank), three lengths of rope, a pulley, and a barrel with both ends knocked out.

The candidates were told: "In this problem you have to use your imagination. Before you, you see a raging torrent so deep and so fast that it is quite impossible to rest anything upon the bottom of the stream. The banks are sheer, so it will be impossible to work except from the top of them.

"You are on a mission in the field, and having come to this brook, you are faced with the task of transporting this delicate range finder, skillfully camouflaged as a log, to the far bank, and of bringing that box of percussion caps, camouflaged as a rock, to this side. In carrying out this assignment, you may make use of any materials around here. When the job is done, all of you, as well as any material you used, are to be back on this side" (OSS Assessment Staff, 1948, pp. 95-96).

The group was to work in an area about 15 feet along the bank marked by two white stakes.

In this exercise one could easily note the difference between asserted leadership and effective leadership, and ample opportunity was given to observe differences among the candidates on such variables as energy and initiative, effective intelligence, social relations, leadership, and physical ability.

A second leaderless group situation was *The Wall*. Here the candidates were led to a wall that was 10 feet high and 15 feet long. Behind the wall, which the candidates could see, was another wall of the same height and length, parallel to it, the two walls being eight feet apart. On the candidates' side of the wall, there were a heavy log, an old board a few inches longer than the log, and a couple of 2x4s, two feet and three feet in length.

The candidates were informed (fancy being mixed with fact as in all situational tests) that although they could not see it, the barrier before them actually consisted of two walls (fact) separated by a 200-foot canyon (fancy). They were escaping from some Japanese soldiers. In order to save themselves they would have to get to the other side of the far wall and, to fulfill their mission, they would have to take their king-size bazooka (the log) with them. They might get across the wall in any way they wished, but they must not walk around the ends of the wall, and, of course, whoever or whatever fell into the canyon would be counted as lost.

The same variables observed and rated at *The Brook* were observed and rated at *The Wall*.

The Brook and *The Wall* gave some advantage to men with marked initiative and assertiveness. To discover real ability when leadership was assigned, five other field tests were employed. The task of the leader in the *Mined Road* was to get his group across a mined road in 10 minutes; in the *Sentry*, to get his group, with one man wounded and unable to walk, across a road guarded by a sentry (played by a junior staff member in uniform) whose regular beat meant that for about 45 seconds of each of his tours he could not see the section of the road where the group would try to cross. In the *Agent's Room*, the leader has just received a radio message that a friendly agent had, in a hurried getaway, left some important papers behind; the task would be to recover the papers. The instructions were given at the entrance to a large, unused carriage house on the second floor of which was a crude living room (the agent's room). Members of the group were told that they had been passing as natives, had forged credentials, were dressed in native costume, and could speak the native tongue. Midway through this exercise, a German guard armed with a rifle approached the carriage house.

The other two assigned leadership exercises, the *Blown Bridge* and *Killing the Mayor*, like the three just described, provided good opportunity to observe each candidate's leadership skills as well as other variables: practical intelligence, emotional stability, social relations, and physical ability.

An indoor, verbal counterpart of the outdoor, physical *Brook* and *Wall* exercises was a leaderless group discussion. The topic was "What are the major postwar problems facing the United States and (if you have time) along what lines do you think they should be solved?" The dimensions observed and rated in this situation were leadership, effective intelligence, energy and initiative, and social relations.

To measure resistance to stress and frustration tolerance, important facets of "Emotional Stability," two situational tests were devised. *Construction*, which came to be known as *Behind the Barn* (for that was where this exercise was held), required the candidate to direct two helpers in the task of building a five-foot cube structure with seven-foot diagonals on the four sides, using a huge "tinker-toy" set of materials. The candidate had 10 minutes in which to accomplish the task. All the physical work was to be done by the helpers, junior staff members who played the role of Kippy (passive, sluggish, and something of a stumblebum) and Buster (aggressive, critical, constantly making impractical suggestions). Both were insulting, faultfinding characters. In the history of Station S, this was was never completed in the allotted time. Some candidates gained insight into the problem, but more often they became so involved and so frustrated that they had difficulty in handling their frustration and controlling their anger. A few physically attacked their helpers, and some asked to be relieved from the program after this exercise.

After the *Construction* test, the candidate was taken aside by a senior staff member who, in a *Post-Construction Interview*, provided the candidate an opportunity for catharsis. Some admitted their anger and confessed to having almost hit their "helpers" while others, with quivering lips and trembling hands, denied they had been in any way emotionally upset in the exercise. This interview was also used to test the candidate's ability to maintain cover. Since a person is particularly inclined to break cover in moments of relaxation following stress, the interviewer would inquire about earlier similar experiences which the candidate had had and how he had acted then. If the candidate was not on guard, he would be led into talking about past experiences of a similar kind in which he had performed better and this, of course, was a breaking of cover since X conditions had not been established.

In the *Stress Interview* proper, candidates, one at a time, were instructed that they had just been found by a night watchman in a Government building in Washington going through papers in an office. The candidate was not an employee of the agency, nor did he have any identification papers. The night watchman would be bringing him to the security office for questioning. The candidate was given 12 minutes in which to think up an innocent cover story that would explain his being in the building, after which he was to knock on a designated basement door. Upon being ordered to enter, he was seated in a dark room, the only light being a blinding spotlight directed at his face. For 10 minutes, he would be questioned about his presence in the building. At first quietly and in an understanding, sympathetic manner, he was encouraged to give more and more detail, then suddenly the questioner would turn sadistic, confronting him with inconsistencies and implausibilities in his story with ever-increasing tempo and crescendo of voice. The staff member who questioned the candidates was a New York trial lawyer skilled in techniques of cross-examination. Suddenly the examiner would break in with, "We now have abundant evidence you have not been telling the truth. That is all." Then, after whispered conversation among the staff who had been sitting behind the examiner, observing the candidate but not seen by him except as dim forms, the examiner would announce, "It is our decision that you have failed this test." After five seconds, during which his reactions were observed, he was told to go to a room on the third floor. There he found a staff member, feet on the desk, reading a paper, who would inquire, "How are things going?" In this *Post-Stress Interview* many a candidate would break cover when sympathetically asked if he had ever been in a comparable situation. The *Stress-* and *Post-Stress Interviews* provided ample opportunity to observe and to rate emotional stability, maintaining cover, and motivation for assignment in OSS.

Later in the afternoon of the second day, all candidates under 45 who had passed the physical examination before coming to Station S ran an *Obstacle Course* especially designed to test physical agility and daring.

That evening, candidates were assigned in pairs to act in *Improvisations*. These were role-playing dyadic situations dreamed up by the staff in sessions referred to as "Brain Storms" and tailor-made for each candidate to help resolve doubts which the staff might still have about him. For example, there might have been some question as to how Candidate A could take criticism or rejection, and how much tact Candidate B could muster. The situations they might have been called upon to improvise, the emphasis being put upon what they would actually do if confronted with such a situation rather than acting it out, could have been the following:

"A. moved to a small city about three months ago and opened a business there. He has been doing quite well and one month ago sent in an application for membership in a club in the town. He has heard nothing in response to his application and goes to the home of B., a prominent member of the club, with whom he is pleasantly acquainted. (A. is then sent out of the room and B. is told that A. has received several blackballs.) A. is then called back into the room" (OSS Assessment Staff, 1948, p. 170) and the improvisation begins.

After each improvisation, the participants' reactions were questioned, commented upon, and criticized by the participants and also by the other candidates and staff. Each candidate was observed in two improvisations. At the halfway break, liquor was brought in and continued to be available throughout the evening and as long into the morning as anyone wanted.

After ,*Improvisations*, candidates were divided into two teams to debate the question: "What Shall We Do With Germany After the War?" The debate provided opportunity to observe and rate the dimensions of energy and initiative, effective intelligence, social relations, leadership, and especially, since liquor was still flowing, the ability to maintain cover.

The unmentioned and never named *Liquor Test* led to much behavior which otherwise would not have been observed. During the last months of the OSS, we were grateful for an OSS operator (an Army Captain who had parachuted into France to work with a resistance group) who, staying up as long as any of the candidates wished, relieved the professional staff of this duty.

On the morning of the last full day of assessment, the candidates' opinions of and attitudes toward each other were collected. The *Sociometric Questionnaire* asked candidates: "With whom would you enjoy continuing your acquaintance?" "Which men expressed the most realistic and convincing opinions in the debate last night?" "If you were a member of a group on a dangerous mission, whom would you prefer to have as your leader?" and other questions of the same sort. The *Judgment of Others* test required the candidates to write five personality sketches for the five assessees whom they felt they had come to know best. Data from these two exercises were available to the staff in forming their final impressions of the candidates.

During the rest of the day, while the staff was preparing its S Report on each of the candidates, the assessees were involved in solving the *Murder Mystery*. For this exercise, they were given copies of the mythical *Fairfield Chronicle* which reported the finding of the dead body of a woman on a road near S. Working in competing groups of six, their task was to wring from three junior staff members (standard role players), who were designated as possible informants, the information necessary for them to make proper inferences and thus to solve "the murder."

Athletic Events—broad jump, high jump, and shot-put—more in the spirit of a game than as a serious test, and a *Baseball Game* between the candidates and junior staff members not involved in the conference engaged the interest of the assessees during the last afternoon.

Reports on the candidates' performance in these last-day simulations and games were available to the staff before their deliberations ended.

For each assessment class, usually consisting of 18 assessees, the staff was divided into teams of two senior staff members (professionals with PhD or MD degrees) and one junior staff member (enlisted men who had had some training in psychology). Each team was assigned to a group of five to seven candidates. The senior members conducted the life history interviews; the junior member administered special individual tests and interpreted the projective test protocols. Otherwise, the work of both senior and junior members was the same—namely, to develop as a group as complete a conception as possible of each candidate in the subgroup assigned to them.

During the various situational tests, the behaviors of each participant were carefully noted by both senior and junior members of the responsible team, each staff member rating each assessee on the variables relevant to the particular exercise. Usually immediately following each situational test, the staff team met to discuss their impressions of the candidates and the ratings they had assigned to them. The purpose of the meeting was to come to agreement upon the ratings to be assigned to each assessee on each of the rated variables.

The staff meeting for the preparation of the Station S Report on the candidates ran from after lunch on the last full day of the assessment until all reports had been finished, which was often close to midnight.

Before the staff meeting, each interviewer had written a first draft of his section of the reports on the men he had interviewed and for whom he was the primary assessor. This was the description of the candidate as a person and of the major events of his past history that seemed to shed light on his present personality, with special emphasis being given to picturing how the candidate might be expected to behave in a variety of situations and circumstances in the future. Also, before the staff meeting, the member of the staff who was responsible for reporting on the behavior of the candidate at Station S as revealed in the various situational tests (the "situationist," as he was known) had written his section of the final report which not only described the behavior of the candidate at S but offered specific support for the statements and predictions made in the first part of the report written by the interviewer.

A huge board, which covered one wall of the staff room, offered a graphic display of how each candidate had been rated by the staff team assigned to him on each of the variables in each of the relevant tests and situations. Ratings were represented by thumbtacks, red if above average, blue if below. While the interviewer and the situationist read their reports, staff members looked at the board and the thumbtacks to see if the reporters' statements were supported by the ratings. If not, there was discussion until general agreement was reached about the changes that would have to be made in the overall rating of the variables on the Station S Report or in the statements in the written report. Sometimes the report could be revised in the staff meeting. If not, it would be rewritten by the report writer after the meeting.

The final report consisted of a face sheet on which the candidate was rated on the nine variables already described, plus other sheets which carried a character sketch of the candidate based upon the interviewer's insights and the staff's observations of the candidate at S, and recommendations concerning overseas assignment made on a 5-point scale: not recommended, doubtful, recommended with qualifications, recommended, highly recommended. A similar scale (not recommended to highly recommended) was used to indicate the candidate's fitness for work at (1) a rear base, (2) an advanced base, and (3) at or behind enemy lines; his fitness for (1) higher, (2) middle, or (3) lower level of authority and responsibility; and, finally, his fitness for different types of assignment—e.g., administrator, intelligence officer, operational agent, etc.

These Station S reports, sometimes worked over long past midnight of the last day of assessment, were already at the OSS Headquarters in Washington when the candidates returned there the next morning.

How effective was the OSS assessment program? We cannot say with certainty, but accepting our validity figures at face value we were forced to conclude that we were not very successful in predicting performance overseas. Were errors mainly in the assessment process, in the appraisal process, or in both? Again, we cannot say with certainty, but we do know that the appraisal process as carried out left very much to be desired. Our appraisal data were of four types:

1. *Overseas staff appraisal.* These were appraisals made by OSS assessment staff members on the basis of interviews with the immediate chief or commanding officer and, if possible, associates of our "graduates" overseas.

2. *Theater commander's appraisal.* From the spring of 1944, each returnee was reported on and his personality traits were rated by his immediate superior.

3. *Reassignment area appraisal.* From the fall of 1944, a center was set up (Area F) for the reassessment or reevaluation of personnel who had completed a tour of duty in Europe or the Middle East for reassignment in the Far East.

4. *Returnee appraisal.* Beginning in the summer of 1945, each returnee was asked to report on others known to him, rating their performance low, medium, or high.

When assessment job ratings were correlated with appraisal job ratings for Stations S and W, validity coefficients were all positive but disappointingly low, ranging from .08 to .53, depending upon the source of the appraisal data, as shown in Table 2-1. Much to our surprise, the one-day assessments at W appeared to have been more effective than the three and one-half day assessments at S.

Table 2-1   Correlations between S and W Assessment Job Ratings and Appraisal Ratings

Type of Appraisal	S Job Rating (Classes S-45 on)		W Job Rating (All Classes)	
	r	N	r	N
Overseas staff appraisal	.37[a]	88	.53[a]	83
Returnee appraisal	.19[a]	93	.21[a]	173
Theater commander's appraisal	.23	64	.15	158
Reassignment area appraisal	.08	53	.30[a]	178

[a]Cases in which correcting r for restricted sample made a significant difference; r given in each case is the corrected one.

Source: OSS Assessment Staff, 1948, p. 423.

We of the OSS staff are indebted to Jerry S. Wiggins (1973) who, making certain assumptions and using improved principles for estimating outcomes of predictions, worked over our data and came up with a more favorable picture than the one we had drawn.

His estimate is that at Station S, if we had used only random selection, our percent of correct decisions would have been 63%, but actually 77% were correct. Corresponding estimates for Station W are that by random selection, 66% would have been correct, but actually 84% were correct. This means that at S, assessment effected a 14% increase in correct decisions over random selection and at Station W, an 18% increment. Considering the crucial nature of the assignments, increments of 14% and 18% of correct decisions are not unimportant.

It is interesting to speculate as to why the briefer (one day) assessments of Station W were more accurate than the longer (three and one-half days) assessments of Station S. It may have been that the procedures used at W were more efficient than those employed at S, although this seems unlikely. Perhaps the staff at W was more competent than the one at S: more psychiatrists served on the staff at W and less use was made of junior assessors than at S. Differences in the populations assessed at the two stations could also have been a determining factor. Those assessed at W were more often high-echelon executives in the organization, women secretaries, and office workers, many of whom had already spent some time in the Washington headquarters, while those sent to S for assessment were either the more difficult cases who were already presenting more perplexing problems or were men destined for more hazardous duty under more stress and danger than would be experienced by the W assessees. Indeed, of those assessed at W, 74% received rear base assignments with only 15% serving behind enemy lines. In contrast, only 29% of Station S graduates received rear base assignments, while 43% operated behind enemy lines. Among possible explanations of the differential success rates of the two assessment centers, the one that seems least plausible is the notion that the staff at Station S suffered from the superabundance of information about their assessees, while the staff at Station W, with less information, had just what they needed and no more to make the kinds of decisions called for in the OSS assessment program. But the fact remains that we cannot say with certainty why the assessments at W surpassed those at S. Indeed, still today the optimal length of assessment center programs remains an unanswered question, one which should long since have been subjected to empirical investigation.

At the end of their report on the OSS program, *Assessment of Men*, the OSS staff made a number of recommendations which it was hoped would remedy some of the defects of assessment as practiced in the OSS.

These recommendations were published 28 years ago, 10 years before the first operational assessment center was established in American industry by Michigan Bell. They were formulated as definite rules, although we recognized that they were no more than a set of hypotheses to be tested in the planning and operating of subsequent assessment centers which it was our hope would be established.

These recommendations are reproduced below with the thought that the readers of this chapter may find it both interesting and informative as they review them to ask themselves such questions as: How many of these recommendations have been carried out in the setting up of assessment centers in business, in industry, in government, and in education? If adopted, have they proved helpful? And if they have been ignored, were they rejected for good reasons? Finally, what further recommendations should now be made for the improvement of assessment centers?

The recommendations as provided in *Assessment of Men* (1948) follow:

1. Select a staff of suitable size and competence, diversified in respect to age, sex, social status, temperament, major sentiments, and specific skills, but uniform in respect to a high degree of intellectual and emotional flexibility. (p. 473)
2. Before designing the program of assessment procedures, conduct a preliminary study of the jobs and job holders of the organization. (p. 475)

2.1. Make an adequate functional analysis of each of the roles for which candidates are to be assessed as well as an analysis of the environments in which each role must be fulfilled. (p. 476)

2.2. Obtain from members of the organization a list of attributes of personality which, in their opinion, contribute to success or failure in the performance of each role. (p. 476)

2.3. After a careful survey, analysis, and classification of the information obtained by these observations and interviews (Recommendations 2.1 and 2.2) make a tentative list of the personality determinants of success or failure in the performance of each role. These determinants will constitute the variables which, if possible, will be measured by the assessment procedures. (p. 477)

2.4. Define, in words that are intelligible to members of the organization, a tentative rating scale for each personality variable on the selected list as well as for the overall variable, Job Fitness. (p. 479)

2.5. Devise a satisfactory system for appraising the performance of members of the organization both at this time and later. (p. 481)

2.6. Obtain appraisals of a properly distributed sample of the present members of the organization. (p. 484)

2.7. Examine the defects of the appraisal system as revealed in practice (Recommendation 2.6), and correct these by revising, where necessary, the lists of variables, the definitions, the rating scales, or the other elements. (p. 484)

2.8. Obtain the figures necessary for a brief numerical statement of the personnel history of the organization over the last four or five years. (p. 485)

3. Design a program of assessment procedures which will reveal the strength of the selected variables; for assessing these variable set up scales which conform to the rating scales that were defined for the purpose of appraisal. (p. 485)

4. Build a conceptual scheme in terms of which formulations of different personalities can be made. (p. 488)

5. Set up an efficient punch-card system which will permit periodic statistical analyses of assessment findings. (p. 490)

6. Assess candidates for a long trial period without reporting ratings or decisions to the organization. (p. 491)

How far and in what directions the state of the art of assessment has moved beyond that which obtained in the assessment program of the OSS is spelled out in the other chapters of this book.

REFERENCES

Office of Strategic Services (OSS) Assessment Staff. *Assessment of men*. New York: Rinehart, 1948.

Smith, R. H. *OSS: The secret history of America's first central intelligence agency*. Berkeley, Calif.: University of California Press, 1972.

Wiggins, J. S. *Personality and prediction: Principles of personality assessment*. Reading, Mass.: Addison-Wesley, 1973.

CHAPTER 3

APPLICATION OF THE ASSESSMENT CENTER METHOD

William C. Byham

INTRODUCTION

The rapid growth and acceptance of the assessment center movement can be attributed to several key factors. These include:

— a process that had considerable scientific research and evaluation prior to widespread implementation;

— a number of organizations with a management climate that fostered research and development in the personnel selection area;

— a scientific and business community which facilitated communication of this idea; and

— the development of software items (manuals, techniques, simulations) which enabled smaller organizations to adapt the method.

Dr. Byham, of Development Dimensions, Inc., describes these as well as other pressures which spawned the assessment center movement. Not the least was the pressure for equal opportunity emerging in the 1960s and 1970s. He also describes a variety of programs currently used from a unique vantage point as consultant and researcher to many organizations using this method today.

* * *

One thousand or more organizations throughout the world are making use of the assessment center method. At least 30,000 individuals are assessed yearly in centers and both the number of centers and number of assessees are rapidly increasing each year. Assessment is most widely applied in business organizations in the United States and Canada but worldwide interest is growing with principal interest in Great Britain, South Africa, Brazil, Japan, and Australia. Government interest in United States and Canada has spurted recently, particularly stimulated by the desire to provide equal employment opportunity and an increased emphasis on career planning and management development for government executives.

FROM THE AT&T TREE

The growth of assessment centers post-1957 can be envisioned as a tree, with the trunk of the tree being AT&T's assessment center and assessment center research programs. Originally there were only a few branches of the tree—IBM, Standard Oil (Ohio), General Electric, Sears—the centers of these organizations resembled their forebearer quite closely. As the tree has matured and branches have sprung from branches, centers have increasingly departed from the AT&T mold, yet the stamp of AT&T's original centers can be seen in almost all centers operating today.

The early history of assessment center applications can also be viewed as an interesting case study in scientific communications. Early applications of the assessment center method resulted almost entirely from informal communications within two groups of industrial psychologists that meet informally twice a year to share research findings and techniques. One group is called the "Dearborn Group" and, believe it or not, the other is the "No Name Group." The representatives of these groups heard early reports on the assessment center method from Dr. Douglas Bray (the AT&T representative) and were informed of the AT&T validity studies years before they were published in the professional literature. Group members representing firms such as IBM, Sears, and General Electric were sufficiently impressed by the early findings to make initial applications in their organizations and start their own research programs. Early applications of assessment followed the AT&T methodology and many actually used AT&T exercises. But, from the beginning, organizations started adapting the materials and methods to their own needs. One of the first to do so was Standard Oil (Ohio), which applied its assessment center programs at higher levels of management and with a greater emphasis on training and placement. After a few years of experimentation, General Electric also began to apply the method at higher levels and changed its emphasis to obtaining training information as opposed to selection information.

The next spurt of growth of the assessment center method resulted from the first professional announcements of the AT&T validity studies and a description of the assessment center method written by Dr. Douglas Bray which appeared in a 1964 AMA book *The Personnel Job in a Changing World*. A small number of psychologists from organizations such as Cummins Engine, J. C. Penny, Olin, etc., became interested and developed centers, again often with the aid and assistance of AT&T representatives. At about this time, the first application of the AT&T pattern of assessment outside the United States came about when a representative of Shell Oil (Brazil) visited Michigan Bell Telephone Company and was impressed enough by the method to take it back to Brazil to make an almost identical application for selection of first-level supervision in Shell Oil. Caterpillar Tractor also made an early use of the technique outside of the United States when it developed an assessment procedure for its Belgian subsidiary. It was for selection of first-level supervision and closely paralleled the American center.

Even with 13 years behind the concept and more than half a dozen professional articles published about the method, only 12 American organizations operated assessment centers by 1969. But interest was growing. Two major conferences on the assessment center method were held in 1969 in New York City, one sponsored by the Executive Study Conference and one sponsored by the Division of Personnel Psychology of the New York State Psychological Association and the Metropolitan New York Association for Applied Psychology. In July-August 1970 the first general article (by William C. Byham) describing and evaluating the assessment center process was published in the *Harvard Business Review*. A number of consulting firms specializing in assessment centers were established. Previously, there were no consultants available with extensive assessment center experience and there were no commercially marketed exercises available. The availability of "packaged" exercises drastically cut the initial investment that an organization had to make to start an assessment center. Previously, organizations starting a center had to spend thousands of dollars on exercise development prior to the first pilot installation. All these events during the 1969-1971 period resulted in a tremendous upsurge in interest and application of the assessment center method. Since 1970, applications have been mounting rapidly.

PROFESSIONAL SHARING OF INFORMATION ON THE ASSESSMENT CENTER METHOD

As the number of organizations applying the assessment center method grew, a need arose for some formal sharing of information and techniques. The first such organization was made up of industrial psychologists who had a heavy research orientation. The group eventually formed an organization, which adopted the name "The Assessment Center Research Group." It meets twice a year. It was from this body that the idea for this book arose, and most of the authors are members of the group.

The need for a broader based group became evident as the number of organizations running assessment centers went into the hundreds. In response to that need, in 1973 Development Dimensions sponsored the first International Congress on the Assessment Center Method, which was held in Williamsburg, Virginia and which was attended by 60 individuals from five different countries. An international congress has been held each year since, with the number of people in attendance and the number of countries represented growing substantially each time, parallel with the growth of assessment throughout the world.

Another important development occurred in 1973 when the first issue of *Assessment and Development* was published by Development Dimensions. This biannual newsletter is specifically for practitioners of the assessment center method and is intended as a conduit for practical operational information, and as an early place for research and other studies to be published prior to publication in professional journals. The newsletter has uniquely served this purpose with almost all of the major innovations and reports of research since that time first appearing in *Assessment and Development*. It has become accepted as the major source of information on the assessment center method, with more than 8,000 copies distributed at each publication.

PRESSURE FOR EQUAL EMPLOYMENT OPPORTUNITY

Since the Civil Rights Act of 1964 was passed, and particularly since the landmark Supreme Court decision on personnel selection (Griggs vs. Duke Power), organizations have continually compared their selection program at all levels against the yardstick of job relevance. As Chief Justice Berger put it in his opinion in the Griggs vs. Duke Power case, "the touchstone of compliance is job relatedness." The first response of many organizations was to throw out nonjob-related selection devices such as many psychological tests. But they soon realized that something must be made available in their place, and many organizations turned to the assessment center method. The assessment center method is particularly appealing to organizations because studies have indicated that it is equally fair for any race or sex and because it lends itself to validation based on "content validity." Basing a selection instrument on content validity allows an organization to put it into operation more rapidly than procedures requiring other forms of validity. The typical pattern is for an organization to base its validity initially on the content of the assessment center and then to establish statistically related predictive validity after the program is in operation and data on the job performance of people who have been through the center are available.

The effect of EEOC pressure has not only been to encourage companies to use the assessment center method; it also has had a marked effect on the application of assessment. One particular result is the increasing use of the assessment center method for "early identification." This again was pioneered by AT&T, but has been taken up by many other companies wishing to find representatives of minority groups and women with talent, so they can push them up through the organization in order to meet affirmative action goals. An example of this program is covered in Chapter 11.

Another effect of EEOC pressure has been to change the method of input into assessment center programs. In the past, the most common way of obtaining people for assessment was through supervisory nomination. More recently, organizations have tended to use self-nomination in order to get around the possible biases of immediate supervisors and make the procedure more open to everyone.

NOTES ON NOMENCLATURE

A result of the increase in assessment center programs has been a proliferation of names for the programs and names for the various people involved in the programs.

Organizations have been particularly unhappy with the name "assessment center" because they feel that "assessment" is a harsh, evaluative term and the word "center" implies a place rather than a method. Therefore, only a very small minority of organizations call their programs assessment centers. Listed below are 20 common names of assessment programs. The particular name an organization chooses depends very often on the developmental orientation of its program and also the names that it has used previously to describe other programs in its organization.

Career Development Center	Career Development Program
Personal Development Center	Management Potential Identification
Management Diagnostic Program	Program
Management Identification Program	Human Resources Identification Program
Talent Identification Program	Personal Evaluation Laboratory
Supervisory Evaluation Program	Executive Development Procedure
Executive Assessment Index	Developmental Planning Workshop
Personal Development Program	Executive Skills Seminar
Executive Opportunities Analysis	Strategic Manager Development Program
Personnel Development Process	Supervisory Talent Evaluation/
Developmental Identification Laboratory	Identification Program

In this book we have adopted the name "assessor" for the person who observes the behavior of individuals as they go through behavioral exercises. This is probably the most common name applied, but also common are "observer," "staff," or "faculty."

The individuals that go through an assessment center we call "assessees" or "participants." "Participant" is the term most commonly used in programs.

SUPERVISORY ASSESSMENT

By far, the largest use of assessment centers is to identify supervisory potential. Bell Telephone Systems alone assess more than 10,000 individuals yearly at this level. The information obtained can be used to make promotional and/or training and development decisions. Concentration of assessment programs at the supervisory level results from organizations following the model established by Bell System Companies and from management's recognition of the difficulty of judging potential of individuals for first-level supervisory positions. Little opportunity is usually available to assess supervisory or managerial skills as a candidate performs a technical or sales job. The assessment center that allows an organization to project how a candidate would perform in a supervisory position before being appointed can make a tremendous contribution. Another reason for the popularity of supervisory assessment is the large number of promotional decisions made at this level in organizations. The cost of assessment can be spread over more people and the likelihood that enough candidates for assessment can be found to make assessment efficient is increased. Assessors are also easier to find for supervisory level assessment, and many organizations find it easier to install experimental assessment programs at lower levels because it requires less involvement of higher management. A recent stimulus to supervisory assessment has come from EEOC pressure on organizations to improve their selection system in those positions.

Assessment for first-level supervision varies greatly between organizations, because the requirements and responsibilities of first-level supervisors vary greatly between organizations. There is a tremendous difference between the job scope and responsibilities of a closely supervised assemblyline foreman and a manager of a small retail store, or between the head of an offshore oil well drilling operation and a sales manager of a highly sophisticated sales force. Yet, they are all first-level supervisors. Also falling in this broad class are airline pilots, newspaper editors, service station operators, and police sergeants. The great diversity of supervisory positions calls for unique assessment centers and the reader should be cautious when generalizing from one supervisory program to another.

MIDDLE MANAGEMENT ASSESSMENT

Experiencing the greatest growth in number of applications is assessment for middle management positions. This growth comes from a broadening of assessment applications in organizations that have previously applied the method at lower levels and from many organizations making initial applications at the middle management level. While middle management assessment can never compare to supervisory assessment in numbers of individuals assessed or number of centers conducted, consultants' records of 1976 assessment center installations indicate that 40% of "new starts" of assessment centers are at the middle management level. Because of the narrowing of the management pyramid, such centers are conducted less frequently in an organization than lower level centers and therefore process fewer people.

The reason for the interest in middle management assessment seems to come from two opposite circumstances. Some organizations have an excess of middle managers due to computerization and to the institution of job enrichment programs at lower management levels, making certain middle management levels redundant. On the other hand, a larger number of organizations are experiencing growth coupled with the dip in the population curve caused by a suppressed birthrate during the Depression. The Depression babies would now be in the age group from which middle managers are usually drawn.

By far the most important reason for the steady increase in middle management applications is the increasing recognition of assessment as a diagnostic technique to guide training and development activities. The original AT&T, IBM, and Sears' applications of assessment involved training in only the most minor way. Training suggestions from assessors were passed on in reports, but basically the centers were designed to make go, no-go decisions. Following the lead of Standard Oil (Ohio) and General Electric, organizations increasingly have recognized the potential advantages of getting a fix on their middle managers' strengths and weaknesses. With this information, the individual can be strengthened in the performance of his or her present job and a systematic, organized training and developmental program can be designed to prepare him or her for future responsibilities.

Middle management assessment centers have much in common. The dimensions are usually quite similar, as are the exercises. Unlike assessment at the first level, which may be for a highly specific foreman's or supervisor's position, middle management assessment typically aims at multiple middle management jobs. Because a particular job cannot be defined, the organization settles on general managerial dimensions typical of the level. Job level, not a specific job, is the aim of assessment.

HIGHER MANAGEMENT ASSESSMENT

To date, applications of assessment techniques for top management positions (vice presidents or general managers) are relatively rare although increasing in popularity. As with many personnel activities, most assessment experts suggest starting assessment at the top of an organization if possible, and this advice is increasingly being followed. Obviously, selection and development decisions at higher level management are the most crucial to the success of an organization. Individuals have more control over profits and greater responsibilities. Mistakes at this level can make a business fail.

An obvious problem of higher management assessment is finding people to do the assessment. This is probably the greatest deterrent to its use. Some organizations, such as the Huyck Corporation, have used the president, executive vice president, and general managers as assessors for the first round of assessment centers. The State of Wisconsin was able to obtain the services of the Secretaries of the various State Departments in its initial assessments. The usual procedure is to assess at the highest level possible, then, immediately after assessment, train the assessees to be assessors so that they can assess the next lower level. That level is then trained to be assessors, and so the assessment procedure works its way down in the organization until it reaches the level where it will be generally applied in the future. An increasing number of organizations use outside experts as assessors for top-level positions. Higher management assessment centers are quite similar, reflecting the need for "general" management skills in high-level positions.

MANAGEMENT TRAINEE SELECTION

A relatively new application of the assessment center method is to aid in the selection of college students to be management trainees. It has been found by AT&T and Sears research that the average performance of trainees can be raised and turnover decreased by making such applications.

Assessment centers for management trainee selection usually take less than a day to administer and are the second step in the selection process—after the student has been secured by a college recruiter.

SALES POTENTIAL ASSESSMENT

As with most other applications of the assessment center method, AT&T pioneered the use of assessment centers to select salesmen. In AT&T centers, prospective "communications consultants" from within and without the organization are put through a one-day center designed to bring out dimensions of sales success. In validation studies comparing assessment center prediction with sales results, the method was shown to be highly accurate.

Only a few other organizations, such as Wickes and Johnson Wax, have followed up on the AT&T example by developing a full-blown sales assessment procedure where a number of applications are processed each week. More organizations, such as Hoffman-LaRoche, Pitney Bowes, Eastern Airlines, and Edgars Stores, Ltd., have used assessment procedures as part of an expanded interview process. In these applications, an applicant is put through several assessment exercises on an individual basis while observed by different executives.

TECHNICAL ASSESSMENT

A major facet of AT&T's emphasis on early identification of employee potential for better maximization of the work force is the development of a series of early identification programs, including the sales and managerial programs described above. Another part of the program attempts to identify engineering skills.

EDUCATIONAL ASSESSMENT

By 1976, five colleges and universities were using the assessment center method as part of their regular curriculum. First to apply assessment was the Graduate School of Business at Stanford University, which developed an assessment program for career counseling of second-year business students. Other business schools that are using the method for counseling are Brigham Young University and Baylor University.

A unique application of assessment methodology was developed at Alverno College in Milwaukee, Wisconsin, which uses assessment center techniques for its criterion-referenced educational program. Rather than taking traditional kinds of tests, students at Alverno must pass competency examinations, many of which are based on the assessment center method.

Another unusual application of assessment is by Nova University in Florida, which uses the assessment center as a mid-career evaluation and counseling tool for its PhD program in educational administration. This is particularly unique in that its program is an off-campus program operated in various cities throughout the United States. The data for assessment are collected by a single individual with television equipment who administers the material and collects the televised responses of the group and individual exercises. Assessors in Boston analyze the videotape and written responses to reach their decisions.

NONMANAGEMENT ASSESSMENT

Three organizations—Proctor & Gamble, Rohm and Haas, and the Tennessee Valley Authority—have applied selected assessment techniques to developing work teams in newly opened plants. Obviously, the dimensions and the exercises differ considerably from those that usually are used during assessment. The organizations are typically not looking for a highly controlled assemblyline worker. Rather, they seek an independent worker—yet one that must work with others as a member of a team. This is the kind of worker for whom many highly automated plants are designed.

Assessment applications for selection have much similarity to the "work sample" method of employee selection which is gaining popularity in industry and government. To the extent that the simulation is a sample of what will be required on the job and is administered and evaluated consistently and fairly, the technique is job related and would seem to meet government requirements in this area. Whether the methodology is called "assessment center" or "work sample" seems to be dependent on the exercises used. The intent is exactly the same. Organizations that use exercises similar to those used in assessment centers, such as leaderless group discussions, interview simulations, and analysis problems, tend to call their programs "assessment centers."

GOVERNMENT ASSESSMENT

The first government center to capitalize on AT&T's assessment research and to utilize exercises similar to those pioneered by AT&T was the Internal Revenue Service, which started an assessment center program in 1968. The original program was to identify supervisory potential. A second application within the Service in 1969 identified potential for a special high-level executive development program. The Federal Aeronautics Administration followed in 1969 with an assessment center to assess supervisory potential. The first Canadian Government application of the method occurred in 1970 to aid in the identification and selection of candidates for a first-line management development and training program. In 1972, a larger, more sophisticated center, aimed at the identification of senior executive potential, was inaugurated.

Assessment solely for the purpose of developmental counseling was first tried in 1973 by the United States Social Security Administration in a program that assessed upper middle managers as they began an 18-month executive development program. The purpose of the assessment center was to make individuals aware of their developmental needs so that they could structure self-development programs and experiences during their 18 months away from their jobs. No members of higher management saw the report. This application was also a situation where outside "experts" were used as assessors.

Also in 1973, the United States Army and the United States Air Force both began pilot applications of the technique. Late in 1973, the Office of Management and the Budget developed a pilot program to do for all federal agencies what the Internal Revenue Service program was doing within its own organization—to help identify people for intensive, high-level management development programs. The first program conducted by the Civil Service Administration for the Office of Management and the Budget evaluated 150 key executives throughout government for higher management positions.

By 1975, most major government departments were making some application of assessment—usually for selection, but some for career planning. In 1975 the Civil Service Commission contracted for the development of the first set of standard government exercises to be used for evaluating management trainees in a wide number of government departments.

State government got its first taste of assessment in 1972 when the State of Illinois made an initial try at assessing for first-level supervision. This was very much an experimental program and in the first two years of operation only 50 people were assessed. The first major application within state government occurred in the State of Wisconsin which replaced psychological tests with assessment procedures for determination of advancement into high-level civil service positions. In a two-day center, applicants for the "Career Executive Level" of state government were assessed on 18 dimensions by higher level state executives. The program started with appointed officials assessing the highest civil service level, and the program has worked its way down through all the incumbents in the top four levels of government (Career Executive Levels). They are now assessing 12 people every 10 days in the middle management ranks. The Quebec Police Department developed an assessment program, and the Province of Manitoba started a supervisory level assessment program in late 1973.

The first application of the assessment center method within city governments was in police and fire departments. The New York City Police Department was the first to apply assessment. Policemen are assessed for potential for top-level management positions. Applications in other cities followed and now cities such as St. Louis, Kansas City, Rochester, and Richmond use the method to aid in promotion with their police and/or fire departments.

NONPROFIT ORGANIZATION ASSESSMENT

While some nonprofit organizations, such as Junior Achievement, Inc., have made sporadic applications of the assessment center technique, the first large-scale application was made by Blue Cross of Illinois, which developed an extensive assessment procedure aimed at identifying potential for first-level supervision. This was followed by other Blue Cross Organizations, and now there are nine programs in operation.

An unusual application is the assessment program established by Forty-Plus of Toronto. They offer assessment as a service to members wishing insight into their managerial strengths and weaknesses.

CENTERS OUTSIDE THE UNITED STATES

The growth of assessment in Canada has paralleled that of the United States, and it would seem that the penetration of the method in Canadian industry approximates its penetration in the United States. Early users of the assessment center method in Canada were Northern Electric Company (first-level supervision), Canadian Kodak Ltd. (first-level supervision), Steinberg's Ltd. (store managers), British Columbia Telephone Company (first-level supervision), and British Columbia Hydro and Power Authority (first-level supervision).

Outside the United States and Canada, assessment has had a rather spotty application, which seems to be more related to the availability of consultants than any other factor. Largely because United States' consultants were brought to South Africa, many of the largest organizations there are using assessment techniques with some of the strongest total organizational commitment to assessment. Assessment is being applied to all levels in organizations, often with a heavy developmental emphasis.

Shell continues to operate its assessment program in Brazil for first-level supervision. In addition, some government organizations have adopted the method.

In Asia, Japan has the only operating assessment centers. They place more value on the positive training effects for the managers trained as assessors than they do on the assessment center results themselves.

Mexico has only one operating center in Grupo Cydsa, but there is much interest.

Australia has three centers (Qantas Airlines, Hill Samuel Insurance & Shippings Holdings Ltd., and Ingham's Enterprises Pty. Ltd.).

In European countries, a small number of organizations have centers, including Eli Lilly (Germany), Mobil Europe, Inc., Timex, Mont Edison (Italy), the British Post Office Corporation, and a number of Scandinavian companies.

This does not include the early users of assessment centers such as the Civil Service Commission of England.

IBM is the major international user of assessment. It operates centers in nine countries. Generally, these centers are quite similar, with the material translated and adapted for the local country. IBM has conducted multinational research into the impact of its centers and has received much encouragement from the results.

CHAPTER 4

ISSUES IN ESTABLISHING AN ASSESSMENT CENTER *

Thomas A. Jeswald

INTRODUCTION

Putting the cart before the horse is often the sequence by which many new programs in the personnel world are implemented. This situation often results from a lack of significant preparation for change on the part of an organization. As pointed out in this chapter, simply purchasing an assessment center program intact from a vendor does little to professionalize the sponsoring organization.

As with any popular technique, there are many consultants and "experts" who jump on the bandwagon. The message to the reader of this chapter is clear—let the buyer beware. There are many critical steps in implementing an assessment center strategy.

In this chapter, Dr. Jeswald pulls together many of the critical issues each organization must face *prior* to starting a center. These include whom to assess, the purpose of the center, who sees the results, how are they communicated, and so forth. The use of consultants in establishing centers is also discussed. The reader is encouraged to review the "Standards and Ethical Considerations" found in the Appendix while reading this chapter.

An issue raised in this chapter, which is repeated in a number of other sections in this book, is the nature of the characteristics or dimensions of performance assessed. There are, as we shall see, considerable similarities in the lists of assessment dimensions used by different

---

*This chapter was prepared while the author was associated with the Ford Motor Company.

companies. This apparent similarity, Dr. Jeswald notes, should not be taken as a license to adapt popular dimensions as universal examples. Rather, the process of identifying these characteristics is what is important. This process requires analysis of the behaviors of managers to establish the job relatedness of specific dimensions. A number of excellent techniques are described in this chapter.

Again the message is clear—the assessment center process should be designed to be an integral part of the organization, not simply a fad which is "purchased." Ownership requires development. The fact that there are so many different assessment applications testifies to the robustness of the technique in adapting it to fit an organization's needs. This, as the present chapter so aptly points out, requires considerable care and effort before one attaches the horse to the cart.

* * *

This chapter concerns the management decision to implement an assessment center. Our purpose is to present the major questions that must be answered and the decisions that must be made in planning and implementing a center.

When a new assessment center is being planned, some decisions may seem distant. For example, consider the questions of how quickly participants will receive assessment results and what type of information will be given to them concerning their performance and career prospects. Addressing these questions is sometimes delayed by the planners until after the first session of the center is held. The consequences of this delay may be confusion and disappointment among the participants. Failing to tell participants how long they must wait for results creates not only anxiety, but a suspicion that management is not in control of the process. Likewise, if they expect to receive detailed performance information or career plans and hear only generalities, dissatisfaction is likely to result.

There is an important need for complete prior planning of nearly every aspect of an assessment center, even if it is probable that some aspects will require changes after initial experience. Almost all the problems that organizations have encountered applying the method could have been avoided with more detailed planning. A center generally is given high visibility among employees, especially those with potential for advancement. It is fitting that as much care and thoroughness be exercised in its development as with compensation systems or organization design.

OBJECTIVES OF ASSESSMENT CENTERS

The most fundamental decision about the establishment of an assessment center concerns its objectives. These will determine the center's procedures, expense, and impact on the organization. The objectives can be categorized as personnel selection, individual development, and appraisal of management potential. Each of these objectives addresses a different management need. We will examine them in turn.

Personnel Selection

Probably the most common objective of assessment centers in operation today is to select personnel to fill immediate and specific position openings. Candidates for these openings are drawn from the organization's normal sources, including new applicants as well as present employees in lower level jobs. An example of this is the Foreman Assessment Center (FAC) developed by the Chassis Division of Ford Motor Company. The FAC is operated at irregular intervals, as the number of openings for new production foremen reaches a particular level. Participants in the FAC come from three distinct sources: new college graduate recruits with an interest in manufacturing supervision, present hourly paid employees, and present salaried nonsupervisory employees. Some companies operating centers of this type intentionally form assessment groups of participants from diverse employment backgrounds. This may lessen effects of acquaintance with participants and permits different values and viewpoints to be represented.

An assessment center used for selection is distinguishable by its primary end product—a decision to select or not select each participant for a specific position. A number of additional outcomes may result, but these are less relevant to the organization's expressed need. For example, the center performance of participants may be individually reviewed with them, and some developmental actions may be suggested. Also, placement possibilities other than the target assessment job may be suggested by the assessors observing participants' behavior. The effectiveness of this type of center, however, must be judged in terms of its validity as a selection system.

Considerable evidence exists for the validity of assessment centers as an aid in selection decisions. Validity, demonstrated in a wide variety of organizations, is certainly an important reason for the growing use of assessment centers. But, regardless of the published statistical validities, there are several factors which must be considered to determine whether an assessment center for personnel selection will meet the organization's needs. These include:

1. *Accession rate.* Are there enough position vacancies to justify the development of a center, or any new selection system?
2. *Base rate of job success.* Is the proportion of "successful" performers already so high that a center could not select them more accurately?
3. *Selection ratio.* Will the number of position vacancies, compared to the number of applicants, allow management to accept only the best qualified?

These factors traditionally have been considered in determining the utility of a personnel selection system. They are still relevant in evaluating the potential gain from adopting an assessment center.

Individual Development

A clear trend in the field of supervisory and management training over the past decade has been the increasing use of behavioral science concepts and techniques. It is not surprising to find that assessment centers have been adapted to serve the objective of individual development. Specialists in training and development have been quick to realize the value of assessment information in their work.

With increasing frequency, organizations are designing assessment centers with at least a secondary objective of facilitating development of the assessed managers' skills. A few centers are conducted in which development takes precedence over selection and some are conducted solely for development, such as the program conducted for the Social Security Administration. Participants in this center are selected for a special rotational development program on the basis of ratings of past performance. They are drawn from each of the various bureaus which comprise the Administration. The assessment center is conducted as the first step of the development program. Since they already have been identified as possessing potential, anxiety about the program is not high. The program includes three days of exercises and a full day of oral performance feedback. A written report also is prepared and is given to each participant; the report suggests self-developmental actions. Career development specialists also examine the report to determine what kind of developmental assistance on the organization's part might be appropriate.

Chapter 11 includes additional information about the role of assessment centers in career development systems.

Appraisal of Management Potential

A third objective for which assessment centers might be used concerns the identification of individuals for longer term progression into middle and upper management. Many organizations pursue this objective through supervisor ratings of "potential" based upon present job performance. Such ratings will be valid if several conditions are present—e.g., raters use uniform standards and skills required in higher level positions are substantially the same as those required of ratees in their present positions. Furthermore, the prediction of potential requires the consideration of nonperformance factors such as age, education, and extent of developmental opportunities available. Two individuals, one age 25 and the other 55, might perform the same job equally well; realistically, however, their potentials may differ because of age alone.

Because "potential" is such an elusive concept, some organizations have adapted the assessment center to augment management judgments. Ford Parts Division's Management Career Planning Center (MCPC) was created for this purpose. In the MCPC, the skills assessed are based on analyses of the requirements of two executive positions—Parts Distribution Center Manager and District Sales Manager. These target jobs are several levels above the MCPC participants, who generally are first- or second-level supervisors or staff specialists. The intent is not to identify any participant for immediate promotion to one of these managerial jobs, but rather to give individuals the opportunity to display their abilities to deal with higher level management problems. This becomes input to the organization's estimate of an individual's "potential." Although the assessment information may be used in making some immediate promotional decisions, it is more likely to be used to plan developmental experiences for the participants, such as special projects or rotational assignments. Ultimately, promotability to executive positions will depend not on MCPC performance, but on actions taken by participants to strengthen weaknesses identified during the MCPC and level of performance demonstrated in various developmental assignments.

In a sense, the appraisal of management potential combines the objectives of personnel selection and individual development. This type of assessment center permits the fullest use of the information collected. In the case where only selection is of concern, an absence of performance feedback to the participants, beyond a "pass or fail" judgment, deprives them of the basis for meaningful self-improvement. A purely development-oriented center deprives the organization of unique and probably valid evaluative information. These points, however, should not blind one to the fact that each objective meets a different management need, and choice of an objective should be based on management priorities.

Table 4-1 Differences in Assessment Center Design According to Assessment Objective

Aspects of the Center Design	Objective of Assessment		
	Selection	Development	Appraisal of Potential
Basis for selecting target job	Immediate need for qualified personnel	Immediate need to upgrade skills or broaden experiences of present managers or those identified as possessing "potential"	Long-term need to identify and develop a pool of qualified management personnel
Eligibility for participation	Those qualified by experience or education for a specific position	Those identified as having skills deficiencies or narrow experience	Those performing well on supervisory or staff specialist jobs
Nature of the skills assessed	Specific: limited to skills critical for performance of the target job	May be specific or general	Generalizable to a family of management jobs
Time required for assessment	Minimum necessary to stimulate critical tasks and maintain reliability of measurement	Minimum necessary to simulate critical tasks, provide immediate feedback and/or counseling	Minimum necessary to simulate critical tasks, provide immediate feedback and/or counseling
Difficulty level of assessment exercises	No more difficult than the most difficult tasks required in the target job	Various levels of difficulty, so that participants with different degrees of competence can be challenged	Various levels of difficulty, so that participants with different degrees of competence can be identified

Type of decision reached	Select or reject for the target job	Need for other developmental experiences	Need for developmental experiences, eligibility for future promotions
Extent of feedback given	Limited	Detailed: may include peer and self-evaluations	Detailed: may include peer evaluations; emphasizes goal setting with the supervisor, career planning, and self-development
Reports generated	Brief: retained by the personnel office	Detailed: retained by the participant and training specialists	Detailed: retained by the participant and the personnel office
Follow-up research required	1. Validation, as required by government regulations 2. Continuous monitoring of reliability 3. Development of new exercises and alternate forms	None: measurement of behavior change is highly desirable	1. Validation, as required by government regulations 2. Continuous monitoring of reliability 3. Development of new exercises and alternative forms 4. Measurement of behavior change

OBJECTIVES AND ASSESSMENT CENTER DESIGN

The choice of an objective for an assessment center implies a number of decisions about the center's design. There is no universal agreement among professionals as to how and which specific parameters are determined by each of the objectives. The viewpoint of the author is represented in Table 4-1.

If personnel selection is the objective, the principles which should guide the design of the center are the same as those used in the development of other psychological selection instruments such as selection tests. For example, to establish the content validity of the center, exercises must be chosen or created on the basis of job analyses. The difficulty level of exercises should be uniform and equal to the difficulty of tasks that are critical to effective performance on the target job. This approach gives assessors the best opportunity to differentiate between participants who can and cannot perform adequately.

Follow-up research is an important aspect of personnel selection systems. No matter how well an instrument of prediction may have been researched during its development, periodic evaluations of its effectiveness must be made. At a minimum, compliance with federal guidelines for selection procedures must be periodically examined. Other research needed to ensure the quality of the assessment center may involve the monitoring of assessor reliability (agreement) and the development of new exercises to reflect changes in the nature of the target job.

In the case where individual development is the greater concern of the organization, the center design should be consistent with a different set of principles—those dealing with the conditions of human learning. As Table 4-1 indicates, *feedback of performance information* to participants is an extremely important principle which must be considered. Videotaping participants is an effective means of allowing participants to examine their various styles of problem solving, communicating, etc. Video observation is an effective supplement to formal assessment center feedback.

The *transfer of knowledge* acquired in the center to on-the-job situations is facilitated simply because the exercises are simulations of the job and the discussion of the behavior in entire exercises is extremely meaningful to participants. Exercises used in the center need not be abstract; they may deal directly with real problems facing management. Participants who develop outstanding solutions in such exercises might be given the opportunity to present the solution to higher management, or perhaps to be assigned to work on the problem on a full-time basis.

An assessment center used to appraise management potential combines design features from both other types. If assessment reports are used to make promotional decisions, the center is subject to the same governmental regulations which apply to the pure selection situation. The same is true if the center is considered to be only one part of a system of management development; all parts of the system must conform to the regulations.

Most of the measurement issues related to appraisal of potential would be dealt with in a manner similar to the personnel selection case. Two exceptions are worthy of mention. If potential is being appraised for higher management jobs, the center probably should simulate certain critical tasks which are common to a family of managerial jobs. Therefore, the skills assessed must be derived from the analysis of a cluster of jobs, and must generalize to all of them. The second point concerns the difficulty level of exercises. This type of center should be able to differentiate among candidates at several levels of competence. This can be accomplished by including various exercises (or parts of exercises) requiring low, intermediate, and unusually high degrees of competence.

STEPS IN IMPLEMENTING AN ASSESSMENT CENTER

There are numerous decisions to be made in the course of establishing an assessment center, but none of these is as far reaching as the decision concerning objectives. Secondary decisions, however, do play an important part in the quality and accuracy of the assessment center findings. The implementation steps described in this section are, wherever possible, defined in terms of the procedural and design alternatives available. The sequence of steps presented is an approximation; a number of them may be carried out simultaneously.

Developing an Implementation Strategy

Immediately after the program's objectives have been set, a strategy must be developed for creating all the necessary conditions for the organization's acceptance and effective use of the program. The following kinds of questions might be addressed in order to fix the elements of a strategy:

1. Does management have any covert objectives for the center (e.g., stimulating mobility between organizational units or getting rid of "deadwood")? How important will these factors be to management in judging the success of the center?
2. Which personnel systems (e.g., performance appraisal or management training) will require change upon introduction of the center? How extensive are the required changes, and how great will be the resistance to change?
3. Which staff departments must be consulted in order to obtain needed approval?
4. Which personnel specialists (e.g., training, manpower planning) should be

involved in the planning of the center? What prior orientation to the concept should be arranged for these individuals?

5. Which organizational units and individual managers might be willing to risk involvement in the center while it is still "experimental"?

6. Should the center be administered internally or through a consultant service? What image of the center will develop among employees in either case?

7. What are the major evaluation points of the program? When will further budget commitments be made?

These questions demand serious thought by those charged with the implementation of an assessment center.

In most cases, a phased implementation strategy is desirable. That is, the center is not made operational immediately, but assesses only a limited number of individuals until some evaluation is conducted. This allows managers to review and react to the program while changes in the center's design can still be made inexpensively. Also, if the center is administered internally, it permits the staff to gain experience and experiment with alternative administrative procedures prior to coping with a high volume of assessees.

Establishing Roles in the Assessment Center

In most organizations, implementation of an assessment center is far too complex to occupy only one person. A steering committee or task force should be established to share the workload. This group should be broadly based, drawing representatives from key staff and line functions. The role of the task force may end at the time of conduct of the first center, or, if the strategy calls for it, the role may extend even beyond the period of evaluation. In the Chassis Division of Ford, such a task force is responsible for monitoring the quality of the Foreman Assessment Center and ensuring that assessment information is properly used.

An early decision confronting the task force is likely to be whether, or how extensively, to use external consulting services in the center. Professional expertise is available to carry out any or all of the tasks associated with the center. Most organizations that operate assessment centers have made at least some limited use of expert consultants, even though competent psychologists may have been in their employ. The technology of assessment centers has become specialized to the point that many organizational psychologists have found it inefficient to attempt to launch a center without the benefit of personal experience. Thus, in most cases, it is a question of which services should be purchased and for what period of time.

An advantage of consultant involvement in the development of a center lies in the considerable time saved in bringing it from the idea stage to the conduct of the first session. A disadvantage is that the consultant is likely to impose on the organization his own preferences for certain measurement and administrative procedures. These may or may not be appropriate for the organization. Ultimately, the decision to use consultant services should hinge on the availability of qualified internal psychologists and the immediacy of management's need to develop the center.

The following are the major functions that can be performed effectively by a consultant:

1. *Orientation of managers.* The image of the consultant as an expert in his field is often helpful in selling the idea of assessment to managers. A joint presentation by the consultant and internal personnel officers can be quite effective. Proposing the establishment of an assessment center may imply criticism of present selection or development systems. For this reason, a consultant can be employed to present certain information which cannot be tactfully presented by internal staff.

2. *Development of assessment dimensions and exercises.* Few organizations have attempted to analyze managerial jobs in the manner described later in this chapter. A consultant skilled in these techniques can speed the collection of this information through some minimal guidance of internal personnel. Following this step, the consultant's experience can be quite valuable in translating job requirements into measurable dimensions and in identifying appropriate types of exercises.

3. *Assessor training.* In many organizations, assessors are trained only a few times per year. In these cases, employing a consultant as a trainer may be more efficient than using internal personnel. The consultant could be expected to provide training on rather short notice and to use high quality training materials and procedures.

4. *Administration.* In some instances, the entire task of ongoing administration of the assessment center is performed by a consultant. While the decision to make use of this type of service might be made on budgetary grounds alone, there are other possible reasons why this arrangement may be appealing. The major reason is the degree of confidentiality that can be maintained. If the consultant conducts all center activities, counsels participants, and keep all records, the chances of the assessment information being abused can be reduced substantially.

5. *Audit.* If an assessment center has been in existence for more than two years, an audit of procedures can be extremely valuable. Like other administrative systems, an assessment center can become routinized and perhaps carelessly handled. A thorough critique of the center might be done jointly by a consultant and internal personnel. Preferably, most of these individuals would have been involved in the establishment of the center. The audit might be limited to the observation of center processes

and records or include research concerning validity of selection decisions, extent of assessor rating agreement, etc.

As most implementation strategies unfold, a key role is played by the line organization (defined here as the unit serviced by the assessment center). In the planning phase, line managers can provide important information needed to establish objectives, the dimensions to be assessed, and administrative procedures. Through discussions of the experiences of these managers, the assessment center planners can gain a better understanding of the present and future demands upon management. There undoubtedly will be differences of opinion among managers as to how effective performance in the target job is defined. It is the task of the planners to listen and seek out the common thread that will lead to effective assessment.

When the center becomes operational, line managers form the pool from which assessors are drawn. For them to accept the dimensions used and the job relatedness of the exercises, they must be involved in program planning.

The staff that administers the center, usually the personnel function, has the responsibility for maintaining the system and ensuring consistency of application. This is distinguished from the personnel research role of evaluation, validation, refinement, and extension of the concept to other target jobs. Maintenance can normally be carried on by individuals with personnel administration experience, but research is more properly the domain of the organizational psychologist.

Defining Assessment Dimensions

The process of defining the dimensions of performance to be assessed has received insufficient attention by practitioners. The writers of some popular articles on assessment centers seem to take the position that there is general agreement as to the tasks managers perform in their jobs and the skills required to perform effectively. If this were true, one would establish assessment dimensions by merely adopting a standardized list of skills.

Literature reviews by Campbell, Dunnette, Lawler, and Weick (1970) and Prien and Ronan (1971) suggest that it is fallacious to assume the validity of generalized assessment dimensions. In brief, the available research evidence leads to the following conclusions:

1. Managers' jobs differ greatly from one another, both in substance and mode of operation.
2. There is little agreement between the job duties reported by incumbent supervisors and their duties as seen by their superiors.
3. Upper level management positions can be distinguished from middle and

lower levels in terms of the amount of decision making and severity of personal demands of the job.

4. The relation between job duties and individual behavior is an important consideration, especially in analyzing higher level management jobs. Different management styles can and do lead to identical results.

In light of this information alone, one would have difficulty in taking assessment dimensions completely for granted. There is, however, an additional point to be made, related to governmental regulations affecting selection systems. Enneis (1970) has been critical of the "chairman-of-the-board" syndrome, which has led some employers to discriminate against minorities. This syndrome refers to the idea that each individual hired must be sufficiently competent to perform the complex work of high-level managers. The implication of the various governmental guidelines for selection procedures is that assessment centers used for selection must generally be job related. The use of jobs two, three, or more levels above candidates or the target for a *selection* assessment center can only be justified if internal promotion is the only method of filling the jobs and if a significant number of people progress to the higher level.

The dimensions assessed must represent skills required on the target job. A responsible and efficient approach to implementing a center must include some effort to analyze and understand the target job.

TECHNIQUES OF JOB ANALYSIS

There are several analytic techniques that have been found useful in the development of assessment dimensions. As with other approaches to behavioral measurement, the results of job analyses are superior when more than one technique is used to study the same behavior.

Byham (1970) suggests that assessment dimensions be derived from discussions among key managers familiar with the target jobs. These may take the form of either group interviews or "brainstorming" sessions. During these sessions, examples of behaviors associated with successful or unsuccessful job performance are brought out with detailed behavioral definitions. The consultant then distills the dimensions underlying the behaviors and comes up with a suggested list of dimensions. The draft dimensions are put in the form of a questionnaire and reviewed by appropriate managers above the target level, or they can be refined and prioritized. This procedure is a variant of the "technical conference" approach to task analysis.

The effectiveness of the conference technique depends both on the knowledge of the participants and skills of the discussion leader. The conferees should be selected to include not only the supervisors of the target job, but also various typical interfacing personnel. For example, if the target job is that of sales manager, the conference might involve representatives of the marketing and finance organizations. Some senior participants should be chosen to give the group an advantage of historical perspective on the target job. Also, some participants must be sufficiently familiar with future technology and business prospects to offer some guidance with regard to future job demands. The task of the discussion leader is to draw out examples of behavior—not favorite lists of "boy scout" characteristics.

The conference technique is especially useful where a single target job can be rather narrowly defined before any analysis takes place. Otherwise, an entire series of conferences is necessary for each target job. This would offset a major advantage of the conference technique—its speed.

Another technique that has been used frequently is the mail survey. The assessment center designer may either assemble a series of questions into a multiple choice or checklist instrument or use a standardized form such as the Executive Position Description Questionnaire (EPDQ). The respondents to the survey would be the same categories of personnel represented in a conference. However, the written format allows many more individuals to contribute. Thus, several jobs may be examined simultaneously, with a rather small expenditure of management time. In this connection, Slivinski and Desbiens (1970) have demonstrated the value of the EPDQ for locating similar patterns of job dimensions within diverse occupational groups.

A significant drawback to using job description surveys alone is the inability to probe for additional information and clarify conflicting ideas. For these reasons, it is often advisable to supplement survey data with some interviews or a limited conference.

The critical incident technique (Flanagan, 1954), although it ranks as a distinct analytic tool, may be present in concept in both the conference and survey approaches. That is, respondents in each of these cases may be asked to recount the details of incidents of notably poor or superior performance of target job incumbents. A major difference between Flanagan's procedure and these adaptations lies in the time of recording. The original procedure calls for observers to record the incidents as they occur. The advantage of this over the various adaptations is that the observers' logs are not as subject to selective memory effects.

The critical incident approach has much to offer the designer of assessment centers. The collection of incidents may require an extended period of time—perhaps three to six months—but this very fact may considerably improve the quality of the data. This could be especially important if relatively little is initially known about the target job. The rich behavioral data may also be used as a basis for designing simulations. Scenarios of some incidents may be directly converted to case studies or in-basket items. Finally, the incidents may suggest criteria against which the center may be validated.

FROM JOB REQUIREMENTS TO ASSESSMENT DIMENSIONS

Once the requirements of the target job are established, they must be evaluated and screened in order to derive a final set of assessment dimensions. The following are criteria which might be used in the screening process:

1. The assessment dimensions should be defined in behavioral terms. For example, "Oral Communication Skills" can be defined in terms of eye contact, enunciation, voice modulation, gestures, etc. Certain other concepts, such as "Character" or "Maturity," may be too vague to permit reliable observation.
2. The assessment dimensions should exclude skills which can be more easily or economically observed outside of a simulation context. This restriction would generally eliminate two types of job requirements: sophisticated technical or academic abilities and mundane background or personal characteristics. Competence in financial analysis or differential calculus can normally be determined while candidates are performing nonsupervisory jobs; in some occupational areas, passing a licensing examination may serve the purpose. Many important background factors can be evaluated through a biographical information blank (e.g., physical handicaps, stress tolerance, or willingness to relocate). In essence, the final dimensions should reflect the management skills which candidates have very limited opportunities to exercise on their present jobs.
3. Since the assessment center may have to co-exist with a performance appraisal system, and perhaps other personnel evaluation schemes, it may be advantageous for the designer to see that the performance dimensions evaluated are similar. Comparisons between new and old systems are inevitable; this approach will make them more meaningful. However, one should not construct the center exclusively to serve the system. Well-researched assessment dimensions should stand on their own merit. Concessions should be made only where minor changes in description serve to align the dimensions with skills used in other systems.

Assembling the Measurement Instruments

Once the final assessment dimensions are decided upon, the designer is in a position to select or construct the measurement instruments. At this stage, there is no substitute for experience and professional judgment. The designer must decide whether each dimension is most effectively measured by a standardized paper-and-pencil test, a commercially available simulation exercise, or a new exercise tailormade for the organization. Various types of exercises and their purposes are described in Chapter 5.

Table 4-2 shows a type of array for the results of the job analysis which may be helpful in assembling the exercises. This is an adaptation of the content/process matrix used by some researchers to construct content valid achievement tests. The column at the left lists three behavioral processes required in the job of field sales manager. These processes have been accepted as assessment dimensions. The top row of the exhibit contains the categories of job content related to each process. For example, as shown, the field sales manager must be skilled in problem analysis. The manager must make analyses and judgments concerning the performance of subordinates, the reliability of vendors, and the validity of consumers' complaints. Also, a number of sources of business data must be monitored as indicators of trends and problems. Occasionally, the manager may offer product design suggestions based upon the data available.

Some quantification is necessary before such a matrix can be useful in identifying measurement instruments. In Table 4-2 an importance rank has been assigned to each assessment dimension and to each category of content related to each dimension. The rankings are based on the consensus of a group of managers familiar with the job.

From the matrix, one can see that organizational ability in dealing with data is of greatest importance. Thus, the most important exercise for the assessment center is one requiring the use of organizational ability in dealing with production and personnel schedules and marketing data. To the extent possible, the exercise should concern the work of subordinates and the activities of independent dealers. It is likely that an in-basket exercise could be developed to fit these requirements. Another important exercise would provide an opportunity for participants to demonstrate leadership in dealing with subordinates. This suggests that an assigned-role group discussion exercise would be appropriate.

Continuing in this manner, one can develop a priority listing of types of exercises. However, each assessment dimension does not necessarily require a different exercise. The priority listing must be revised so that each exercise contains the opportunity for the demonstration of several dimensions. The result is a blueprint for assessment exercises, which should lead to a high quality simulation of the important tasks of the target job.

Table 4-2 Content/Process Description of the Job of Field Sales Manager

Process (Assessment Dimension)	Content		
	People	Data	Things
Problem analysis: seeks out data and determines source of problems *Importance Rank: 3*	Subordinates, vendors, consumers *Importance Rank: 2*	Sales, marketing, warranty costs, personnel costs, daily mail from consumers *Importance Rank: 1*	Office space arrangement, product design *Importance Rank: 3*
Organizational ability: plans, organizes, and controls the work of others; forecasts problems and anticipates changes *Importance Rank: 1*	Subordinates, independent dealers *Importance Rank: 2*	Production scheduling, marketing, personnel scheduling *Importance Rank: 1*	Administrative forms *Importance Rank: 3*
Leadership: directs groups in the accomplishment of tasks *Importance Rank: 2*	Subordinates *Importance Rank: 1*	Sales, operating costs *Importance Rank: 2*	

Developing a Qualified Pool of Assessors

Beyond the design of the assessor training, discussed in Chapter 6, the following additional issues should be resolved during the early stages of assessment center implementation:

1. From what organizational units should the assessors be drawn? In some cases having line managers from diverse units serve as assessors can be productive. This approach permits the involvement of managers who ordinarily would have no such opportunity. Such involvement may lead to interest in developing additional centers in other units. Also, mobility of assessees between units might be stimulated. On the other hand, there is a risk that the line managers who "own" the assessment center may not accept the judgments of the outsiders.

2. From what organizational levels should the assessors be drawn? A rule-of-thumb used in many organizations is to draw assessors from among those currently one level above the target job. This strategy often ensures the availability of a sufficient number of potential assessors. By the same token, higher managers may be prevented from having any direct experience with the center. This ultimately may be detrimental to the credibility of the assessment information at higher levels.

3. Of what size should be the pool of trained assessors? What should be the frequency of service as an assessor? The answers to these questions will be largely determined by the anticipated volume of participants to be assessed. However, when scheduling assessors, one should consider the assessors' need for "ownership" of the center. For example, consider the case of an assessment center conducted for a sales component of a firm. For a variety of reasons, certain managers from the marketing component are pressed into service as assessors. The latter feel that they are rendering a service to the sales unit but contributing little to their own unit's needs. It is not until a few marketing unit employees are chosen as center participants that these managers seem to feel that their efforts are justified.

Developing Administrative Procedures

Administrative procedures for assessment centers will vary widely between organizations, since they inevitably are fashioned to resemble other standard personnel procedures. Listed in this section are some of the items which should be covered by the procedures. Others have been noted previously in this chapter.

The Flow of Candidates

1. The eligibility requirements for employees to become center participants must be defined. Possible factors considered might include organizational level, function, tenure, and age.

2. A nomination procedure must be established. Supervisor nomination has advantages during the developmental phase of a center. Purposive selection of candidates may be desirable to test the difficulty level and relevance of exercises. In an established center, self-nomination may serve to provide an ample supply of well-motivated candidates. This has been the experience of Cummins Engine Company's Foreman Assessment Center. This procedure also eliminates morale problems from people not given a chance to show their competence in the assessment center.

3. Publicity for the program must be carefully planned. Enough has been written about assessment centers in the business press to create some awareness of the technique among the general population. Some individuals have been found to confuse assessment centers with laboratory training or psychotherapy. It is important to frankly explain to candidates exactly what the center is and what it is not. For the purpose of the initial center, a personal letter to candidates from a top manager would be helpful.

4. An appropriate name for the center should be chosen. Some terms (including "assessment") connote evaluation or possible rejection; these may lead to apprehension on the part of participants. Other terms signify learning opportunities and supportiveness. These include "career planning," "talent development," "identification of potential," "advanced management," etc., as noted in Chapter 3.

5. If the outcome of the center includes developmental actions by the organization or self-development by the individual, mechanisms should be established to record the successful completion of such activities. This may take the form of an addendum to the assessment report on file, or perhaps merely a notation in the candidate's personnel file.

6. A posture toward reassessment should be formulated. Many candidates, especially those performing poorly, will inquire about opportunities to repeat the process. The morale of candidates is likely to be better if such opportunities do exist. However, because of the potential expense involved, it may be advisable for the organization to specify some minimum time interval which must pass before reassessment.

Logistics of Center Operation

The actual conduct of the center must be directed by one or more staff members with well-developed administrative skills. Familiarity with all center exercises and other procedures is mandatory for the staff. The following are typical tasks which the administrative staff may be required to perform:

 1)   monitoring the selection of assessors and candidates;
 2)   scheduling of facilities and equipment;
 3)   providing information to assessors and candidates;
 4)   distributing materials to assessors and candidates prior to the center;
 5)   orienting the candidates;
 6)   monitoring the use of facilities and equipment;
 7)   monitoring the conduct of exercises;
 8)   administering psychological tests to candidates;
 9)   monitoring the observation and recording practices of assessors during exercises and providing guidance when appropriate;
10)   monitoring discussion of candidates by assessors;
11)   debriefing candidates following their participation;
12)   writing assessment reports;
13)   giving performance feedback to candidates after final evaluations are made and reports are written;
14)   controlling the flow of final assessment reports and other information generated at the center;
15)   ensuring the security of assessment materials.

PLANNING THE USE OF ASSESSMENT INFORMATION

Several later chapters deal with the various uses of assessment information. Regardless of the center's objectives, candidates should be made completely aware of the particular uses of the information prior to their participation. Figure 4-1 depicts a typical flow diagram of assessment information which may be useful in providing such information to candidates.

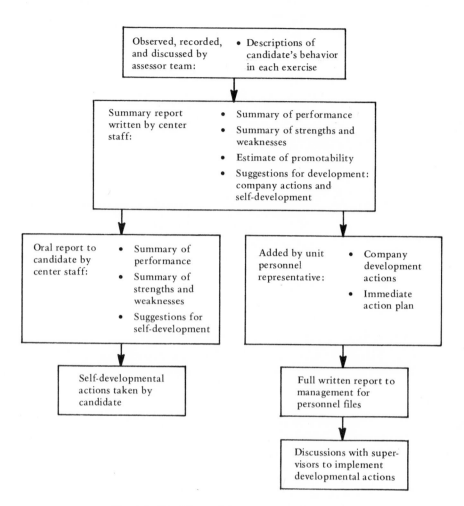

Fig. 4-1. The Flow of Assessment Information

REFERENCES

Byham, W. C. Assessment centers for spotting future managers. *Harvard Business Review*, 1970, *48* (4), 150-160.

Campbell, J. P., Dunnette, M. D., Lawler, E. E. III, & Weick, K. E., Jr. *Managerial behavior, performance, and effectiveness.* New York: McGraw-Hill, 1970.

Enneis, W. H. Minority employment barriers from the EEOC viewpoint. In B. R. Anderson & M. P. Rogers (Eds.), *Personnel testing and equal employment opportunity.* Washington, D.C.: Government Printing Office, 1970.

Flanagan, J. C. The critical incident technique. *Psychological Bulletin*, 1954, *51*, 327-358.

Prien, E. P., & Ronan, W. W. Job analysis: A review of research findings. *Personnel Psychology*, 1971, *24*, 371-396.

Slivinsky, L. W., & Desbiens, B. Managerial job dimensions and job profiles in the Canadian Public Service. *Studies in Personnel Psychology*, 1970, *2*, 36-52.

PART TWO

IMPLEMENTATION

CHAPTER 5

THE SELECTION AND DEVELOPMENT OF ASSESSMENT CENTER TECHNIQUES

Lois A. Crooks

INTRODUCTION

In this chapter, Lois Crooks, of Educational Testing Service, describes the most common exercises used in assessment centers and gives examples for each of the dimensions commonly observed in those exercises.

Two illustrations of assessment center programs are given. The illustration of the Northern Illinois Gas Company assessment center is like typical programs in operation throughout the world. It uses commercially available exercises but is based on detailed job analysis which relates the exercises to dimensions determined important in the organization's first-level supervisory jobs.

The other illustration is of a more complicated assessment procedure which was especially developed for the Canadian government. It is unique in a number of ways, most particularly in regard to the extensive research that went into the program prior to its establishment and the interrelatedness of the exercises. In that program a participant continues in a role through all subsequent exercises, gaining information about the organization and its problems as he or she goes along. This has the advantage of adding realism and depth to the assessment process, but the possible disadvantage of allowing a poor performance in an early exercise to affect performance in later exercises. Another unique feature of the Canadian government program described in this chapter is its use of "actors" as stimuli in two of the assessment exercises. This is an additional commitment of manpower and cost.

69

New Developments

The easy availability of videotape equipment is having a marked effect on assessment center exercises. Organizations have developed programs which capture assessment data exclusively via videotape or in written form. In these centers no assessors are present while the assessees go through their exercises. The participants either produce written documents or their actions are recorded on videotape which are later evaluated by assessors, usually in another city. These programs are increasingly popular because they materially cut down the travel and time requirements of assessment and allow a smaller staff to evaluate a larger number of assessees.

The job analysis and planning for these programs are exactly the same as for any other assessment center. The exercises used are often similar in concept to those described in this chapter, but differ in ways which make it easier to capture data without assessors actually being present. For example, the fact-finding exercise used in most assessment centers is operated as a one-to-one exercise with the participant asking an assessor questions in order to determine the facts necessary to make a decision. In other programs, assessees submit written questions and receive written responses from a pool of answers. This format not only eliminates the need for multiple assessors but it also affords the possibility of objectively scoring the analysis. It also adds realism to the exercise. Rather than having 15 minutes to ask questions, the participant has all day to think of questions, both during specific times allocated for this and in between other exercises. Throughout the day, the participants submit questions to the administrator, and the administrator responds with written answers from a pool of common answers.

Videotape is also increasingly being used as a stimulus in assessment centers. In one such exercise the assessors watch a group discussion on videotape and then answer key questions aimed at evaluating their observational ability relative to the dynamics of the group, the standing of the group and each of its members on the issues being discussed, etc. It is possible to evaluate listening skill, problem analysis, judgment, observational skills, sensitivity, and other dimensions.

Another common exercise is the Sales Call Simulation Exercise. This is used in assessment centers where candidates for a sales manager position are being evaluated. The assessees watch a simulated sales call on videotape and then are asked to prepare a written critique of the salesperson observed on the videotape. They then hold a simulated interview with an assessor playing that salesperson. This is a direct simulation of a major portion of a sales manager's job and has proven to be a very effective exercise.

* * *

BACKGROUND

As described in earlier chapters, the assessment center format developed by AT&T has been the model for most of the programs initiated by other companies, organizations, and agencies in the years since the Management Progress Study was initiated. John Hemphill, then at Educational Testing Service, worked with AT&T on the design and instrumentation for this first assessment center application. Three types of simulation exercises were used: What is believed to be the first business in-basket exercise was developed by the management training group at AT&T, with the help of ETS, for the assessment program. The miniature business game was a manufacturing team exercise using tinkertoys. This had been developed for use in small group research in leadership and the nature of group *Process* conducted by Hemphill and others at Ohio State. The other type of simulation was in the leaderless group discussion format (Bass, 1949), where in a structured or unstructured small group situation the interpersonal effectiveness and roles of participants in group process can be observed.

In addition to the simulation exercises, a general ability test, an adaptation of a projective-type test, various experimental pencil-and-paper tests, and a personality inventory were administered. The in-basket exercise was not scored objectively. Ratings of performance on the in-basket were made by assessors who read the responses. A narrative report was written which included observations from an interview conducted with the assessee on his in-basket performance shortly after he finished taking it. Evaluation of performance on the other two simulations included peer ratings or rankings, observer ratings, and narrative descriptions of participant behavior. Final ratings on the assessees were made on the basis of reports from all assessment techniques, and a summary report was written on each individual.

After AT&T published favorable research results, visitors from other companies flocked to AT&T to observe their assessment centers and to ask for copies of their exercises, rating forms, manuals, and whatever else was available. Even today, in observing programs from company to company, the basic AT&T format described above is readily discernible. However, many companies have developed or adapted materials to fit their special needs, or have purchased materials from other sources. Consultants are available who will come in and conduct an assessment program on a onetime or continuing basis, provide or adapt off-the-shelf materials, and either train company staff members as assessors or use trained assessors from outside sources.

NECESSARY RESEARCH FOR NEW PROGRAMS

To be able to demonstrate job relevance and content validity in the selection or development of appropriate assessment exercises, an analysis of the target jobs should first be undertaken. The reader should review Chapter 4, "Issues in Establishing an Assessment Center."

Various lists of dimensions have been defined and used in assessment programs, ranging from as few as seven or eight to 26 or more. AT&T uses eight to 25 dimensions, depending on the level being assessed. It is difficult to observe, record, and make discrete judgments on so many dimensions, no matter how carefully defined, and statistical analysis discloses considerable overlap. A recent catalog of assessment and development exercises (Development Dimensions, 1975) contains a representative list of 26 dimensions commonly used by organizations in assessment programs. It is not suggested that all of these will be utilized in a typical assessment program.

The selection or development of methods or techniques by which to assess the factors decided upon as important to performance at the target job level depends to a great extent on development time and resources available to the organization and staff. The decision to tailor-make exercises in the context of the company or a prototype of the company setting may call for an investment in time, cost, and creative effort, which may not be readily forthcoming, even with consultant help. If this is the case, selection then depends on buying or borrowing from others. Such materials can then be adapted or used according to needs. There are strong arguments for "tailor-made" rather than adapted or off-the-shelf exercises, particularly on the basis of face and content validity, direct job-relatedness, and acceptability to those being assessed.

TYPES OF EXERCISES COMMONLY INCLUDED
IN ASSESSMENT PROGRAMS

The types of exercises commonly included in assessment programs will be described briefly in the following section, with the dimensions usually considered to be measured by each suggested. This is not an exhaustive list—additional exercises and permutations of them depend on the ingenuity of the staff, the realism desired, and the limitations of time and logistics.

In-Basket Exercises

An in-basket exercise of some kind is included in the majority of assessment programs. Early developmental and experimental work utilizing the in-basket technique was done by Frederiksen, Ward, Hemphill, and others at Educational

Testing Service (Frederiksen, 1962; Hemphill, Griffiths, & Frederiksen, 1962). The person taking the exercise is provided with selected background material and references and a package of problems which have built-in priorities, relationships, and required decision making. The assessee is asked to work on the problems in a specific time period as if actually on the job as described in the instructions. In this way, a sample of the person's administrative behavior is obtained. It has been demonstrated that the written record of this behavior can be scored or evaluated on a number of dimensions to yield measures of performance (Hemphill et al., 1962).

Many companies have developed their own in-basket exercises, some of them with the help of ETS and other consultants. Others have used "off-the-shelf" materials. The majority of assessment center programs are directed toward identifying potential among assessees for higher level jobs within an organization, rather than for selection from a pool of job applicants. Thus, from the standpoint of face and content validity, and perhaps acceptability, the tailor-made version in the company's own or similar setting may have the advantage. The role assumed by the assessee can be set at the target level and a realistic mix of problems can be developed to be handled in terms of company policies and procedures. In-basket exercises have been developed at the foreman or first-line supervisor level, at the lower and middle management levels, and at the senior level. It is possible to develop this type of exercise for any job where administrative activities involving planning, organizing, and decision making are important elements.

In the interest of expediency, most users do not score the in-basket test used in their assessment centers. Assessors read the protocols and make notes of areas to follow-up in a structured interview. In such an interview, the individual's handling of the in-basket is discussed and the assessee's understanding of problems in the in-basket probed. Ratings of the performance are then made by one or more assessors or other staff members on such factors as organization and planning, decisiveness, use of delegation, etc., and a description of the performance and the interview is written in narrative form.

Where in-baskets are scored, analysis of the responses to the in-basket problems is done by a trained scorer who codes in a systematic way what action was taken, how it was taken, and why it was taken. Scoring dimensions are related to factors in in-basket performance found in early research (Frederiksen, 1962) and to recognize aspects of administrative behavior. They include stylistic as well as quantitative and qualitative variables. Such dimensions as "Taking Leading Action to Solve Problems," "Exercising Supervision and Control," "Problem Analyzing and Relating," "Delegation," "Systematic Scheduling," "Quality of Actions Taken," and "Amount of Work Accomplished" are derived from the scorer's analysis of responses. The scorer also makes a subjective rating of overall performance and writes a narrative report describing characteristics of the performance. The "Quality of Actions" score is derived by comparing actions taken by the assessee with actions judged appropriate or inappropriate by consensus of a group of experienced managers. (The disadvantage of detailed scoring is the time involved and the need for a specially trained scorer.) It is advantageous, even with a scored in-basket, to add an interview with the assessee to probe for additional insights or analysis, but some of the characteristics observed in such an interview can be observed in other exercises.

One consulting organization (Development Dimensions, 1975) suggests that by use of the reader-interviewer method of in-basket evaluation, such dimensions as impact, energy, written communication skills, sensitivity, planning and organizing, management control, use of delegation, judgment, and decisiveness may be observed and rated. The reliability of these judgments, when made by more than one assessor, has not been tested. Little research evidence exists which compares evaluations made by the two methods. In one study (Huse, 1968), in which ratings of in-basket performance made on the basis of reading and interview were correlated with scores derived by detailed scoring by the method described above, relationship between the two types of evaluation was low. Research in this area is needed.

Management Games

AT&T first used a team exercise involving manufacture of prototypes using tinkertoys. AT&T later developed a stock market game and other management exercises for assessment programs at higher levels. Such games or simulations can be developed in the company context or at least adapted for face validity, if desirable, although there is no research evidence as to whether face validity makes a difference in eliciting the desired behaviors. The usual format of a game is a team situation involving buying and selling, where objectives must be set and the team must organize to meet them. In a game in which component parts are bought to manufacture prototype products, teams can be given the instruction to maximize profits, which would involve deciding what parts and how many to buy and which products to manufacture, depending on prices offered. Dimensions suggested as possible to assess, depending on conditions set, are planning and organizing skills, leadership behavior, communication skills, problem analysis, judgment, initiative, decisiveness, and flexibility, again with cautions as to the difficulty of sorting out behavior on so many dimensions.

Leaderless Group Discussions

Leaderless group discussion problems may be classified as having nonassigned roles and assigned roles. In the first type, the group of participants (three or six) is handed short case studies or management problems. As consultants, they are asked to resolve the problems and present a written recommendation. Problems dealing with supervision, business judgment, conflicts between departments and employees, job dissatisfaction, and setting of priorities among alternative actions are examples, depending again on important factors in job performance at the target level. Both quality of thinking and group process variables can be observed.

An example of the second type of leaderless group discussion with assigned roles is one used by a number of companies. Each of six assessees in a group is given a description of a fictitious subordinate he or she is recommending for promotion. The descriptions are formulated so that the candidates are about equally qualified. The assessees study their candidate descriptions and each is then allowed five minutes to make a pitch for the candidate the assessee is sponsoring. After all six assessees are heard, a period of free discussion is followed by a rank-ordering of the job candidates by the assessees from most deserving to least deserving. Assessors observing the group (each assessor commonly observing two assessees) judge the assessees on ability to sell their candidates and what they have done to aid the group in reaching a decision. Here again individual skills and group process variables can be observed.

It is fairly easy to formulate problems which have face validity not only for the level being assessed but also for the company context. Whether setting problems in the company context is an important aspect of such exercises is not known, but formulating situations which are appropriate for the level being assessed is important to assure involvement and to elicit the behaviors of interest.

Analysis/Presentation/Group Discussion Exercises

At the lower and middle management levels and above, managers may be required to analyze complex situations and data, to consider alternatives, and to make presentations before groups of peers, their superiors, or to outside groups. If this activity is found to be an important element of the target level job, such an exercise might be included in the assessment program. It can be built around financial analysis, new products and sales strategy, or proposals for new programs in the personnel area (i.e., an assessment program), according to usual practices of the company. The assessee usually receives unorganized data that must be analyzed in order to prepare a presentation. This is sometimes a homework assignment or time to set aside in the program.

It may be effective and realistic to combine oral presentations with questions from the group. In the latter case, assessors not only may observe the ability to analyze, organize, and present data in an orderly way, oral communications skill, and judgment in focusing on issues, but also personal characteristics such as stress tolerance impact, flexibility, and the like.

Interview Simulations (Role Playing)

These exercises are particularly relevant where the incumbent in the target job spends considerable time dealing with others on a one-to-one basis, either in the organization or outside it. Interaction with the public may be in a sales, public relations, or trouble-shooting function. Within the organization, the incumbent may be responsible for hiring, counseling, or appraising. Most of these simulations involve role playing, with the assessee placed in the target role. An assessee in a customer service role might receive an irate telephone call or deal with a disgruntled customer face-to-face. Another situation might involve having the assessee take the role of the supervisor or foreman and discuss a personal or performance problem with a subordinate. In a role reversal, the assessee may be interviewed by his or her superior the first day on a new job or may receive counseling. In these situations, the assessee's ability to think and communicate in a stress situation, impact, energy, listening skill, tenacity, flexibility, and the like, have been suggested as characteristics to be observed.

Other Interviews

The in-basket interview has been discussed previously. In some assessment programs, an in-depth personal interview with the assessee is also included to allow discussion of career expectations, work standards, and motivation. This presents an opportunity to observe a number of personal characteristics.

Fact Finding and Decision Making

A variation of the Analysis/Presentation/Group Discussion format is one in which the assessee collects data on a problem verbally by asking questions of a resource person then has to present the problem and his or her conclusions either verbally (during or after which session he or she submits to questioning) or in writing. Such an exercise again depends on requirements of typical target jobs for which candidates are being assessed. Reasoning ability, thoroughness in gathering data, defensibility of conclusions, and written communications skills may be observed and evaluated. If report is oral, other variables enter in such as persuasiveness, stress tolerance, oral communications skills, and the like.

Writing Exercises

These may be in the nature of filling out forms, writing an essay, or writing an autobiography. Ability to fill out forms accurately from unstructured information received in writing (or orally) may be an important element in some kinds of lower level jobs. Written communication skills may be important in others.

Pencil-and-Paper Tests

In many assessment programs no pencil-and-paper instruments other than the in-basket are used. In others, a general ability test is administered. Also, a personality inventory measure of creativity or other special tests might be included. Some programs administer such tests only for research or counseling purposes, and do not include results in final assessment data; others use them to measure job-relevant aptitudes or characteristics not readily measurable in other ways.

ASSESSOR OBSERVATION FORMS AND ASSESSOR MANUALS

Many areas of the assessment process have changed over the years, but some of the most dramatic changes have been in the forms and in the manuals describing how assessors should record their observations during an assessment program, how to organize their observations after a program, and how to describe them in a written report. Observation forms and manuals differ widely from program to program in detail and sophistication, but it is generally agreed that such materials must be provided for assessor training and use.

In the early AT&T programs, the assessors had only tablets of paper for recording data and were given little direction on the form of their final behavioral observations. That is in contrast to the sometimes elaborate forms and manuals used in many programs which give assessors step-by-step guidance on what to observe during an exercise, provide an organized way of categorizing the observations relative to the dimensions being measured, and guide the assessor in describing the total exercise for the use of the other assessors who will read or hear the report.

While no research is available, it would seem that the detailed forms and manuals provide more reliable behavioral observations. They assure that more meaningful data are communicated to the assessment discussion, because they help assessors focus on the relevant data from the exercises under observation. Guidance is particularly important when assessors are trained for only a few days, as in some instances, and serve only occasionally.

A SENIOR LEVEL ASSESSMENT PROGRAM

The basic types of assessment exercises used in assessment center programs, with the number, type, and content dependent on the target job level, time constraints (one day to as many as four days), and the characteristics or dimensions identified as most important and most feasible to assess have been described in the previous section. In this section, an assessment program will be described in which some types of assessment exercises have been combined in an innovative manner.

The process of deriving dimensions to be assessed and the selection of components for assessing these dimensions may be observed in the description below of the development of an assessment center program at the senior level which has been in operation for several years.

The objective of the program is to identify potential candidates for senior level management in the Canadian government. Those identified in the assessment center and recommended by a selection review board on the basis of other factors (such as education, experience, and job performance) undergo an intensive three-month training program away from the job, and then follow a course of job rotation and counseling with expectation of reaching senior level at some time in the future. The candidates are usually three or four levels below entering senior level positions at the time they are assessed, and are nominated for the program by their superiors in the various departments of the government.

The development of this program followed quite closely the steps suggested above, beginning with analysis of the work of senior executives by use of the Executive Position Description Questionnaire, selected interviews and daily activity logs, and survey of characteristics of present senior level population (amount and type of education and experience, age and sex distribution, functional areas of work, perceived relative importance of a range of abilities, skills, and personal characteristics to performance at the senior level). With the assistance of an advisory committee of senior executives, research staff identified a list of attributes considered most important to performance at the senior level in the Canadian government.

Consideration was then given to which of these could be measured or observed in an assessment program. Twelve dimensions were selected: intelligence, motivation, analyzing and synthesizing skills, quality of judgment, leadership qualities and skills, planning and organizing skills, oral communication skills, appropriate delegation to subordinates, stress tolerance, interpersonal relations and awareness, independence (of thought and action), and creativity (fluency, flexibility, and originality). These attributes were then defined in behavioral terms in relation to the work of senior executives. The design of job relevant exercises was undertaken to measure these dimensions.

The survey of the senior executive population had shown that 75% of the jobs were in the general management category, and the remaining 25% were in policy-making roles or were technical or subject-matter specialists. Given this emphasis, the decision was made to focus on the general management role in the assessment program. The point was made that management is an activity that everyone gets into at some time at some level, whether or not the individual's primary function is management.

Integration of Content of Exercises

The first exercise to be developed was an in-basket test. The role simulated was that of Director General of Personnel and Administration, these two functions having generalizability and impact across most management jobs. The simulated organization was a prototype government agency. A set of typical problems was developed with the help of an advisory committee of senior executives and from material gathered in interviews. This in-basket was pre-tested by eliciting the cooperation of nearly 150 senior executives. They also took another in-basket test with the role set at a lower management level, on which data had been gathered in early research in the government (Crooks & Slivinski, 1972), and a number of other measures to provide some additional benchmark data. Performance ratings were obtained from deputy ministers on these executives, with their consent, for concurrent validation purposes. A scoring procedure for the new in-basket test was developed which provided detailed scoring data for research purposes as well as specific scores to be included as assessment center data.

It was decided fairly early in the planning that the other exercises in the assessment program would grow out of the simulated setting in the in-basket test. The intent was to provide a continuous build-up of information and realistic experience for the assessee by reproducing and expanding on critical elements and problems in the simulated senior executive's job in all assessment exercises.

The most frequent patterns of interaction found in activity logs of senior executives were with subordinate staff, with superiors, with other government agencies, and with peers. These patterns were incorporated into the situation simulated in the in-basket and were then utilized in designing the other exercises.

Design of the Assessment Center

A walk through the assessment center will illustrate the way in which the exercises develop. Twelve individuals are assessed in a two and one-half day program. After orientation in the first afternoon, they take the in-basket test in a group (two and one-half hours). When this is completed, they are told that they will retain the role they assumed in the in-basket throughout the program. They are given a folder and the opportunity to make notes on any in-basket problems or situations "they may wish to follow up." They also each receive a memo from the President, their superior in the simulated organization, setting up a personal meeting "to discuss problems and to offer assistance." Prior to this meeting, they are instructed that they are to have a meeting with their staff (five division heads introduced in the in-basket), who will brief them for the meeting with the President.

Beginning the following morning, the assessees are divided into two groups of six. Three assessors (senior executives who have undergone a week of intensive training in all aspects of the assessment program) are assigned to each group of six, and these two modules proceed concurrently and separately through the center.

Each assessee meets with the staff. This is a live meeting. The staff members are played by actors who have been carefully briefed and rehearsed in a prepared script, according to the personalities and roles described for them in the in-basket. The assessee is handed materials, is asked questions, is asked to make decisions by the staff, and is given the opportunity to assume the leadership role prescribed according to his ability to understand and adjust to the situation. This meeting lasts one hour, and an assessor observes and records the process. The assessee then has a period to prepare for the meeting with the President. This meeting takes place, also live, with the role of the President played by an actor. The President has an abbreviated script with prepared questions. An assessor, present at the meeting, is introduced as an assistant. The dimensions to be observed in these two exercises are oral communications, stress tolerance, quality of judgment, interpersonal awareness, leadership and analysis and synthesis, as defined in behavioral and job-related terms in the Assessors' Manual. The assessors write reports describing behavior and process on dimensions to be observed.

The next exercise is a meeting with representatives of the agency responsible for reviewing and approving budget allocations. This meeting is set up to occur immediately upon the return of the assessee from a hypothetical business trip. The staff has prepared a file of information which the assessee has to assimilate and organize for a presentation of the preliminary budget forcast. The file includes a lengthy proposal from one of the division heads, estimates of staff and other expenses for the next three years from each division, and supporting memos from each division head. In preparing this presentation, the assessee may also incorporate information gathered from previous exercises. At least two hours are set aside for the assessee to prepare for this presentation. Two assessors play the roles of the program planning officers of the agency to whom the presentation is made. They have an abbreviated script and prepared questions, as needed. The behavioral dimensions to be observed in this exercise are stress tolerance, motivation, independence, analysis and synthesis, oral communication, and quality of judgment.

In the final exercise, the President sets up a task force of the six assessees in their role as the Director General of Personnel and Administration to work on organizational problems first emerging in the in-basket, reinforced and enlarged upon in the staff meeting, the meeting with the President, and in the budget presentation. The assessees are given a period of time to prepare individually for this meeting, and come to it prepared to present and back up their individual points of view. They do not appear to find it unusual to be in a meeting of five others in the same role, and essentially view it as a meeting of peers. They are asked to reach consensus on a plan of action in a two-hour discussion and to prepare a written document for the President's consideration. The three assessors in this module are present, with each one responsible for observing and recording behavioral data on two assessees on the dimensions being measured in this exercise. Behavioral dimensions observed are stress tolerance, motivation, independence, leadership, interpersonal relations and awareness, analysis and synthesis, oral communication, and quality of judgment.

In addition to the exercises described, assessees are asked to complete a number of pencil-and-paper measures primarily for career counseling and research purposes, including the Strong Vocational Interest Blank, a General Intelligence Test, the Structure of Intellect Model Test (of creativity), the Administrative Judgment Test (U. S. Civil Service), and a Personality Research Form. These are scheduled into the assessment center as the flow of the exercises permits. At the final integration stage, assessors get results on the In-Basket Test, GIT, and SIM only, in terms of normative data from the senior executive pre-testing.

In this assessment center program, there is great involvement by both assessees and assessors because of the realism and the continued integration of information and interaction. The descriptions of each assessee's elicited behavior in a variety of circumstances provide the assessors with ample evidence on which to base their consensus rating on each dimension and overall. These ratings are made on a 7-point scale with the midpoint representing the minimum level required for performance as a senior executive. The assessors are senior level executives and apply judgments from their experience in making these ratings. Norms for the tests involved were established from testing of a senior executive sample prior to the initiation of the program. Three hundred candidates, both men and women, have gone through this assessment program at date of writing. The program has been conducted in both the English and French languages, with translations of all materials. A report is in progress describing in detail the dimensions measured, planning and scheduling of the program, the feedback process, and research findings (Slivinski, Crooks, Grant, & Bourgeois, in press).

Another kind of format, representing a more typical center is described in the next section.

A FOREMAN SELECTION PROGRAM

In contrast to the complexity of the program at the senior level in the Canadian government, Northern Illinois Gas Company has developed a one and one-half day assessment program for the identification of first-level supervisory talent. The program is primarily designed to help the organization make more accurate decisions on who should be selected for first-level management and, secondarily, to aid the organization in identifying the developmental needs of those promoted.

The program is divided into two days. On the first day, self-nominated candidates are interviewed and are given an in-basket exercise. On the second day (the actual assessment center), the assessees participate in five activities, all of which fit into a regular 8 to 5 day. The assessors take two days to evaluate their findings. A report is prepared for higher management, and the participants are given the option of an individual interview concerning their performance.

The exercises included in the program are the following:

Background Interview

Background interviews are conducted with each candidate by assessors who are specially trained. The interviews are primarily to assess the following dimensions:

Oral communication skill	Initiative
Oral presentation skill	Independence
Written communication skill	Planning and organization
Stress tolerance	Delegation and control
Career ambition	Problem analysis
Leadership	Judgment
Sensitivity	Decisiveness
Flexibility	Reading and understanding
Tenacity	

In-Basket Exercise

The in-basket exercise simulates the problems a newly appointed foreman might encounter. The in-basket contains 14 items and takes one and one-half hours to complete. During the assessment day, each participant is interviewed for one hour relative to his or her performance on the in-basket.

The following dimensions are assessed from the in-basket performance:

Oral communication skill	Planning and organization
Written communication skill	Delegation and control
Stress tolerance	Problem analysis
Leadership	Judgment
Sensitivity	Decisiveness
Flexibility	Reading and understanding
Initiative	

Leaderless Group Discussion (Nonassigned Role)

A nonassigned role, leaderless group discussion puts groups of four participants into the role of consultants whose function is to aid the organization in making decisions toward solving typical supervisory problems.

The following dimensions can be observed from this exercise:

Oral communication skill	Tenacity
Oral presentation skill	Initiative
Stress tolerance	Independence
Leadership	Problem analysis
Sensitivity	Judgment
Flexibility	Decisiveness

Competitive Group Exercise

Contrasting to the cooperative group described above, a competitive group exercise is given in which each participant is told that he or she is a department manager and has a candidate in the department who is being considered for a pre-supervisory training program. The participant is told that the goal is to attempt to get his or her candidate nominated for the program while still helping the organization make the best decision.

The following dimensions can be observed from this exercise:

Oral communication skill	Initiative
Oral presentation skill	Independence
Stress tolerance	Planning and organization
Leadership	Problem analysis
Sensitivity	Judgment
Flexibility	Decisiveness
Tenacity	

Superior-Subordinate Interview

A superior-subordinate interview situation is simulated where the participant is assigned the role of a newly appointed supervisor and given a number of facts about a hypothetical subordinate whose performance is deteriorating. After one-half hour to prepare, the participant actually conducts an interview with an assessor who role plays the subordinate, while another assessor evaluates the participant's behavior.

The following dimensions can be observed from this exercise:

Oral communication skill	Planning and organization
Stress tolerance	Delegation and control
Leadership	Problem analysis
Sensitivity	Judgment
Tenacity	Decisiveness
Independence	Reading and understanding

Staff Allocation

Since a major aspect of a foreman's position in Northern Illinois Gas is to allocate staff members to various projects, this task is simulated. The participant is put into the position of a plumbing foreman who must allocate people to various projects throughout the day. After the participant has made his or her initial allocations, emergencies arise, and people have to be reallocated. The participant then must explain actions taken to an assessor role playing his or her superior.

The following dimensions can be observed from this exercise:

Oral communication skill	Initiative
Stress tolerance	Planning and organization
Leadership	Problem analysis
Sensitivity	Judgment
Flexibility	Reading and understanding

The Northern Illinois Gas Program illustrates how an assessment center can be conducted from 8 to 5 on company premises with minimum disruption of work and still have enough exercises in the assessment program to achieve adequate reliability from multiple observations of behavior on most dimensions. The possibility of making clear-cut observations of behavior on so many dimensions in each short exercise can be questioned, however.

RECOMMENDATIONS

1. The dimensions to be observed and measured in an assessment program should stem from factors demonstrated to be inherent in job performance at the target level.
2. Assessment exercises or techniques to measure the dimensions identified should be selected and developed wherever possible in the context of the organization instituting the program for face and content validity and to demonstrate job relevancy.
3. Research has produced such techniques as the in-basket, the leaderless

group discussion, management games, and role playing, as well as methods of achieving reliable observations of individual and group behavior. Published theoretical and applied research should be continually monitored to seek out ways to identify and measure these and other factors found to be relevant to job performance.

4. Assessment programs should be preceded and followed by research, not only to satisfy EEOC guidelines but to be able to demonstrate the validity of the technique and the long-term benefits to the organization in terms of improvement in overall performance of staff.

BIBLIOGRAPHY

Bass, B. M. An analysis of the leaderless group discussion. *Journal of Applied Psychology*, 1949, *33*, 527-533.

Bentz, V. J. Validity studies at Sears. Symposium on "Validity of Assessment Centers." American Psychological Association, Washington, 1971.

Bourgeois, R. P., Leim, M. A., Slivinski, L. W., & Grant, K. W. Evaluation of an Assessment Centre in terms of its acceptability. *Report AC-6*. Managerial Assessment and Research Division, Career Assignment Program, Public Service Commission of Canada, Ottawa, 1973.

Bray, D. W., & Campbell, R. J. Selection of salesmen by means of an assessment center. *Journal of Applied Psychology*, 1968, *52*, 36-41.

Bray, D. W., & Grant, D. L. Situational tests in assessment of managers. In *Proceedings of the Executive Study Conference: Management Games in Selection and Development*. Educational Testing Service, Princeton, N.J., 1964.

Bray, D. W., & Grant, D. L. The assessment center in the measurement of potential for business management. *Psychological Monographs*, 1966, *80* (17, Whole No. 625).

Bray, D. W., & Moses, J. L. Personnel selection. *Annual Review of Psychology*, 1972, *23*, 545-576.

Bullard, J. F. An evaluation of the assessment center approach to selecting supervisors. Mimeo. Report, Caterpillar Tractor Co., Corporate Personnel Department, Peoria, Ill., May 1969.

Byham, W. C. Assessment centers for spotting future managers. *Harvard Business Review*, 1970, *48* (4), 150-160, plus appendix.

Campbell, J. T., & Crooks, L.A. Content validity of job sample measures. Symposium on "Content Validity." American Psychological Association, Montreal, 1973. RM-73-26, Educational Testing Service, Princeton, N.J., October 1973.

Campbell, R. J., & Bray, D. W. Assessment centers: An aid in management selection. *Personnel Administration*, 1967, *30* (2), 6-13.

Carleton, F. O. Relationships between follow-up evaluations and information developed in a management assessment center. Paper presented at the meeting of the American Psychological Association, Miami Beach, Florida, 1970.

Cohen, B., Moses, J. L., & Byham, W. C. *The validity of assessment centers*. Pittsburgh: Development Dimensions Press, 1974.

Crooks, L. A. Issues in the development and validation of in-basket exercises for specific objectives. Research Memorandum 68-23. Educational Testing Service, Princeton, N.J., November 1968.

Crooks, L. A. The in-basket study: A pilot study of MBA candidate performance on a test of administrative skills as related to selection and achievement in Graduate Business School. ATGSB Brief No. 4. Educational Testing Service, Princeton, N.J., October 1971.

Crooks, L. A., & Slivinski, L. W. Comparison of in-basket test score profiles of four managerial groups. *Studies in Personnel Psychology*, Spring 1972, *4* (1), 19-30.

Development Dimensions. 1975. *Catalogue of Assessment and Development Exercises*. Pittsburgh: Development Dimensions, 1975.

Dodd, W. E. Will management assessment centers insure selection of the same old types? Paper presented at the meeting of the American Psychological Association, Miami Beach, 1970.

Dodd, W. E. Validity studies at IBM. Symposium on "Validity of Assessment Centers." American Psychological Association, Washington, D.C., 1971.

Dunnette, M. D. Multiple assessment procedures in identifying and developing managerial talent. In P. McReynolds (Ed.), *Advances in psychological assessment*. Vol. II. Palo Alto: Science & Behavior Books, 1971.

Finkle, R. B., & Jones, W. S. *Assessing corporate talent*. New York: Wiley-Interscience, 1970.

Finley, R. M., Jr. An evaluation of behavior predictions from projective tests given in a management assessment center. Paper presented at the meeting of the American Psychological Association, Miami Beach, 1970.

Frederiksen, N. Factors in in-basket performance. *Psychological Monographs: General and Applied*, 1962, *76* (22, Whole No. 541).

General Electric Company. Talent Development Program (Supplement for potential staff members). Mimeo. Report, Corporate Personnel Department, 1969.

Grant, D. L., & Bray, D. W. Contributions of the interview to assessment of management potential. *Journal of Applied Psychology*, 1969, *53*, 24-34.

Grant, D. J., Katkovsky, W., & Bray, D. W. Contributions of projective techniques to assessment of management potential. *Journal of Applied Psychology*, 1967, *51*, 226-232.

Greenwood, J. M., & McNamara, W. J. Interrater reliability in situational tests. *Journal of Applied Psychology*, 1967, *31*, 101-106.

Hemphill, J. K. Dimensions of executive positions. *Research Monographs No. 98.* Bureau of Business Research, Ohio Studies in Personnel, The Ohio State University, 1960.

Hemphill, J. K., Griffiths, D. E., & Frederiksen, N. *Administrative performance and personality: A study of the principal in a simulated elementary school.* New York: Teachers College Bureau of Publications, Columbia University, 1962.

Hinrichs, J. R. Comparison of "real life" assessment of management potential with situational exercises, paper-and-pencil ability tests, and personality inventories. *Journal of Applied Psychology*, 1969, *53*, 425-432.

Holeman, M. G. An assessment program of OCS applicants. *HumRRO Technical Report No. 26*, 1956.

Huse, E. F. Evaluation by structured interview as compared with quantitative scoring of in-basket test performance. Symposium on "The In-Basket Exercise—Test or Technique?" American Psychological Association, San Francisco, 1968.

Kraut, A. I., & Scott, G. J. Validity of an operational management assessment program. *Journal of Applied Psychology*, 1972, *56*, 124-129.

MacKinnon, D. W. An assessment study of Air Force officers. Part V: Summary and applications. *WADC Technical Report 58-91 (V)*. Wright Air Development Center, 1958.

McCormick, E. J., Jeanneret, P. R., & Mecham, R. C. A study of job characteristics and job dimensions as based on the position analysis questionnaire. *Journal of Applied Psychology*, 1972, *56* (4), 347-368.

Meyer, H. H. The validity of the in-basket test as a measure of managerial performance. *Personal Psychology*, 1970, *23*, 297-307.

Moses, J. L. Assessment center performance and management progress. Symposium on "Validity of Assessment Centers." American Psychological Association, Washington, 1971.

Moses, J. L. The development of an assessment center for the early identification of supervisory potential. *Personnel Psychology*, 1973, *26* (4), 569-580.

Slivinski, L. W., Crooks, L., Grant, K. W., & Bourgeois, R. P. The development and application of the Career Assignment Program Assessment Centre. Public Service Commission, Ottawa, Canada (in press).

Wollowick, H. B., & McNamara, W. J. Relationship of the components of an assessment center to management success. *Journal of Applied Psychology*, 1969, *53*, 348-352.

CHAPTER 6

ASSESSOR SELECTION AND TRAINING
William C. Byham

INTRODUCTION

There are striking differences in various assessment programs in the amount of training given assessors. Surveys of assessment center operations have found variations ranging from no training to three weeks of training.

For those organizations that conduct assessor training, there is usually a relationship between the length of the assessment center and the length of assessor training. The mode of assessor training for a one-day assessment center appears to be three days (32 hours), with the mode for a two- or two and one-half-day center being five days (48 hours). But there are many exceptions to these figures, particularly at the lower end of the scale.

In this chapter, Dr. Byham has set a high standard for the content and the conduct of assessor training programs. Because of his influence in the field and because of the high standard maintained by the AT&T programs (three weeks of training), the majority of organizations starting assessment center programs are investing in substantial training. While there is general agreement on the need for training, there is disagreement on the kind and duration given.

There is also some disagreement about some of the actual training suggested—particularly the emphasis on interviewer training if the background interview is to be included in the assessment center. Some organizations feel that such emphasis on interviewing training is not required because the necessary skill level is already available in assessors.

Not covered in this chapter is the training of individuals to be assessment center administrators or to provide the assessment center feedback. Both of these areas require specific training programs.

An assessment center administrator must be able to administratively schedule the assessment center (facilities, assessors, and participants), administer the exercises, chair the assessor discussions, and write up the final assessment reports. Occasionally, report writing is delegated to assessors. Special training to handle this responsibility must be provided to the assessors as part of their assessor training if they are adequately to write final summary reports. Such training usually includes having model reports available and giving assessors the opportunity to record data from a standardized discussion, write up a report, and then compare those reports with each other.

Feedback of assessment center results to the participant is usually handled by the administrator or a member of the personnel department. Occasionally, it is handled by an assessor. This is more often true when the assessors are highly trained or are used for an extended period of time such as in the AT&T programs. In all cases, the feedback of assessment center results is a difficult task requiring considerable skill, and the individuals who are to perform this task must be trained. Usually it takes about three days of specific training to develop the necessary skills. Yet, many organizations provide no feedback training. Unfortunately, the result of not providing such training may be ineffective use of the data in terms of follow-up training or problems in turnover or morale resulting from poor communication of data.

* * *

Assessor training is one of the most important, yet often most poorly handled, aspects of assessment center operations. The best laid plans, the most perfect exercises, the highest quality administrative staff cannot overcome the lack of proper training. On the other hand, the reverse may be possible—extremely skilled assessors can get the most out of even a poor exercise, and often they do not really need any assistance from an administrator. The need for assessor training is immediately obvious to anyone who observes an assessor training program. There are great differences in assessor observational skills at the beginning as compared to the end of a training program. Research at IBM (Hinrichs & Haanpera, 1975) has shown that a lack of emphasis on assessor training can lead to unreliable judgments by assessors and thus lower the validity of a program.

There is no unanimous agreement on how assessor training should be conducted or how much is required. Very little research data are available, with most practitioners making judgments on "intuition" and "feel." No organization has conducted comparative research into various assessor training procedures. Few can even define what a "well-trained" assessor is—at least not beyond a vague generalization.

The only real experimentation in assessor training techniques, methods, and designs has resulted as a response to pragmatic situations encountered by practicing consultants. Forced by organizational and situational constraints, consultants have had to experiment. They have had the luxury of trying out many new training methods as they have run assessor training programs week after week for different organizations with different needs. This has provided an opportunity to try out new ideas and methods and also to learn from mistakes. The suggestions in this chapter are thus written from the perspective of a practicing consultant. In most of the areas we cannot prove we are right. In cases of substantive disagreement by our peers on issues, we will make a special effort to present all sides of the issue.

PLANNING ISSUES

Before one can design an assessor training program, a number of planning issues must be considered. A few of the most important are discussed below, with recommendations where appropriate. One must always remember, however, that there are many exceptions to all the comments made because, as mentioned many times in this book, the assessment center method must be adapted to the particular needs of the host organization.

Importance Placed on the Development of Nonassessment Skills in Assessors

It is universally accepted that the combination of participating in assessor training and subsequently being an assessor is a powerful developmental experience for managers. Organizations using the assessment center process have continually observed greater behavioral changes resulting from assessment centers than are typically obtained from other management training programs. While this "extra benefit" of transfer of skills to the job results from any use of managers as assessors, it can be heightened if the development and transfer of new skills are designated as major purposes of an assessor training program and the program is adapted accordingly. Thus, a basic decision to make is how much emphasis is to be placed on the assessors acquiring transferable job skills.

Organizations feel that managers who have completed assessor training programs and have served at least once as assessors improve markedly in their abilities to interview, counsel, and coach subordinates as they develop skills in observing and communicating behavior. Assessors also learn the importance of withholding judgment until adequate information is gathered. Because of the concentrated effort assessors make in analyzing and studying behavior in the exercises, they gain skill in delegation, planning, and controlling plus new skills in understanding groups and in leadership.

Let us consider why the combination of assessor training and acting as an assessor is such a powerful developmental tool. We know that management skills can be developed through a process of self-awareness, followed by analysis of alternative methods of dealing with situations and continued practice and reinforcement of the newly developed or learned skills until they become automatic. This paradigm is met in the assessor training/assessment center process. By participating in assessment center exercises themselves, by reading information on alternative solutions furnished in the printed assessor training material, and by observing practice subjects and relating the practice subjects' behavior to their own behavior, assessors gain self-awareness into their abilities. This was shown by Byham and Thoresen (1976), in a study of hundreds of managers which demonstrated that the managers' (assessors-in-training) self-evaluation of their skills decreased during an assessment center. That is, they realized, as a result of participating in a center, that they were not as good as they thought they were in many managerial areas.

The second step in the paradigm—analysis of alternative methods of dealing with situations—is provided through experience with the exercises where alternative methods are discussed. Assessors have the opportunity of sharing with each other their handling of the problems, and the printed assessor training material provides bountiful data on alternative actions.

For some skill areas, participating in an assessor training program and being an assessor in an assessment center provide the practice and reinforcement necessary for the third step in the paradigm. Certainly this is true of the skills of observing and recording behavior, interviewing, etc. Other skills, such as conducting appraisal interviews and administrative skills, are learned but are not really practiced in an assessment center. This explains why not as much positive change in these skills is recorded as in the more basic skills (Byham & Thoresen, 1976).

Desire to Expose Large Numbers of Managers to the Assessment Center Process

Many organizations use assessor training as a means to increase commitment, knowledge, or support of the assessment process and to help assure the effective follow-up of developmental recommendations.

Support is important to any personnel activity and organizations have typically found that one of the best ways of gaining the support of managers for the assessment center method is to involve them as assessors. Managers who have been trained as assessors are more willing to give up their people to be assessed and also their subordinates to be assessors. The latter is particularly important as will be discussed later under staffing. It is also generally assumed that managers who act as assessors will, when asked to nominate people for the assessment center program, be more critical of their own subordinates' skills and thus provide a higher number of "successful" participants for the assessment center. Their knowledge of the assessment procedure helps them decide which individuals would benefit the most.

Probably the most important argument for involving large numbers of managers as assessors is their increased ability to effectively use the results of the assessment center process. The difficulty with psychological testing has always been that managers would over- or underrely on test results and seldom put the proper emphasis or weight on the results relative to other information about candidates. This problem is lessened in the assessment center procedure to the extent that managers are intimately aware of how the assessment center data are derived because of their training as assessors. They are more likely to put the proper weight on the results in terms of selection, and they are more apt to take meaningful action in terms of development. With this in mind, some assessor training programs provide, as an extra, discussions of follow-up developmental activities to widen the repertory of developmental actions available to the manager.

Many organizations make a conscious effort to get all managers at the assessor level through assessor training within a year after beginning an assessment program. This is the most important level because these individuals will have the most to say about nominating individuals for the assessment center and the most to say about the subsequent developmental efforts deriving from the diagnosis provided by the assessment center. As a secondary priority, organizations try to get higher managers through assessor training because they will see and use the assessment center reports, and of course their backing of the program is important.

Because of the desire to expose as large a number of managers to the assessment center concept as possible, many organizations run frequent assessor training programs the first year they start to use the method in order to process as many managers as possible. Organizations also usually make an effort to use each trained manager at least once as an assessor to "set" the training. The nearer this actual experience is to the assessor training, the better. Participating in an assessment center soon after training materially increases the effect of the training because real skill practice is provided and all elements of the training and the assessment center process are pooled together for the assessor.

Subsequent Uses of Assessment

If an organization plans to use assessment methods at several levels in the organization, it must plan the order of the applications in order to minimize the possibility that a person might be trained as an assessor, and then later be assessed in an assessment center. While this situation has arisen many times and has not caused great difficulty (assuming different exercises are involved), it should be avoided for psychological reasons if for nothing else. Center participants feel that fellow participants who have been trained as assessors have an advantage even if they do not.

While there is often concern over the value or accuracy of assessing someone who has already been trained as an assessor, there is no indication that simply serving as an assessor, in and of itself, will help a person who subsequently becomes a participant. If the only thing a person needs to do to perform well in an assessment center is to be trained as an assessor, then we should quickly forego most other management training efforts and train all managers as assessors. Unfortunately, it is not that easy. A manager's ability to assess or to evaluate others does not necessarily imply the ability to perform the assessed skills. This is demonstrated in the world of athletics and the arts, where many of the best critics or coaches are not themselves fine artists or athletes. Further, simply knowing what skills are being measured and how they are measured does not imply that the person will automatically be able to perform. This is not unlike knowing that the "trick" to passing a typing test is to type accurately. That knowledge does not allow a person to walk in and "beat" the test.

Some improvements should be expected. Assessor training may, and probably does, increase managerial skills in some areas. These behaviors should carry over onto the job, making the managers more effective in their day-to-day operations and more effective as an assessee in an assessment center.

If plans develop so that trained assessors subsequently are assessed, they should certainly be exposed to a different set of simulations. This should happen automatically since they are at a higher level in the organization, and thus should be evaluated against a different set of dimensions with a higher level of expected performance.

Organizations planning applications of the assessment center method at several levels typically start at the top of the organization, training the appropriate level of management who assess the next level down. This level is trained as assessors to assess the next level down, and so forth. This was the approach taken by the State of Wisconsin. Nearly every upper level manager and Department Secretary was trained as an assessor and served at least once in a center for the purpose of his or her own personal developmental exposure to the process and to obtain assessment information about their subordinates, the top rung of civil service managers. After obtaining assessment information about the top professional management within the state, that level of managers was then trained as assessors so that they could assess the next lowest level and so forth, until the ultimate use of the assessment center to identify middle managers for entry into the state's Career Executive Development Program was obtained (Byham & Wettengel, 1974). It took one year to work the assessment center process down from the top to its ultimate use. In addition to the developmental benefits derived from the program, it acquainted all levels of management within the organization with the assessment center process, thus assuring effective use of the results by the people who would receive the assessment center reports.

As an organization moves the assessment process down the hierarchy and assessees become assessors, another benefit develops. The previously assessed assessor will have an even more heightened developmental experience from assessor training. By virtue of attendance as an assessee, there is more awareness of weaknesses which should receive concentrated attention. It will also take less time to train them because they are already familiar with the general type of exercises and the flow of the center and do not need as much orientation. Even though the content of an in-basket or group exercise changes to reflect lower level job demands, the process remains virtually unchanged.

Level of Assessor in the Organization

In most assessment programs, the assessor is two levels above the candidate population. Assessors who are involved thus have an intimate knowledge of exactly what is required for success in the target position or position level which is usually one level below the assessors. As an example, if hourly employees are being assessed for foremen positions, the assessees would usually be drawn from the ranks of general foreman or superintendent. Since they constantly observe the relative effectiveness of their subordinate foremen, this is the most appropriate level for assessors. They have an accurate knowledge of the degree of each dimension needed at the target level. They are also the real decision makers regarding promotion of hourly workers to foreman.

When assessment is used at high levels in the organization, perhaps at the director or general manager level, it is usually impossible to get assessors two levels higher in the organization. In these cases the assessors are drawn from the next highest level. Even then it may be difficult to gain necessary time commitments for fulfilling the role of an assessor. In cases of this nature, it is common for assessors to be drawn in increasing numbers from high-level staff positions or from outside the organization. The latter is frequently done by federal government agencies in the United States.

Rotating or Semi-permanent Assessors

Because of the large number of individuals to be assessed in the Bell System Assessment Centers, AT&T has set up its operating assessment programs to utilize line managers who are taken from their job for a six-month period to work full time as assessment center staff members. Due to this extended assessment center commitment, AT&T can afford to spend three weeks in training the assessors, and they reach near professional levels in their ability as they gain experience with the technique. Two other organizations staff their assessment centers in this way. By far, the majority of organizations, however, train a pool of line managers from which three to six managers are drawn to staff individual assessment centers. The number of centers in which an individual manager is used depends, of course, on the number of centers run by the organization and the size of the pool. It has been our experience that the maximum number of times a manager can be taken from the job to serve as an assessor is approximately four times a year, although there are many exceptions to this. Most organizations promise not to use assessors more than once or twice a year. Obviously the decision as to whether to follow the AT&T model or the rotating model is a key decision as it affects all other aspects of the utilization of assessors in an assessment center and assessor training. While the number of people to be processed in an assessment center is probably the prime determinant in making this decision, one must also consider the developmental impact on assessors. The rotating method exposes more assessors to the assessment center procedure, thereby expanding the positive developmental effects and also orienting more people to the assessment center system.

Ratio of Assessors to Participants

Some organizations utilize a one-to-one ratio of assessors to assessees in order to capitalize on the developmental experience available to the assessors, to train as many managers as possible, or to minimize the work required of an individual assessor at a center. Most centers assign assessors at a one-to-two ratio. The one-to-two ratio has been found to be the most efficient ratio for most assessment centers. While assessors can physically observe more than two participants in a group exercise, the one-to-two ratio produces almost the maximum amount of paper work that an assessor can be expected to accomplish in an assessment program.

Where efficiency and productivity are the prime requisites, where there is limited staff available, or where only a limited number of dimensions are sought and there is little need for extensive documentation, centers have been run very successfully on a one-to-three ratio. In these cases steps are often taken to capture some exercises on videotape to allow a more thorough analysis without tying up candidates for unreasonable periods of time. Observation forms also need to be more exact and standards of behavioral recording often must be lowered. Certainly, the greater the ratio of participants to assessors, the more highly trained the assessors need to be because they must be more efficient in both their observation and their recording skills.

Line Versus Staff Assessors

Most organizations staff their assessment centers with line managers because line managers seem to benefit most from the experience, and because the line managers' positions in the hierarchy allow them to have previously developed standards of performance at the target level for which the participants are being considered. But, for various reasons, line managers are not always available so organizations are forced to supplement the line managers with personnel department, development staff representatives, or even outsiders. This has both advantages and disadvantages. Obviously staff representatives do not know the job as well as line managers, and they do not have as well-developed standards of performance on the dimensions. On the positive side the "outsider," be he or she a staff member or a consultant, may keep the assessors on their toes and "keep them honest" in their assessment discussions by forcing the other assessors to prove points to him or her. There is no evidence that outside "professionals" are better at assessment than trained line managers, but there is also no evidence that they are any worse. Their main disadvantage lies in the fact that outsiders and to some extent company staff personnel may have different standards of acceptable performance due to their lack of familiarity with performance of incumbents at the target level.

The facts of life are that many times it is literally impossible to get a sufficient number of line managers, so if one is to conduct an assessment program, one must settle on having a certain proportion of assessors from staff positions or from outside the company. The question is how large this proportion should be. Most centers make it a general rule that no more than 50% of the assessor population will be nonline. This maintains the aura of the assessment center as a line management activity and maintains line management's "ownership" of the process.

A few companies and government organizations conducting assessment centers use recently retired line managers as assessors. They have the advantage of a thorough knowledge of the organization and of the target job or the target job level. They often desire this kind of work and are far less expensive than consultants. The disadvantage is that they require considerable training, and they may lack credibility in the organization. Participants in the assessment center may feel that the changing values of the organization are not adequately reflected in the assessors' judgments. In addition, they do not bring the aura of objectivity and professionalism obtained from an outside assessor. Most importantly, the use of retired executives eliminates the developmental opportunities for younger managers who still have years to contribute to the organization.

Time Requirements

The fact that assessors are drawn from at least second-level supervision, and often from as high as general manager, places a premium on their time and creates the need for assessor training and the assessment center operation to be as efficient as possible. The typical design of assessor training requires from three days minimum to one week maximum. In addition, it then takes two to five days to conduct a center depending on the number of exercises, number of dimensions, and ratio of assessors to participants.

Only the organization can determine the value of this time commitment. There is a growing feeling, however, that as the moral and legal ramifications of manager selection become more important, the cost of making a poor selection is becoming so great that few organizations can afford not to invest the extra effort and time in this regard.

Some methods have been tried to minimize the time requirements or at least reorganize them to the advantage of the managers (assessors). Organizations may be able to utilize weekends for training or assessment. They may make use of videotapes to store information on presentations or group exercises, thus allowing the assessors to fit their assessment responsibilities more easily into other activities. They may increase the ratio of assessor to assessee if the assessors are experienced.

Some modifications of the evaluation period may be introduced to reduce time. For example, in some centers where there are 12 candidates and six assessors, the six assessors are divided into two teams of three, each evaluating six of the candidates. If desired, the entire staff of six assessors can meet at the end of the evaluation to share findings and to gain concurrence on all evaluations.

By introducing some of the above scheduling innovations, Chevrolet was able to reduce a traditional five-day assessment center program processing 12 candidates with a staff of six to a four-day center assessing 18 candidates with a staff of eight. The resulting increase in productivity and reduction in time commitment is obviously a major benefit.

An additional time conserving practice involves training a large pool of assessors from numerous departments, locations, or operations. They are trained at one time and then drawn from that pool as the need arises. This is especially valuable when the resources for conducting training are scarce or when outside consultants are used to conduct training and expense is a consideration.

Center Design and Geographic Dispersion

One of the major uses of assessment centers is in the identification of management potential in organizations with widely dispersed employee populations. This situation may demand the transportation of large numbers of assessors and/or candidates to a central location or to various geographic locations. Of course, transportation adds additional time and expense. Extreme distance can add as much as a day or two to the time managers are away from work.

Travel problems may be solved to some degree by establishing regional centers and exchanging assessors from nearby areas, plants, or offices. Careful scheduling of the center's beginning and closing hours to take maximum advantage of flights without cutting into an additional day should also be considered. Starting a center at midday Sunday, as an example, may allow assessors to travel Sunday morning and return Thursday in the late evening. Starting the center Monday morning would still require people to leave their homes early Sunday but would keep them from returning until Friday, a full day later.

Most center administrators prefer to move assessors rather than assessees so that it is not unusual for assessors from the West Coast to assess participants on the East Coast and vice versa. As travel factors are considered, staff selection may become obvious as the alternatives of who travels where, the availability of staff personnel in home offices, and the demands of their time are considered.

Acquaintance with Candidates

So that biases, prejudices, and the influence of outside information are avoided, it is advisable that an assessment center staff and participants be unknown to each other. In most large organizations, this presents little or no difficulty, and even many medium sized organizations can arrange this when assessing lower levels of personnel.

It becomes a more significant problem when working at higher organizational levels where previous relationships or knowledge of performance become almost inevitable. Nevertheless, the administrator should avoid acquaintances as much as possible. Many have achieved this through exchange programs—assessors from different plants, offices, or geographic locations go to another location to assess. When avoiding acquaintanceships is not possible, safeguards to keep assessors and assessees who know each other well from interactions in one-on-one assessment exercises (i.e., personal interview, in-basket interview, interview simulations, or other similar exercises) should be instituted. This is important both from the standpoint of the assessee who will generally be more comfortable and less anxious in situations where the assessor is unknown and

How Well Do You Know These People?

	Very well. Have known or worked with for years.	Quite well.	Acquainted on casual basis.	Have met but can't say I know.	Not at all. Have never met this person.
Candi-date

Assessor_____

1) ____
2) ____
3) ____
4) ____
5) ____
6) ____

also from the standpoint of the assessor who will be better able to achieve objective observations. A simple form similar to the one partially reproduced here, "How Well Do You Know These People?" can serve to get this information in advance of actually scheduling the center. Once this information is obtained, a schedule can be made so that assessors who know particular assessees can be scheduled to avoid any direct interaction with them.

Racial and Sex Mix

The available evidence suggests that there are no differences in observations or ratings when assessors of one race or sex assess their own or another race or sex. Also, racial or sex differences have no effect on the validity of the assessment center process (Huck & Bray, 1976). When minorities or women are in the participant population and are to be included in centers, the usual procedure is to organize the assessment center so that a black or a woman does not find that he or she is alone. Many times individual women or minorities are assessed with no ill effects but most administrators try to avoid the situation if possible. The grouping of minority participants (not to be interpreted as having centers exclusively made up of minority candidates) also allows the maximum utilization of minority assessors, who are often in short supply. If minorities or women are included in an assessment center, most organizations try to have at least one member of the assessment staff represent the racial or sex group. Their principal aim is to support or encourage the minority or women participants through the example of a model in management. This also assures that any particular point of view of the minority or sex group is represented in the assessor discussion.

ASSESSOR TRAINING

Assessor training focuses on the following key skills required in the assessment process:

- Understanding the organization's dimensions
- Observation of behavior in exercises
- Categorization of behavior by dimensions found important to the organization
- Rating behavior by dimensions
- Processing information from various exercises to reach consensus among the assessors for a quality or quantity rating on each dimension
- Determination of overall judgments relative to participants, promotability, training needs, etc.

Other tasks performed by an assessor in order to generate the desired behavior in the exercises are also covered in the training. These tasks include:

- Conducting a background interview
- Playing the role of an irate customer in a simulation
- Playing the role of an employee being interviewed in a simulation
- Conducting an in-basket interview
- Playing the role of a resource person in a fact-finding exercise
- Playing the role of a top executive receiving a report from a subordinate (participant) in an analysis exercise

In these behavior generation tasks, the job of the assessor is to act as a positive magnet for behavior. He or she acts in such a way that the maximum possible behavior is brought out from the participants.

Assessor training programs should contain the key skills and as many of the assessor tasks as are required by the exercises chosen.

Understanding the Organization's Dimensions

In order for assessors to categorize observed behavior under the dimensions determined important by the organization so that they can efficiently compare observations from different exercises, the definitions of the dimensions must be thoroughly understood. If a thorough understanding is not achieved during assessor training, a great deal of time in the first assessment center in which the new assessors participate will be spent developing an understanding. It is a false economy to cut down on the formal training of the assessors on the dimensions, because the organization will pay double for the time cut in lengthened assessor discussions while the assessors argue about the meaning of the dimensions rather than about the behavior of the individual being discussed. The key elements in training assessors on dimensions are:

1. Use dimensions based on a sound job analysis which is understandable by the assessors-in-training and in which they took part and thus have commitment.
2. Have as few dimensions as possible.
3. Have clear, short definitions of the dimensions.
4. Give clear, behavioral examples of observations obtainable in each exercise that relate to each dimension.
5. Provide practice for assessors in categorizing behavior under dimensions.

The latter step is probably the most important. Up to that point, it may be possible for assessors to nod their heads in seeming understanding. The real nuances of the definitions are brought out when the assessor is forced to actually say that certain behaviors illustrate this dimension or that dimension. Training procedures for classifying behavior are discussed in a subsequent section.

Observation of Behavior in Exercises

The fundamental skill taught in assessor training is observing and recording behavior—what the person says or does during the actual exercise. Assessors are asked not to initially classify or interpret this behavior in any way.

The validity and usefulness of the assessment center method is based on the accurate recording of behavior. What separates an assessor discussion about an individual from a discussion held by six managers about an employee is the behavioral anchoring of the assessor discussion. An assessor discussion operates very much as a court where evidence in the form of observed behavior must be introduced in order to convince the other assessors. It is not acceptable for an assessor to say, "Mr. X was definitely the leader in the group." He or she must give behavioral examples of how that leadership was shown. This situation is in marked contrast to the usual managerial meeting where generalizations about individuals are shared in making personnel decisions.

Another advantage of basing the assessment process on observed behavior is that it brings out nuances of style and situational responses. For example, an individual's oral communication skill may be excellent in stress-free situations but may deteriorate markedly under stress. Another individual might show excellent judgment in all cases except where he or she is dealing with people. In these cases the individual might see people as all good or all bad—overlooking the faults of people seen as "good guys" and enlarging on the faults in the people seen as "bad guys." These insights can only be obtained from comparing behavior from multiple exercises, each of which was observed by a different assessor. The observations in any one exercise would not be enough to even hint at such insights, but as the reports are read in the assessor discussion and the pieces of information are put together, a larger, more detailed picture of the total individual can be seen.

Most importantly, having behavioral records of performance allows the two end products of the assessment center method—the report to management and the feedback to the participant—to be based on behavior. Management usually does not want a go/no-go decision nor a report consisting of a series of numbers. It wants some indication of the behavior on which the assessor decisions were made. Management wants to be able to compare the observations of the assessment center to its own on-the-job observations. The more the manager can understand the reasoning behind the assessment center recommendations, the better he or she can integrate the data into his or her own perceptions of the individual and the more useful will be the developmental recommendations that can be made.

Feedback discussions with the participant based on assessment center data are usually more effective than those based on appraisal data because of the great amount of behavior which can be cited in the assessment feedback discussion. Specific behavioral observations can be given as evidence in each of the areas discussed. This behavioral backup increases the probability of acceptance by the participant and makes feedback much more useful and meaningful.

Neither of these two positive outcomes (a behaviorally based assessment report or a behaviorally based feedback discussion) can result if behavior is not caught when it occurs during the exercise. But observing and recording behavior is not easy. Individuals must be trained to do it effectively.

The immediate reaction of a new or untrained assessor confronted with watching an assessment center exercise is to:

1. Make general classificatory statements: "She was the leader in the group" or "He was sensitive."
2. Interpret actions: "He asked for more money than he wanted to give himself room for maneuver."
3. Impart feelings to or reasons for the actions: "He was disappointed about his performance."
4. Describe the individual's underlying personality structure: "He had a need for closure," "She wants to be a leader like her father," or "He is paranoid."

To overcome these problems, one of the first steps in many assessor training programs is to use a "Behavior Example Exercise" to help participants understand the difference between a clear, behavioral description of behavior and an unclear, nonbehavioral description. A portion of such an exercise is shown below.

Behavior Example Exercise*

Imagine yourself in an assessor discussion session. Suppose an assessor makes the statement provided below and offers no further data on the behavior in question. If you consider the statement a good example of behavior (i.e., you would be willing to use it in arriving at your evaluation of the dimension being discussed) place a mark in the "good example" column. If you consider it too vague, general, judgmental, etc., and not something you should use in arriving at a conclusion about a participant's skill along a dimension, place a mark in the "poor example" column.

Good Example	Poor Example	Statement
_____	_____	1. Led the group to accomplish its goal.
_____	_____	2. Told the foreman to go ahead and fire the tardy employee.
_____	_____	3. When the arguments became heated, he broke down under the pressure.
_____	_____	4. Was very creative in his solutions to the in-basket problems.
_____	_____	5. Suggested that they not invest all of their money during the first trading period.

©Copyright 1974, Development Dimensions. Inc.

While parts of the skill of behavior observation can be trained individually (by using techniques such as a "Behavior Example Exercise," which teaches assessors-in-training what "behavior" is), there is no substitute for giving an assessor the opportunity to put all of the training elements together in an actual exercise. This practice is the mainstay of most assessor training programs. The assessors are given the opportunity to observe an exercise, using practice subject(s) or videotape. They record behavior as if they were assessing the individual(s) and then complete the observation forms. Then the assessors meet to share their observations. Usually the training is culminated by affording the opportunity for the assessors to watch the exercise again on videotape to see what they missed.

---

*Answers to the exercise are: #1-poor example (PE), #2-good example (GE), #3-PE-didn't describe how heated or what "broke down" means, #4-PE, and #5-GE.

Classifying Behavior

After behavior has been observed, it must be organized by dimensions in order to be useful in the assessment center. This classificatory process is both important and potentially difficult. It also is a true test of the assessors' understanding of the definitions of the dimensions.

The dimensions used in an assessment center have been derived from on-the-job behavior. They are often illustrated by on-the-job definitions. For example, when used in the selection of a pharmaceutical salesman, the dimension "initiative" might have the definition—"Actively influencing events rather than passively accepting; self-starting; would be expected to think of unique ways of getting into a doctor's office." Assessors must translate the meaning of the dimensions from job terms to assessment center terms and fully understand how the dimensions can manifest themselves in behavior observable in the exercises.

Several training techniques seem to work well in teaching behavior classification:

1. Provide multiple examples of observable behavior related to each dimension for each exercise. Examples such as the following for each dimension are usually included with the assessor instructions for each exercise included in Observer Manuals furnished all assessors.

    Leadership—Effectiveness in getting ideas accepted and in guiding a group or an individual to accomplish a task.

    > "Provided initial organization and got the group started on the task by deciding how long each could speak (3 minutes) and assigned order of talks."

    > "Pushed group to get task finished on time; i.e., reminded group of time constraints four times in last 7 minutes."

    > "Looked to for reaction and approval (eye contact) by other group members. Often responded with comments expressing agreement or disagreement—which problem to work on first, final disposition of all proposals, what order participants were to speak, etc."

    Use of Delegation—Ability to use subordinates effectively and to understand where a decision can best be made.

High

"Believes most decisions should be made at the lowest level by the people directly involved."

"Delegated clearly by suggesting courses of action and whom to contact for more information; e.g., 'Tom, see Bill before you. . . .' "

"Used staff to collect data on problems so he could make careful decisions."

"Had secretary hand-carry important letter to his boss first thing Monday morning."

Low

"Did a lot of noncritical work that should have been done by subordinates; e.g., analyzed the attitude survey data."

"Delegated eight items to Rogers, but no items to Smith or Jones."

"Claims that he often becomes overworked because he doesn't trust subordinates to 'do it right'."

2. Provide special guides to the type of behavior usually classified under each dimension for each exercise. These guides are usually included in Observer Manuals along with the instructions for assessor for each exercise. A portion of such a guide is reproduced below.

ORAL PRESENTATION
—Was the participant persuasive in presenting own case?
—Did the participant show enthusiasm and liveliness?
—Did the participant make a special effort to direct the presentation to individuals in the group?
—Was the presentation well organized with an introduction, a body, and a summary?
—Did the participant use good voice modulation, tone control, etc., to emphasize points?

PLANNING AND ORGANIZATION
—How effective was the participant in planning own presentation?
—Was the participant aware of time?
—Did the participant participate in a haphazard manner or follow a predetermined strategy in participating or making suggestions?
—Did the participant consider long- and short-range objectives and/or have long- and short-range plans?
—Did the participant set priorities?

Behavior Classification Exercise

City Council

Below are examples of behavior recorded from the City Council Exercise. Using the dimensions provided in your Observer Manual, your task is to indicate the appropriate dimension under which the behavior would be classified and indicate if it is an effective (with a "+") or an ineffective (with a "-") behavior. A specific example of behavior may appropriately be classified under more than one dimension. Write the appropriate dimension(s) beside the description of behavior in the space provided on the right side of the page. Limit yourself to a maximum of 4 dimensions for each behavior.

Dimension(s)

1. In discussion, made clear concise comments. Used little verbiage, was direct, and to the point.

---

2. When he contributed to the group discussion, it was only to "sell" his department. He made no suggestions or recommendations as to how the group could better accomplish its goals.

---

3. Although representing the Department of Water and Sewers, she identified areas of common concern with other members in the group discussion. Attempted to use this to establish a liaison with 2 other participants (who were promoting Fire and Public Health) by suggesting that an abundant source of clean water would benefit all three departments.

---

4. When his department was challenged by two participants simultaneously, he answered by using good logic, bringing in points he had not mentioned before and tying in positive aspects of his department to the negative aspects of other participants' departments.

---

5. When the group was at a 2-2-2 deadlock in the voting, he suggested a voting procedure which allowed the group members to both vote and rank at the same time. This broke the tie and the issue was resolved.

Dimensions represented are: (1) + Oral communication skill; (2) – Leadership; (3) + Problem analysis; (4) + Stress tolerance and problem analysis; (5) + Problem analysis, creativity and initiative.

3. Provide practice in classifying behavior by using instruments such as the "Behavior Classification Exercise." This is a half-hour programmed instruction, individual training exercise which provides immediate feedback to participants as they practice categorizing samples of behavior. The reader might be interested in trying his or her hand at classifying behavior by taking a portion of the "exercise" shown on p. 107. These "exercises" are available for most of the commonly used assessment exercises from the publisher.

4. Provide practice in categorizing observed behavior and the opportunity to share judgments.

Rating Behavior By Dimensions

After assessors have categorized observed behavior under the organization's dimensions, the next step in most assessment programs is for the assessors to rate the dimensions according to the observed behavior. The following 1 to 5 rating scale is the most commonly used.

> 5—a great deal of the dimension was shown (excellent)
> 4—quite a lot was shown
> 3—a moderate amount was shown (average)
> 2—only a small amount was shown
> 1—very little was shown or the dimension was not shown at all (poor)
> 0—no opportunity existed for the dimension to be shown

Principal use of the dimension ratings for each individual exercise is to aid communication of the observations during assessor discussion. In the assessor discussion, assessors announce the dimension on which they will report and then give their rating. This is followed by a recitation of the observed behavior that supports the rating. The rating prepares the listener for the data to follow. The listener would expect a lot of positive examples of behavior to follow a high rating or many negative examples of behavior to follow a low rating.

Ratings are made relative to an absolute outside criterion which is usually defined as "successful individuals at the target level for which the assessment center is designed." If the assessment center is designed to help select individuals to be first-level supervisors in an automobile assembly plant, then the target level criterion is "an average successful supervisor in that position." As with the users of any rating scale, assessors must be trained in the meaning of the rating so that their evaluations can be as consistent as possible. The use of an outside criterion for comparison must be stressed because the natural reaction of new assessors is to use other individuals in the assessment center as the criterion for comparison. In assessor training programs, the administrators emphasize that in any 12-person assessment center all 12 individuals could rate very high on a dimension or all 12 could rate very low.

Surprisingly, there is very little attempt in most assessor training programs to provide information on the normative group against which ratings are made. It is a basic assumption of most assessment centers that the assessors are familiar with this normative group because they are drawn from the level of management which generally supervises the group (two levels above the assessees). They know how the normative (or target) group behaves on the job; their only problem is hypothesizing how the group would behave in the actual assessment exercises.

A few organizations put a sample of people drawn from the normative group through a pilot assessment program to help the assessors further obtain normative data. For example, if the assessment center were assessing hourly workers for first-level supervisory positions, the organization might arrange for six current supervisors to participate in the exercises to provide "normative" information. This is relatively rare (except for AT&T assessor training programs where the third week of the three-week program is devoted to such a practice session) and no research into its need or effectiveness is available.

Observations of assessment center administrators indicate fairly clearly that assessors in a one-week assessor training program reach good consensus as to appropriate ratings of behavior. A legitimate question arises as to whether groups of assessors trained in different assessor training programs come up with the same set of norms. Two studies, reported by Byham (1976) and Moses (1973), point toward a positive answer to this question.

Little formalized training is provided assessors in rating other than a general discussion using practice data. Such a discussion is facilitated by asking assessors to rate categorized observations of behavior. This can be accomplished by using training aids such as "Behavior Rating Exercise," a portion of which is shown below.

Behavior Rating Exercise

Below are examples of behavior from the Conglomerate Game categorized by dimension. Remember, your rating is relative to successful people at the target level for the assessment center in your organization.

5—a great deal of the dimension was shown (excellent)

4—quite a lot was shown

3—a moderate amount was shown (average)

2—only a small amount was shown

1—very little was shown or the dimension was not shown at all

0—no opportunity existed for the dimension to be shown

Leadership

Active throughout all phases of exercise. During planning period #1, divided up holdings and worked out group strategy. When convinced of a strategy, he actively pushed it to the other members trying to convince them. Active trader during trading period #1; made two deals independently. During planning period #2, he was again on top of the exercise. Knew what other groups held and told group what they should attempt to buy and what they must hold.

Sensitivity

Seemed at times to be frustrated when own group members didn't follow the rationale of his suggestions. He showed this by his nonverbal gestures and his comments; e.g., "You don't understand *that*!" However, he would usually take time to explain his rationale to them in a manner which was not a put-down. When he interrupted others, he always excused himself.

Planning and Organization

From beginning of exercise, he was very conscious of both offensive and defensive strategy. After developing the first plan of attack, he determined how much of each stock his team should attempt to buy, recalling that to buy all stocks in a conglomerate would probably not be possible. During planning period #2, he planned for the upcoming trading session by identifying stocks to sell and to keep. During the trading period #2, he stayed at the trading table for an extended period, tallying the results of trading and making sure the group stayed with its plan. On three occasions, he recalled group members to the table to review the situation and coordinate activities. He also developed a plan for an anticipated last minute trading flurry.

Problem Analysis

Realized early in the exercise that it would be impossible to get all of the stock in four companies. He deduced from questioning that Table #1 did not know his group's (Table #2) holdings in a given stock. He recognized soon in trading period #2 which stocks should be gotten rid of and which stocks held on to. He also recognized the defensive value in holding Great Northern and insisted that it not be sold in the last trading period.

Decisiveness

Although he made a number of decisions, he would often "try them out" on other group members before actively supporting them. When he got agreement from at least one other group member, he would push the decisions hard to the rest of the group. At no time did he really try to convince his group of a strategy until he "tested" it. Although he made two trades independently, the trades had been already decided upon by the group. On two other occasions, he was in a position to make trades, but before doing so, called his group back together to see if they had any objections. Both trades were rational in terms of strategy.

Common Behavior Ratings:

> Leadership—5
>
> Sensitivity—3
>
> Planning and organization—4
>
> Problem analysis—5
>
> Decisiveness—2

© Copyright 1975, Development Dimensions, Inc.

The principal method of instruction is to allow the assessors to observe the same individual in an assessment center exercise and then classify and rate the behaviors. Their ratings are then written on a blackboard and discussed. It always amazes the author how great the agreement is among assessors, once they get over the problems of misclassification of behavior. A leveling of standards quickly develops that can be observed even within an assessor training program. The reliability of ratings increases markedly over the training program, indicating assessors achieve a consensus judgment of the meaning of the ratings.

As with any rating system, there is difficulty in getting the assessors to use the entire rating scale. New assessors tend to use only the middle portions of the scale. Discussion of what behavior it would take to make "1" or "5" helps to alleviate this problem.

Processing Information from Various Exercises and Determining Overall Judgments Relative to the Participant

The last two steps in the flow of information from the observed behavior to a final overall assessment decision typically receive the least emphasis in assessor training. Even the most elaborate assessor training programs give the assessors only one experience in the process of coming to a group consensus on each of the dimensions and on overall rating. This practice is often intended to act more as a final illustration of the need for explicit behavioral observations than to really train assessors in how to integrate the data from the various exercise observations into overall judgments for each dimension. Assessors seem to be able to do this well and therefore there is very little training given outside of a brief lecture on the relative importance of the various dimensions, their interrelationships, and the role of the assessor in the final discussion of each individual.

In their final assessor discussion, assessors must weigh the individual ratings given a dimension in each exercise and come up with an overall rating for that dimension representing all of the available data. The process itself is a very interesting one somewhat akin to taking an aerial photograph of a city. The assessors have observed the dimension in different exercises, which is similar to taking multiple pictures of a city from an airplane. Then they must put those together to form some conclusions about the overall dimension. This is like the lab technician's job of fitting the photographs to each other and overlapping those portions that are similar. Just as a total picture of the city eventually emerges from the multiple pictures taken from the plane, so does a total picture of the individual on a dimension emerge from the multiple insights gained from the various exercises. It is important that assessors have a familiarity with how this process operates and their role in it. It is particularly important that they understand that observations from some exercises are more important than observations from other exercises relative to certain dimensions. For example, in a situation where an individual was seen as being excellent in problem analysis in a complicated analysis exercise and as being only average in problem analysis in a group exercise (where problem analysis is quite difficult to observe), the assessor should put more weight on the analysis exercise finding.

Assessors are told to look over the dimensions and weigh the behavior observed in each dimension on each exercise relative to such factors as:

1. How good the exercise is in bringing out behavior on that particular dimension.
2. The strength of the behavior that was actually observed.
3. The consistency of the behavior over a number of exercises.

The final judgmental act of most assessment centers is when the assessors look over the dimensional profile of strengths and weaknesses of an individual and make some judgment as to potential for advancement. Here again this is an act that most assessors handle very easily, but training is still important. Just as all exercises would not contribute evenly to a final judgment on a dimension, all dimensions are not of equal weight when it comes to the final decision. Most organizations have excellent evidence of that from the job analysis research conducted when starting their assessment program. In that research, management of the organization is usually asked to rate a tentative list of dimensions in terms of importance. Major differences in the relative importance of the dimensions are usually found.

As discussed in other chapters, it is usually not the practice of organizations to give the weighting obtained in the job analysis or other research studies to the assessors. Because of the interrelatedness of the dimensions and the fact that the dimensions are interactive, research studies have tended to show that assessor weightings of the dimensions for a particular individual are superior predictors over a mathematical interpretation of the data derived from empirically defined weights (Huck & Bray, 1976; Moses, 1973).

When the assessors are coming to an overall judgment based on the profile of strengths and weaknesses on the dimensions that they have determined for the individual, the assessors are admonished to do more than add up the dimensions to come to an overall agreement. Instead they are instructed to weight the dimensions relative to the importance of the dimensions, their interrelationship, the degree of assurance with which each of the dimensions was evaluated (some dimensions may be based on a great deal of behavior and other dimensions based on relatively little behavior) and the amount of training that would be needed to overcome weaknesses (and the probability that change could occur). These admonitions are given in a mock assessor discussion during assessor training, and they are the same as those given by most good administrators in every assessment center.

The last major portion of most assessor training programs is devoted to a mock assessor discussion where assessors practice reaching decisions on dimension ratings and in making overall judgments (followed by training recommendations). In two- or three-week assessor training programs, this practice takes the form of a complete mock assessment of six candidates. In the more typical three- to five-day program, only one candidate is assessed. If live practice subjects were used to teach assessors observation skills for each exercise, it is not difficult to arrange for one subject to take part in all the assessment exercises. Then at the end of the assessor training program, it is possible to conduct a mock assessor discussion of this individual using the assessor exercise reports generated in the practice observations. The same thing can be accomplished if an integrated set of model videotapes is used (all with one common practice subject) in training assessors.

Another common device for providing experience in the handling of the final assessment discussion is to watch specially prepared videotapes of assessors in such a discussion. The tape is stopped after the presentation of the exercise reports so that the assessors-in-training can practice integrating the data and reaching final decisions. The final portion of the tape can then be played to show how the model assessors integrated the data.

Any way it is done, some practice in the processing of information from various exercises and determining overall judgments must be provided.

Assessor Training Aids

The accuracy and efficiency of assessor training has markedly increased over the last few years through the use of observer manuals, in-basket manuals, and other aids.

In many centers each assessor is given an Observer Manual. It contains general information about the assessment center process, schedules, the organization's dimensions, instructions for handling each part of each exercise, answers to questions that might be asked of an assessor by a participant, copies of all necessary forms with instructions, copies of all material provided to participants, guides on what to observe at different times during each exercise, hints on being an effective assessor, etc.

In-basket assessor material is often published in a separate manual because of the large amount of data provided. In both manuals the essence of the assessor training program is provided so the assessors need take no notes during the program. The manuals provide a reference for the assessors every time they are called upon to serve. This reorienting function is extremely important when assessors are used only occasionally.

ADDITIONAL GOALS OF ASSESSOR TRAINING

Assessors in most assessment centers must play a dual role in both observing behavior and in stimulating the behavior to be observed. This is, of course, true when the assessor conducts a background interview of the individual, conducts an in-basket interview, acts as a subordinate in the interview simulation, or acts as a supervisor hearing an analysis problem being presented.

In interview situations such as the background interview and the in-basket interview, the assessor is usually obtaining the information from the participant alone and recording that information for later interpretation. In other exercises such as the interview simulation, fact-finding exercise, etc., assessors are often double-teamed so that one assessor "role plays" while the other observes behavior. Experience indicates that keeping the assessors' minds strictly on observing behavior and not on worrying about the role facilitates observation of behavior. Only assessors who are extremely familiar with the exercises are assigned to both tasks.

Positive Model + Practice = Training

The training of assessors to fulfill nonassessment roles varies extensively but most effective programs have two parts: a positive model and a practice session.

In the modeling portion of the training, the trainer acts as a positive model by conducting an interview or acting the role of an irate customer. Videotape can also be used to provide a model. Sometimes several models are shown using several practice participants in order to show the assessors how to perform the function when faced with different kinds of situations (e.g., different styles of leadership in an interview simulation exercise or different avenues of questioning in a fact-finding exercise). This model, of course, is supplemented by a large amount of written data about the role which has previously been supplied (e.g., role-playing instructions, instructions on how to conduct an in-basket interview, etc.).

The practice portion of the training gives the assessors the chance to practice the role playing or interview assignment and be critiqued on their performances. Usually assessors are divided into groups of three with two assessors critiquing the third as he or she practices the assignment.

Background Interview Training

One of the most common tasks of an assessor is to conduct an interview into the background of assigned participants. Special skills must be provided the assessor so that the necessary data are elicited. Training assessors on how to conduct the background interview is one of the biggest challenges of many assessor training programs and one to one and one-half days are often given to this kind of training, which focuses primarily on how to generate the behavior needed so predictions of future behavior can be made. The background interview in an assessment center treats background data as a source of behavior in a way similar to data collected in an exercise. The challenge is to get an accurate understanding of the past behavior. Thus, a large amount of assessor training time is spent in teaching assessors how to ask effective questions and follow up on leads to gain the necessary information.

The assessment interview differs significantly from the selection interview in that the purpose of a selection interview is to make a decision. The purpose of the background interview in an assessment center is to record information on the dimensions being measured—not to make a decision. The assessor is at no time required to make an overall evaluation of the participant based on the interview. He or she must only decide whether there is evidence of the designated behavioral dimensions in the participants' responses and to what degree the dimensions are present. Interviewers in a selection interview usually seek negative evidence about applicants. Interviewers are not evaluated relative to the good people they did not hire but by the poor people they do. This leads them to be particularly sensitive to negative information. The assessor in a background interview focuses on positive, concrete indicators of both positive and negative behavior and on clarifying reasons for behavior rather than on seeking out only negative indicators.

Interview training often begins with a lecture, reading, or other technical input about the interview process. This is followed by a group exercise that develops nonleading questions to elicit information on the dimensions being sought. The purpose of this exercise is not only to develop a list of good nonleading questions to serve as a resource for the assessors but, more importantly, to show the assessors the difficulty of coming up with good questions during an interview and the need for planning an interview.

All participants then develop questions and plan an interview for a practice subject. The practice subject is then interviewed by the trainer or a videotape of an interview is shown. All assessors record observations during the interview as if they were conducting the interview. They then individually categorize and rate the dimensions. This is shared and the effectiveness of the interviewer in bringing out the needed information is discussed.

Practice interviewing usually follows. In many training programs, arrangements are made for assessors to interview an unknown person. These may be local college students or others who have been brought in specifically for this training program. Each assessor has the opportunity to conduct one interview and receive a critique from one or two of his or her fellow interviewers.

Another common design is to divide assessors into groups of three, allowing one assessor to interview another with a third as an observer. The experience is repeated three times until each has had an opportunity to practice.

Whenever the role playing or practice situation is used, it should be done on the basis of "situational playing," which is an adaptation of the role-playing method. In situational playing, the subjects or interviewees develop a situation to "play out," but they are themselves in all other respects. For the purposes of the practice situation, they may decide they are highly motivated by status, passed by too often, very creative, dissatisfied with the competence of their boss, or other situational variables. In the interview they answer questions to reflect these feelings but in response to any other question regarding background, education, etc., they are actually themselves. This increases their ability to provide a believable role and also gives hidden information for which the interviewer may probe. This will also dramatically increase the face validity of this interview practice session.

In-Basket Interview Training

One of the most important exercises of most assessment centers is the in-basket exercise. While excellent insights can be obtained from merely evaluating a participant's completed in-basket exercise, far greater insights are obtainable through a discussion with a participant about his or her handling of various items. In this way assessors are able to clarify and validate hunches obtained from reviewing the written material.

A significant portion of most assessor training programs is devoted to the in-basket exercise. First assessors are provided with a feel for the various approaches to each item. This is accomplished by allowing the assessors to report on how they handled each item and by their reviewing of their in-basket manual, which contains lists of possible courses of action for each item.

Assessors are trained in how to categorize the observed behavior by dimensions using especially developed forms and how to construct appropriate, nonleading questions to follow up on the item in the interview. For example, if a participant wrote on the bottom of a memo "Jane, see me about this," the assessor might want to ask questions such as "What are you going to tell Jane?" "What is the priority you attach to this item?" "Why did you choose Jane?" The questions are designed to further illuminate the dimensions sought and to assure the assessor's understanding of the participant's actions.

The conduct of the in-basket interview itself is usually quite easy for assessors if they have properly prepared. Most training programs provide a positive model of how the interview should be handled and the longer programs allow the assessor/trainee to conduct a practice interview.

When forced to make a decision between allowing the assessors to practice preparing for an interview and actually conducting it, the author usually opts for the former as the preparation is the more difficult task.

Interviewee Training

Many assessment exercises call for an assessor to respond to a participant in some way. The assessor may play the role of an employee with whom the participant must conduct an appraisal interview, an irate customer whom the participant must interrogate and appease, a customer whom the participant must sell, or a top executive receiving a report of an analysis delivered by a subordinate employee (assessee). Detailed instructions on how to play these roles are provided assessors. The opportunity for assessors to practice role playing prior to acting as an assessor is a must. Assessors exhibit a marked tendency to overplay roles unless well trained.

Resource Person Training

A popular assessment exercise is the fact-finding exercise where the participant is given a small amount of information and is allowed to ask questions of a resource person prior to coming up with a decision. The resource person must be trained in how to handle the questions both in terms of answers and in generosity of data provided. The resource person does not volunteer data but only provides data in answer to specific questions.

Several models and the opportunity to practice several times usually makes up the training.

EXAMPLE OF A TYPICAL ASSESSOR TRAINING PROGRAM

For the purpose of this model, let us assume that we are training second-level managers or superintendents whose task will be the assessment of technical/professional employees for promotion to the first level of management. The center is a "typical" one which includes an analysis exercise, an in-basket exercise, a background interview, two group discussion exercises, an interview simulation, and a fact-finding exercise.

The first day of assessor training is always the busiest as it must be devoted to developing an understanding of the assessment center process, learning the dimensions to be measured and their exact definitions, understanding the meaning of "behavioral observations" and how they can be recorded, and training in at least one exercise.

Most programs start out with an overview of the process and a discussion of the dimensions. The dimensions are not only provided and discussed, they are related to the exercises where they will be observed. For example, in a detailed discussion of the dimension "Leadership," effective/ineffective behaviors are explored and typical patterns of behavior are discussed in each exercise.

A valuable part of the first day's experience is the orientation of the staff to how the final assessor discussion is conducted. It is much easier for people to learn a series of tasks if they can learn early in the training how each step in the process relates to the final product. Videotapes of an assessor discussion, or actually holding such a discussion using previously prepared exercise reports, provide this orientation.

Because the ability to recognize significant behavior and to record observations is so critical to the assessment process, a training exercise such as the Behavior Example Exercise is usually used the first day to point out the difference in behavioral versus nonbehavioral statements.

The Behavior Example Exercise might be followed by a videotaped exercise with the entire assessor group focusing on one participant. As the assessors watch the exercise on the TV screen, the appropriate behavioral observations are shown on a movie screen from an overhead projector. Transparencies showing what an assessor would record while watching a videotaped exercise are available from the publishers for many exercises and are very useful. Once the trainer is confident that the assessors are recording most behaviors, the tape is allowed to finish without interruption with each assessor individually making notes. The assessors are then given a positive model of what should have been recorded. It is often helpful to rerun the videotape to check out learning and provide each assessor with feedback on the quality of the behavioral recording.

Another important training element that must be covered the first day is the categorization of behavioral statements by the appropriate dimensions. Again, this must be explained, practiced, critiqued, and practiced again. The half-hour Behavior Classification Exercise using programmed instructional techniques is available for this purpose.

Sometime on the first day, most administrators arrange for assessors to try observing and recording the behavior of a group of practice subjects (usually college students) or a videotape of a group exercise. Many administrators set up the training schedule so that the assessors have the evening to practice summarizing observations under the dimensions and rating those dimensions. The exercise is then continued the next day either by pairing the assessors, working with teams, or working with the whole group in critiquing those reports. This practice and critique should be done two or three times at a minimum during the course of the first few days of assessor training.

Training individuals in handling the in-basket is very important. To save time, the in-basket is usually completed by the assessors in advance of the actual training session. A well-designed assessment in-basket will consist of both independent and interrelated items. An understanding of the items and their relationships to each other is critical. Assessors are taken through the in-basket, item by item. A thorough analysis is made of alternative courses of action for each item and the dimensions indicated. In those cases where a scoring system is used, it is important to go through each item so that the rationale for the scoring is understood.

Because the in-basket is generally one of the most important assessment center exercises, maximum understanding of its use is vital. It is also the most time-consuming exercise for an assessor to evaluate, and practice greatly increases efficiency.

After the trainer has gone through a sample in-basket, item-by-item, showing assessors how to complete the evaluation forms and how to prepare for the interview, the trainer conducts a model interview (or shows a videotape). The assessors all practice making observations and classifying data. They then get a chance to compare their observations and ratings and discuss how the interview was conducted as they watch a replay on videotape. Finally, individual assessors, or small teams of assessors, are given a sample of a finished in-basket for evaluation and practice on preparing for the interview.

In the middle of the training program, assessors are trained in conducting the background interview. This training is most appropriate at this time because it provides a significant change of pace compared to the other training provided. Time spent on this portion of the assessor's training is seen by many organizations as having extremely high value, not only in terms of providing the assessors with needed skills for the assessment center but also by providing assessors with skills they can use on their everyday jobs.

The experiences which fill the remaining two or three days include completion of and training on the analysis exercise, individual exercises, etc. Because the need for experience with assessment will be felt by all of the assessors before they actually conduct a "real life" center, part of the last day is most profitably spent in a simulated center. One model for doing this is to employ a "subject" candidate. This subject goes through most of the exercises while the assessors observe behavior and write reports. The subject participates in the group exercises (with other subjects), does an in-basket, the analysis exercise, and the other one-on-one exercises. He or she is the subject of a background interview in front of the entire group of assessors. The practice assessor discussion then focuses on those assessment reports generated by the assessors after each of the demonstration exercises. Such practice serves to reinforce, review, and strengthen the assessors' skills and makes them more comfortable in their roles before assessing the first group of actual candidates.

When development is a prime objective in assessor training, it is important that all of the assessors have a chance to complete as many of the simulations as possible in addition to utilizing practice subjects to complete the exercises. This is not as critical when the prime objective is only to train them as assessors.

During the training, the assessors themselves are solicited to develop answers, alternatives, various strategies, and answers to be considered. Assessors develop lists of questions to be asked of candidates in interviews. Again, they learn more by developing their own lists of nonleading questions than they will if given a list of "questions to ask." (In some cases where absolute consistency from one center to the next is important, prescribed questions may have to be provided.)

The impact of a total assessor training program on assessors is far greater than the sum of the parts. While the practice provided relative to the various exercises is different, the basic, underlying skills are the same especially that of observing and recording behavior accurately. Thus, one must caution anyone from taking a piece out of an assessor training program and using it alone. If only one exercise were to be used alone (e.g., in-basket), far more practice would have to be provided in the use of that exercise than is normal in an assessor training program where there is overlap in learning from other exercises.

In summary then, a typical five-day assessor training program for middle management would look like this:

CAREER DEVELOPMENT PROGRAM
Assessor Training Schedule

Monday

8:00 - 8:30	Introductions
8:30 - 9:30	Description of assessment center program and dimensions
9:30 - 10:45	How to observe behavior, Behavior Example Exercise, preparation for Compensation Committee Exercise
10:45 - 11:00	Break
11:00 - 12:30	Demonstration of Compensation Committee Exercise (videotape)
12:30 - 1:30	Lunch
1:30 - 2:30	How to categorize behavior, Behavior Classification Exercise
2:30 - 3:45	How to rate behavior, Behavior Rating Exercise, model of final report on subject observed in exercise
3:45 - 4:00	Break
4:00 - 5:00	Watch Compensation Committee Exercise a second time (videotape)
5:00 - 6:00	Write reports
6:00 - 7:00	Dinner
7:00 - 9:00	Read and compare reports

Tuesday

8:00 - 8:30	Introduction to background interview
8:30 - 10:00	Development of nonleading questions for background interview
10:00 - 10:15	Break
10:15 - 11:00	Preparation for background interview
11:00 - 12:30	Demonstration background interview (videotape)
12:30 - 1:30	Lunch
1:30 - 2:30	Write reports
2:30 - 3:30	Discuss reports
3:30 - 3:45	Break
3:45 - 4:30	Discuss reports
4:30 - 5:30	Watch portions of background interview on videotape
5:30 - 6:00	Free
6:00 - 7:00	Dinner
7:00 - 8:30	Assessors participate in Management Problems Exercise
Homework	Prepare for practice background interview

Wednesday

8:00 - 12:00	Practice background interview
12:00 - 1:00	Lunch
1:00 - 1:30	Final discussion of background interview
1:30 - 4:30	Discussion of in-basket items and preparation of in-basket interview
4:30 - 5:30	Group discussion of sample in-basket
5:30 - 6:30	In-basket interview demonstration (videotape)
6:30 - 7:30	Dinner
7:30 - 8:30	Write reports

Thursday

8:00 - 9:00	Compare reports on in-basket interview
9:00 - 9:30	Preparation for interview simulation
9:30 - 9:45	Break
9:45 - 11:00	Demonstration of interview simulation (videotape); discussion of behavior observed
11:00 - 12:00	Practice being an interviewer in interview simulation
12:00 - 1:00	Lunch
1:00 - 2:00	Discussion of analysis problem
2:00 - 2:30	Example of analysis presentations (videotape)
2:30 - 3:30	Write report on behavior observed in analysis presentation
3:30 - 5:00	Discussion of analysis presentation

Friday

8:00 - 12:00	Demonstration of final assessment discussion
12:00 - 1:00	Lunch
1:00 - 2:30	Final questions and answers
2:30 - 3:30	Assessor Certification Exercise

ASSESSOR TRAINING DURING AN ASSESSMENT CENTER

Because organizations often train a pool of assessors at one time, it is not uncommon for six months to one year to pass before a manager gets to try out his or her newly acquired skills as an assessor. Obviously, this should be avoided if possible. But whether the time between assessor training and the first assessment center is one year or one week, the administrator of the assessment center must retrain the assessors before each assessment center. This is usually accomplished by scheduling a meeting each evening where the next day's exercises are discussed, hints on what to do and what to look for are given, etc.

Retraining is particularly important when assessors are to be used for the first time. There is no question that the more an assessor serves, the more efficient he or she becomes and the easier his or her chore becomes (although an open issue relative to this point is how long an assessor can serve before becoming bored). There are no data to suggest that first-time assessors are any less able to carry out their responsibilities than are the experienced assessors; it simply takes them longer. They have to struggle a bit more, and they feel somewhat less confident. An experienced administrator will take these feelings seriously and offer as much support as possible, without overly influencing the decision process.

In the Bendix Corporation, for example, where most assessors serve a limited number of times (in many cases only once) because of their very high level in the organization, great effort has been taken throughout the design of the centers to spend time with the assessors to help them through the process. A meeting is held in advance of the center where the first few exercises are reviewed in detail, and where anxieties are reduced by assuring the close participation of the administrator. As each exercise report is completed, it is turned in to the administrator, critiqued in some detail, and returned to the assessor before the assessor goes on to another report. Regularly throughout the progress of the center, meetings are held with the assessment staff to prepare them for coming exercises and to be sure that they are organized in their own mind with regard to their role, the expectations of the exercise, the dimensions that should be watched for, and other similar factors. It has been found that this is extremely helpful in both increasing the final product of the center as well as reducing the anxieties of the inexperienced assessor.

In general it is advisable to balance an assessment center staff between experienced and inexperienced assessors so that the less experienced assessor can learn "tricks of the trade" from the more experienced. This has been accomplished effectively by Chevrolet Sales. Their teams of assessors include five to seven experienced and one or two new assessors. The new assessors are actually assessors-in-training. During the center, the experienced assessors each carry a workload heavier than normal, while the newly trained assessors carry a half load and work alongside an administrator who helps them. All assessors serve three times; as they serve, they are developing their replacements. This has allowed the assessment of a large number of people in a very short time using only three weeks of an assessor's time.

Overcoming Assessor Anxiety

Attendance at an assessor training program is usually accompanied by a degree of anxiety common to participation in most developmental programs. Managers feel uneasy in the application of new techniques to their usual decision process.

More importantly, there will probably be underlying anxiety present about the possibility that they themselves are being assessed (by the administrator or senior managers present). Assessors often make jokes about this. The problem usually solves itself as they experience the training program and they see that they are not put on the spot.

The managers in an assessor training program feel the weight of their responsibilities to candidates and at the same time are often confused by a myriad of new administrative details and new jargon. This increases their anxiety, making them more highly motivated learners. Those with experience in adult education know that anxious, highly motivated adult learners are also often defensive, questioning, stubborn learners and need more than the average reinforcement. They also need adequate opportunity to assimilate all of the new ideas and new skills. As in any case where people are required to make critical decisions, they can become irritated by details or by confusing procedures. A good administrator will recognize the anxieties of the manager-in-training and will do everything possible to reduce or eliminate any additional tensions that might be created by poor or loose organization or by unclear administrative details.

Other factors may also be operating during assessor training. If managers have been assessed themselves prior to serving as assessors, there may be a need to rationalize their behavior or to further examine their strengths or weaknesses. Even though, as participants, they received feedback regarding their performance at a previous center, this might be the first time that they will receive detailed orientation about the methods of measurement and the dimensions that have been identified. This will leave them with natural questions as they recall their own experiences and activities when they participated in similar exercises. An effective trainer will allow the feelings of the assessor-in-training to surface openly. This can be accomplished by drawing from the assessors their experiences and reactions as they go through a center as participants. This can also be accomplished by allowing full discussion, sharing of experiences, and disagreement on concepts as they are discussed.

ASSESSOR TRAINING AS AN INVESTMENT

The best planned assessment center and the most professionally written exercises are wasted if assessors cannot adequately perform their job of recording and classifying observed behavior. It is false economy to cut back on the training of assessors if the intent of the program is to sharpen behavioral observations.

Extensive training may even allow an organization to have a shorter assessment center than would otherwise be possible. Extremely well-trained assessors can get more out of three exercises than untrained or partially trained assessors can get out of five exercises. There also is a marked difference in the level of sophistication of observations. Assessors who are skimming the behavior in exercises are relating to only gross differences while some of the more subtle and often more important differences may be missed.

Another reason why assessor training is a good investment becomes immediately obvious when assessors meet to discuss their assessment center observations and reach conclusions on the dimensions and overall potential. To the extent that the assessors base their ratings on meaningful behaviors and communicate these observations effectively, the discussion can go very quickly and be extremely efficient. To the extent that this does not happen, the assessor discussion is slowed as assessors try to draw from each other examples of behavior to illustrate the ratings provided. Thus, any time saved in cutting back on assessor training is lost on a much larger scale in needlessly extended assessor discussions.

Why Companies Do Not Conduct Assessor Training

The most common rationale of those organizations that minimize assessor training is that manager/assessors in assessment centers are only asked to do what management does all the time—observe and evaluate people, interview people, etc. The fallacy of this argument lies in the fact that just because managers do these tasks all the time does not mean that they do them well. Another argument sometimes made is that the assessors are so guided by the administrator and the observation forms that training is not necessary. While the supplemental observation forms now available for many exercises do ease the assessors' job and help organize observations, training is still necessary in how to use the forms.

It is the author's observation that the most skilled managers using the most advanced forms cannot perform adequately without substantial training. This view is supported by the "Standards of Assessment Center Operation" adopted by the 1975 International Congress on the Assessment Center Method.

Understudy as a Substitute for Assessment Training

Some of the better, more extensive assessor training programs arrange for newly trained assessors to understudy experienced assessors in an assessment program before they become full-time assessors. They observe the same participants as the more experienced assessors, write up their observations, and compare their reports with those produced by the experienced assessors. This is a fairly expensive process in that it calls for double-teaming assessors.

A few organizations that provide no formal assessor training use the understudy method as the sole method of training new assessors. While this method of training is certainly better than nothing, it does not, in the author's opinion, substitute for formal assessor training. The amount of critique and feedback provided is necessarily much less than that provided in formal assessor training. While no evidence exists, we would certainly recommend that the time could better be spent in a formal training program than in an understudy program if one had to choose between the two.

RESEARCH NEEDS

One should not be surprised by the dearth of research on assessor training when one thinks of the lack of research into the effectiveness of most types of training. But still one must be disappointed when surveying the literature in this area to find almost no research on training even though companies spend millions of dollars a year on assessor training and the accuracy and usefulness of assessment programs are greatly determined by the success of that training.

The major research problem has stemmed from the fact that until recently there was no commonly accepted method of evaluating the effectiveness of assessors. Because of this lack of criterion, it was therefore nearly impossible to equate the effectiveness of assessor training programs of different lengths, made up of different contents, and based on different philosophies. Lacking quantitative data, one had to fall back on highly subjective observational data, and this is the basis of many of the observations made in this chapter.

Some experimentation is going on. Researchers at Development Dimensions, Inc., have devised a series of pencil-and-paper "Assessor Skills Evaluation Tests" and a "Behavior Observation Test" where assessors watch 10 minutes of an exercise on videotape, record, and rate behavior. Their behaviors are then evaluated in a way so as to produce a score indicating the amount of observed behavior relative to the total behavior possible to observe. While this instrument is used primarily to help assessors to better understand their own capabilities, it has already provided many useful research insights. This and similar instruments can be used before and after assessor training to gauge the effectiveness of various variations in format, content, and staffing of assessor training programs.

A more far-reaching research possibility that is being tried involves the development of standardized videotape input data for all the exercises in an assessment center. These tapes are shown to groups of assessors receiving differential amounts of training or different types of training. That is, teams of assessors who have been differently trained observe each assessment center exercise and ultimately come to final assessment decisions. These decisions are then compared to determine the extra benefits that can be derived from, for example, adding one additional day of training to an assessor training program. At one time, this might have been quite difficult because it would have meant having dual teams of assessors observing assessment activities. With most organizations having videotape facilities, this is no longer so difficult. This kind of research works particularly well for assessment centers that operate routinely using videotape. In those instances, standardized data could be developed, and assessor teams could evaluate the standardized data on, for example, six candidates with no knowledge of whether it was a "test" case or not. Such research becomes less pure when an assessor team that is accustomed to viewing live data is asked to evaluate data on TV. This gives them a clue that they are being tested.

Certainly there are no limits to the kinds of studies that a fertile researcher's mind could invent. The problem is not what to do but trying to get people to do anything.

REFERENCES

Byham, W. C. Reliability of the assessment center method. *Assessment and Development*, March 1976.

Byham, W. C., & Wettengel, C. Assessment centers for supervisors and managers. *Public Personnel Management*, September-October 1974.

Hinrichs, J., & Haanpera, S. A cross national evaluation of assessment centers in eight countries. *Assessment and Development*, January 1975.

Huck, J. R., & Bray, D. W. Management assessment center evaluations and subsequent job performance of white and black females. *Personnel Psychology*, 1976, *29*.

Moses, J. L. The development of an assessment center for the early identification of supervisory potential. *Personnel Psychology*, 1973, *26*, 569-580.

CHAPTER 7

HOW AND WHY ASSESSMENT WORKS *

Douglas S. Holmes

INTRODUCTION

The heart of an assessment center is the evaluation meeting which integrates data from both the assessment techniques as well as from the various assessors. In this chapter, Dr. Douglas Holmes describes the process used in making assessment decisions.

He points out that there are two different kinds of decisions which assessors must make—an evaluation of specific strengths and weaknesses and a determination based on an analysis of these strengths and weaknesses. A key point made is the capability of the assessment center to provide the assessor with concentrated behavior in many different areas which may be more accurate than a supervisor observing an individual performing the same function repeatedly.

It should be noted that each assessment center has a set of decision rules concerning the evaluation of behavior. This includes the sequence of observing data, the scheduling of assessor-assessee combinations, the method of presenting information in the evaluation meeting, the decision rules for discussing and resolving differences, etc. These systematically insure a more reliable and objective process as well.

* * *

---

*This chapter was prepared when the author was associated with the Center for Creative Leadership, Greensboro, North Carolina.

This chapter provides an overview of how and why assessment works in assessment centers. In a nutshell, the assessment center process captures in action much of what has been learned over the years about rating theory and methodology. The process is uncomplicated, thereby precluding many potential sources of error. Special restrictions placed on assessors minimize additional known sources of error. These include, for example, evaluating only individuals unfamiliar to the assessors or mixing the composition of assessors and assessee. Because only *relevant* dimensions *capable of being rated well* are considered, information that is not useful and potentially misleading is held to a minimum.

In this chapter, some of the rationale involved in the assessment center rating procedure is discussed. Also, some of the more important psychological forces and processes that operate in an assessment center are identified and placed in perspective.

Two types of readers have been kept in mind: the reader-in-a-hurry who wants to learn about assessment quickly for immediate, practical purposes, and the reader-with-some-leisure who wants to enrich and deepen his understanding of assessment. Most of the chapter is written for the reader-in-a-hurry. In one section—"The Logic of Assessment Center Assessment"—pauses are advisable. Primarily, this section focuses on a single question: Why is it reasonable to believe that one can make better predictions about a person's performance after a few days of observation than after several years of observation? This section can be skimmed or skipped if the reader is not interested in the question. However, it should be noted that development of an appreciation for the implications of answers to the question may have practical value. Such an appreciation, in the author's view, would provide an important basis for sound judgments about practical questions which arise regarding assessment centers: What are the inherent limitations of an assessment center? What apparently reasonable changes might be introduced in an assessment center which would gradually decrease the center's effectiveness without the reduction being recognized for years? How can an assessor "keep honest" when there may be no experience-based cues which reveal that the assessor is being less than conscientious?

WHAT IS DONE IN MOST ASSESSMENT CENTERS

The most common purpose of assessment is to select or identify individuals for higher level management assignments. As noted in Chapters 1 and 3, assessment center procedures are applied to other populations and used for other purposes as well. Regardless of the immediate project, two kinds of basic assessment judgments are made. These are:

1. A determination of an assessee's strengths and weaknesses with respect to the specific dimensions evaluated at the center. This determination is made on the basis of a continuous rating scale, usually from 1 (low) to 5 (high). Here, assessors must rate an individual's behavior on specific, continuous scales—i.e., leadership, oral skills, etc.

2. A determination of an assessee's strengths and weaknesses with respect to a specific assessment outcome—i.e., a recommendation for promotion, placement in a special development program, reassignment, etc. This determination, known as the overall rating (OAR), is the culmination of the evaluation of performance at the center. It serves as a recommendation for specific action. This rating is made on the basis of a discrete scale—i.e., either an individual is recommended or not.

In order to accomplish the purposes previously discussed, assessors engage in a sequence of planned activities. Probably the most commonly used sequence is that originated at American Telephone & Telegraph Company (Bray & Grant, 1966). Assessees are observed in individual and group exercises following a prearranged schedule. Descriptive summaries of each assessee's performances in each exercise are prepared prior to the staff evaluation meeting. In this meeting, an assessee's performances are described and discussed. Ratings on specific behavioral dimensions (e.g., leadership, oral skills) are then made by all assessors present, and discrepant ratings are discussed. Discussion of ratings, each taken individually, is followed by consideration of and decisions about the larger issues: overall categorization, specific developmental recommendations, and suggestions of specific steps the company might take to optimize fulfillment of the individual's potential (e.g., placement in a special development program, reassignment).

Each step in the sequence of planned activities is designed to permit systematic evaluation of behavior. As noted in Chapter 4 ("Issues in Establishing an Assessment Center"), an analysis of behaviors needed for success and the development of techniques designed to measure these characteristics are needed in order to design an assessment system.

The individual participates in a variety of simulations. These exercises are designed, as noted in Chapter 5, to stimulate behaviors and activities required for success and to provide a focal point for evaluation of specific assessment dimensions.

Assessors are trained (Chapter 6) to observe behavior and to report on participant performance. A number of reporting methods and observational techniques are used to enable the assessor to synthesize performance. This leads to ratings made by the staff on the specific dimensions, the resolution of differences as a function of behavioral performance, and, finally, the determination of an overall rating. As noted earlier, the assessor in effect makes two kinds of judgments in the process: ratings of specific performance and judgments of outcome.

THE LOGIC OF ASSESSMENT CENTER ASSESSMENT

The foundation stone of assessment centers is the assumption that assessors are able to "know a good person when they see one." The "goodness" of a person is not an individual character assessment; it is instead a term related to particular position requirements. Managers in nonassessor roles have seen effective and ineffective performances by incumbents in the target level. They have, also, traditionally made rating judgments. In the role of assessors they are asked to evaluate the meaningfulness of the behavior observed. The judgment process used in the evaluation session enables an individual to focus on relevant behaviors.

The job of the assessment center professional is to enable the assessors to "see" each individual accurately in order to provide a basis for recognition. *Seeing an individual accurately* is the most difficult part of the assessment process; it is an eminently creative act on the part of a manager or assessor and requires the assessor to both assimilate and evaluate data from a variety of sources. Often, this requires judgment on the part of the assessor to determine which source provides the "best" information.

The next section examines this process from a phenomenological point of view. The profound nature of "seeing an individual" at all must first be appreciated in order to grasp the simplicity, elegance, and power of the assessment center process. It is only through appreciating in general how people create meaningful portraits of other individuals that we can begin to understand how a specifically controlled assessment process can result in the creation of more accurate pictures. Fifteen years ago, the Secretary of the Smithsonian Institute wrote eloquently about how we come to know the world around us:

> . . . we all know that inside our head is the brain. The presence of this brain, we agree, is necessary in order that we may hear, see, think or act intelligently. We know that until it has been prepared and hardened by chemicals for the laboratory the brain is soft. In life its consistency and color are something like stiff oatmeal. The brain is amazingly well protected and isolated from the external world by its bony case.

> There is still much mystery about this brain. How can a spongy, wet organ which lives alone in darkness make possible our intelligent actions, the beautiful colored visual world that we know and indeed our whole subtle and complex mental life? . . .

Sir Charles Sherrington, possibly the greatest student of the nervous system in the twentieth century, has said, "Yet nerve and brain are but a skillfully laid train of powder between the muscles it fires and the restless world outside which fires it . . ."

In this quotation the phrase "train of powder" means a trail of gunpowder or a fuse. This fact should be emphasized because, surprising as it may seem, the modern conception of the nervous system and brain suggests that everywhere the activity of the system involves a *progressive* and yet at each point a wholly *local* release of energy. Energy is *not* put into a nerve by the stimulus or even by the sense organ. A liquid or current does not run or flow from the eye to the brain nor does "an image" travel over the optic nerve to the brain . . .

This truly amazing fact concerning the relationship between the brain and the outside world should be faced by everyone who would understand psychology. It has disquieting implications. No one fully comprehends mental life and its limitations who does not keep this basic relationship in view. The separateness of the world and the brain is hard to accept when it is first considered. It seems to deny common sense. The fact is established, however, that the brain is always in certain respects absolutely set apart from the outer world as it functions in its bony case . . .

. . . we—that is, in this sense, our brains—are never directly in contact with the properties of external things, but only with the state of our own nerves as they are ignited, to use Sherrington's vigorous analogy, by the outside world. Brain remains brain and outside world the outside world. The two are in communication only by periodic signals of sensory nerves which are in many respects like the dots and dashes of telegraphy. The red, white and blue flag does not enter the dark brain but our eyes and optic nerves send in, under proper conditions, messages or signals which make the normal person able to differentiate these colors, respond to them appropriately and have what we call the "visual experience" related to them. (Carmichael, 1957, pp. 37-43)*

When reflecting upon the inherent mystery of perception, juxtapose your awareness of the absolute certainty with which each of us perceives the world around us. It is important to recognize that our sense of certainty stems from our general nature rather than from our specific knowledge of the accuracy of the information with which we begin. In an assessment center process, to the contrary, our confidence in categorizations is related directly to our knowledge about the accuracy and adequacy of signals concerning participants assessed.

The creative act of an assessor who is developing a meaningful picture of an assessee is not unlike the creative act of the same manager in the role of observing subordinates on the job. The only difference lies in the amount and quality of information used.

One might suppose that the amount and quality of information a manager collects about a subordinate supervised for two years would be superior to that gained in two days in an assessment center; this is not necessarily the case. Apart from some of the specific, inherently strong points of an assessment center which are discussed further on, there is a very general advantage—that of concentrated observation and collection of data.

In a socialized setting such as a job, casual, unsystematic observations often serve as a basis for forming long-lasting (and often inaccurate) impressions. For example, a subordinate known for two years, according to the chronological log book, may actually be known for two minutes times a thousand recycles of and elaborations of an initial impression. In a job setting, remarkably few factors operate to correct misimpressions of a subordinate, while pressures to converge on a commonly accepted picture of an individual may well abound.

A major advantage of a well-conducted assessment center is the relatively long period of careful observation (e.g., two days) that precedes major behavioral inferences about a person being assessed. If an individual's behavior is sampled in a variety of relevant situations, and if the assessors *delay* in creating a portrait of the person until the totality of observations are assimilated, then the amount and quality of potentially observable information about the assessee may well equal or surpass that which is available in a typical job setting. The important question in either situation is this: How much information—as opposed to confirmation of already created meanings—do observations provide?

To summarize, the logic of assessment centers is this: if the controlled activities of an assessment center provide information about an individual which is sufficient to permit creation of relevant and accurate portraits about on-the-job performance, and if assessors can accurately categorize these portraits, then descriptions and predictions about the assessee should relate to on-the-job performance. An example of the assessment center process related to determination of selling abilities was, you will recall, presented in Chapter 1.

WHY ASSESSMENT CENTER ASSESSMENTS ARE POWERFUL

1. *OARs Are Valid.* Evidence of the effectiveness of overall assessment center ratings (OARs) is positive (Cohen, Moses, & Byham, 1974; Huck, 1973). The success of predictions relevant to a variety of criteria indicates that assessors have successfully categorized effective and less effective performers. Therefore, the information provided to the assessors must have been sufficient for their creation of accurate and meaningful portraits as a basis for categorization.

Why are assessment center categorizations valid? The probable explanation is that the assessment center process permits the assessors to realize their fullest potential as evaluators through the structured convergence of a number of separately powerful forces. If left to chance, these divergent forces would not only individually detract from the effectiveness of assessment but also cumulatively destroy the gains in assessment technology embodied in an operational assessment center.

In the following paragraphs, some of the more important forces affecting assessment center measurements are outlined.

2. *Predicting Behavior from Behaviors.* From the point of view of the assessor, assessing has only two parts: observations and creations of meanings through the process of *inferring* from observations. Abilities to observe and to infer are central to the activity of assessing.

The concept of *time* is irrelevant to the process of making inferences. It makes no difference to an assessor whether the inferences are about the past, present, or future (e.g., "I bet this person is/was/will be a good supervisor"). What *is* relevant to the process of making inferences is the assessor's skill and storehouse of relevant information. When an assessor moves from stating observations to describing meanings, inferences are utilized and the process is unaltered whether past, present, or future meanings (imagined or created) are described.

The distinction between the psychological process of inferring and time-related concepts such as predicting is important because errors in assessment occur only at the psychological levels of observing and inferring. Most of the inferences made in assessment centers never see the light of day in the form of written predictions or descriptions. However, because of the importance of the products of assessment—OARs, behavioral ratings, and final written predictions and descriptions—assessors must fight a natural tendency to overassess product-related statements and underassess the many elemental observations and associated inferences which lead to final conclusions. Care must be taken, for example, not to infer that a person was silent for 10 minutes in a group discussion because he felt intimidated, but rather that the person was silent. The participant may be silent for many reasons, which include both situational and personal factors.

3. *Safety in Numbers.* The desired products of an assessment center are accurate categorizations. The act of categorizing, with some justification, can be performed by one assessor after five minutes' exposure to an assessee. The only reason that more than this is done is to increase the accuracy of categorization which, operationally, amounts to decreasing errors of categorization.

One way to decrease errors is to increase the number of chances of being right. As the number of behavioral dimensions and situations observed increases, the chance of overlooking an important facet of an assessee's qualifications decreases.

Many duplications exist in an assessment center to serve as a form of "checks and balances." These provide the judge with multiple inputs which minimize the possibility of unreliability of individual judgment.

4. *Advantage of Working in Groups.* Working in groups does more than provide safety in numbers. Assessees, being all in the same boat, provide group support for one another, as well as the impetus of competitive stimulation in an evaluative atmosphere. Further, the degree of respect that assessees show for one another provides an astute assessor with information about peer evaluation.

In the assessor group, a little recognized fact is the degree to which supervisory functions are accomplished by a team atmosphere. Because assessors must count on each other for reliable, observational information, each assessor is motivated to "stay on the ball" and to pay careful attention to work quality. The assessor is "kept honest" by the awareness that anything reported is open to challenge and must be defensible. The assessor soon finds it necessary to take careful notes on behavior in order to adequately discharge this responsibility to other team members.

5. *Practice Makes Perfect.* If you practice something the right way, practice makes perfect. With assessment center assessments, "the right way" is determined in large part by the controlled sequence of exercises and procedures. With standardized procedures, each repetition amounts to practice and improved ability to perform assessments. Assessors develop a frame of reference with experience that enables them to sort the behaviors observed.

6. *Use of Behavioral Data.* Assessment reports are based on observable behavior rather than conjecture. Observable behavior can always be described by a verb and an adverb—"The individual *spoke well.*" If several repetitions of "speaking well" are observed, we might reasonably use an adjective and a noun as part of a characterization—"The person is a *good speaker.*" Ultimately, we might wish to use a generalized noun—"speaking *ability*"—in referring to a quality "possessed" by a person.

The preceding grammatical analogy describes an assessment ladder of abstraction, beginning with verbs, which are most concrete, and ending with nouns, which are most abstract. At each successive rung of the ladder *errors* are *introduced*. Observers can usually agree that an individual *spoke*, or *decided*, or *summarized*. Observers agree somewhat less often whether an individual spoke, decided, or summarized *well* or *poorly*. More judgment, hence more possibilities for disagreement, is required with the use of adverbs than with verbs. Both verbs and adverbs, however, are rooted in observations of behavior.

Underlying the use of adjectives and nouns are inferences, or created meanings. The conclusion from several observations that an individual is a *"good* decision maker" logically involves two steps: the application of verbs and adverbs to actions which are *abstracted* from ongoing behavior (e.g., decisions being made well or poorly) and the use of adjectives and nouns as a means of generalizing from the observed behaviors to the more enduring characteristics of the individual (e.g., "This person is a good decision-maker" or "The individual has lots of decision-making ability").

One of the major strengths of assessment center assessments is that they are based on the use of verbs and adverbs to an unusually high degree. Because assessors are required to speak in terms of concrete behaviors, most of the discussion among assessors has a factual, observable basis.

For those familiar with the history of psychological assessment, this concern with concrete behaviors can be seen to be a potent advantage indeed. In assessment center discussions, for example, one hears very little talk about an assessee's strong need for dominance being balanced with a strong need to be liked by everyone he meets. Instead, one hears about how the individual retreated from a strong line of argument when personally attacked by another group member, and about how adaptive or maladaptive this sort of behavior would be in the position for which the individual is being considered. The problem with using nouns and adjectives when assessing individuals is that the potential advantage of increased generalizability is too seldom realized due to inadequacies in their factual basis.

The emphasis upon behavioral observations in assessment center discussions places assessment categorizations on a factual basis. The nature of these assessments can be described as an "eyes-on" process, featuring discussions about an assessee which literally minimize nonsense. Thus, assessors remain close to their behavioral information, thereby maximizing the likelihood of extracting useful meanings from their observations.

7.   *Behavioral Dimensions.* If the concepts previously mentioned can be relied upon to maximize the utilization by assessors of information available in an assessment center, what can be relied upon to maximize the utility of final categorizations for the ongoing work environment? Part of the

answer has already been provided. Assessors are usually line managers; they can be counted upon to see relationships with the work environment. This is especially the case where the exercises provide a representative work sample of the work environment.

Even when the work sample is only metaphorically representative of the actual work environment, good assessment categorizations can be accomplished if the behavioral dimensions have been carefully chosen and if behaviors relevant to these dimensions are elicited by the exercises. It is, after all, the individual's behavior, not the work environment, which is being assessed. The validity of assessment center categorizations depends in large part on appropriate exercises eliciting measurable behaviors relevant to dimensions which are operative in the work environment.*

8.   *Better Vision.* Two important characteristics of perception are used advantageously by the assessment center process. First, much of what we see is relative, or determined by *relationships* among things seen. For example, look at Fig. 7-1 and decide which man is large, which man is

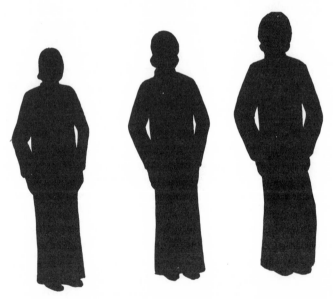

Fig. 7-1 Representative Sketch

---

*The author and his colleagues have developed a week-long interplanetary simulation which was used to assess leaders from many walks of life (e.g., business, education, government, and military). The exercises, behavioral dimensions, and concepts underlying development of the simulation are documented in eight monographs available from the *Catalog of Selected Documents in Psychology.* (Holmes, 1975a, provides an overview of the monographs; Holmes, 1975b, discusses issues related to assessment centers.)

small, and which man is medium-sized. None of us finds this difficult because we automatically compare the men with one another. Are any of the men large when compared with the size of this page? Again, none of us experiences difficulty in responding because both the size of the page and the sizes of the men are easily perceived; their relative sizes are obvious. But to answer the question, "Are any of the men large?" is to be forced to respond, "Compared to what?"

An advantage of an assessment center is that assessees provide concrete comparison points for one another. Observers automatically perceive differences along behavioral dimensions among assessees as a function of actual behavioral differences among assessees. As shown by the example of size comparisons in the paragraph above, although there is no warning bell that sounds for us when we switch comparison points, our answer "large" or "small" depends on which invisible frame of reference we employ. Because those invisible frames of reference have a natural way of shifting, a tremendous advantage is provided by any assessment situation that can provide concrete comparison points (e.g., six persons simultaneously engaged in the same task).

In the judgment of many experienced assessors, the point made in the paragraph above is the greatest advantage that an assessment center process has over an individual assessment process. The importance of comparison points in perception is amply documented in the scientific literature.

The second fact about how we perceive that is advantageously used by assessment centers concerns *perceptual differentiation* or the enriching nature of multiple perceptions. Figure 7-2 portrays an undifferentiated four-cell box. Examining it for a moment suggests nothing spectacular, and

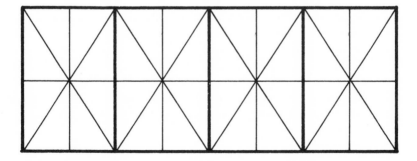

Fig. 7-2.

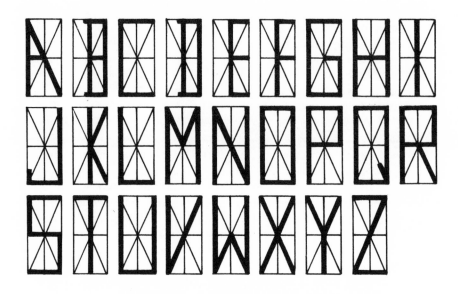

Fig. 7-3.*

results in a global impression of a symmetrical, rather uninteresting box. However, it is a fact that all of the letters of the alphabet can be traced within each cell of the box. This seemingly insignificant box actually contains all of the four-letter words in the English language. If one were to spend an hour tracing the individual letters and again examined the unaltered box, it would no doubt appear far more interesting in retrospect. One would be able to see the many letters and words concealed within it, and would undoubtedly make some aesthetic judgments concerning shapes of individual letters. A way of lessening the detective work is to proceed to Fig. 7-3, an expanded version of the box where the letters have been outlined, and then return to Fig. 7-2. Your first impression of Fig. 7-2 is analogous to the assessor's first impression of an individual being assessed. The traceable letters of the alphabet are analogous to behavioral dimensions manifested by an individual assessee. Your last impression of Fig. 7-2, after having examined the traceable letters, is analogous to the overall impression, or categorization, of an assessee at the completion of assessment.

---

*From INDIVIDUAL BEHAVIOR, Revised Edition by Arthur W. Combs and Donald Snugg (Harper & Row, 1955).

Measuring an assessee's performance along behavioral dimensions does more than supply information about important types of behaviors. It insures that significant aspects of functioning are not overlooked. It also provides a basis for the creation of a more highly differentiated or more complex portrait of an assessee, thereby permitting a categorization based on a richer appreciation of an individual's potential performance.

Summary. Assessment center assessments are powerful because they are based upon concrete, undeniable facts about an individual and make excellent use of the experience, wisdom, and information-processing capabilities of managers. The assessment center technique represents a compatible marriage among the skills of human observers and decision makers, the recognition capabilities of humans, and a structured set of procedures which appropriately separate and order nonevaluative observation, creation of meanings, and judgmental decision making.

THE IMPORTANCE OF PROPER SEQUENCING IN THE ASSESSMENT PROCESS

The sequence of activities in an assessment center can be divided into two major phases. The second, or concluding phase involves the creation of a portrait of the assessee, agreeing on an overall categorization, and conclusive identification of strengths and weaknesses. It is most vital that these processes be *delayed* until all of the facts about an individual have been assimilated.

The first, or preliminary phase of the assessment sequence includes making behavioral observations, forming impressions or gaining insight concerning an individual, and rating along behavioral dimensions. An important consideration is the degree to which observers, as they proceed in the assessment process, share information about behavioral observations, impressions, and numerical ratings. The advantage of sharing is that each assessor's fund of information is increased and is subject to early correction or revision. The major disadvantage is that observers may unduly influence one another, thereby decreasing the desired independence of observation during exercises.

Observer discussions should be continuously monitored, their quality being evaluated by each observer as well as by the assessment team leader. The natural social tendency to share feelings immediately following observation of an exercise, for example, must be controlled because of the likelihood of biasing influence.

HOW ASSESSMENT CENTER ASSESSMENTS COMPARE
WITH OTHER WAYS OF PERFORMING ASSESSMENTS

Fundamentally, assessment descriptions and judgments can be formulated in two ways: by using human judgment every step of the way or by using mechanical or clerical procedures such as actuarial tables or mathematical formulae. The arguments in favor of one or the other are similar to the arguments about the relative merits of manned versus unmanned space exploration.

It would appear, in theory, that mechanical assessment can succeed as well as or better than judgmental assessment. A number of research studies have been reported in which computers, using mathematical formulae or actuarial tables, have outperformed human assessors in certain nonassessment-center situations. Furthermore, highly knowledgeable, experienced psychologists have constructed, at great cost, computer programs interpreting the profiles of specific psychological tests; and thereafter the psychologists responsible have preferred the computer printout to their own spur-of-the-moment interpretations of test responses. The functional superiority of actuarial tables, mathematical formulae, and computer programs over human judgmental assessments can be attributed to two factors: in the design stage of these mechanical devices, great care can be taken to insure that each component is based on comprehensive, accurate information; through a process of trial-and-error, the decision-making procedures of the device can be perfected.

Although mechanical assessment can, in theory, do a creditable or even superior job, in practice it may not work so well. Most of the scientific studies purporting to demonstrate the superiority of mechanical assessment to judgmental assessment have been found lacking with respect to their research design and rationale (Holt, 1970). Judgmental assessments have demonstrated validity when "expert" assessors have put themselves to the test (Cronbach, 1970) and when assessment center procedures have been used (Cohen et al., 1974). Ultimately, a choice between mechanical or judgmental assessment depends on practical considerations. Are necessary personnel and facilities available? What are the relative costs and benefits? How coarse or fine a screening of assessees is required? A quick, preliminary assessment of "acceptable" and "questionable" categories might call for mechanical assessment if the possible consequence of misclassification is not too serious. Other issues as well are covered in Chapters 13 and 14.

Broadly conceived, within an assessment center framework practically any form of assessment can be utilized. Nothing prevents mechanical assessment procedures from being used, as indeed they typically are, in the form of intelligence tests, current events tests, and the like. Likewise, some judgmental assessment techniques requiring interpretations by a highly trained professional assessor are included in some assessment centers—interpretations by a clinical psychologist of projective test results.

Because the assessment center technique can include practically all forms of assessment, its future viability would seem to be assured. Professional assessors, familiar with judgmental assessment, prefer it primarily because of the advantages described earlier. A single assessor working with a single assessee is at a disadvantage because of the assessor's inherent inability to exceed personal limitations. In addition, there is the impediment of the intrinsic difficulties of inferring a range of interpersonal behavior in diverse situations without access to actual observed samples of such behaviors.

Although assessment center assessments appear both in theory and in practice to be of substantial merit, their demonstrated validity may vary with both the situations and the times in which they are performed. For example, it might be argued that assessment centers as currently operated are successful at identifying the degree to which individuals are motivated to learn and to perform the role of manager, and the degree to which they possess those potential abilities required for effective role performance. If the nature of managerial roles were to change markedly—perhaps in the direction of greater self-expression and individuality—the balance of assessment techniques and procedures might also have to change in order to retain a capability for creating portraits of assessees which relate accurately to on-the-job performance. For instance, projective techniques and interviews are relatively more useful than leaderless group discussions in assessing directions of self-expressive tendencies, while the opposite is the case with respect to leadership performance in groups.

It may be that optimal assessment of individuals for upper level management positions currently requires more emphasis on measures of self-expressive tendencies, because self-expressions by upper level managers have greater impact in a work situation than do self-expressions by middle- and lower level managers. In any event, the broad range of assessment technologies feasible within an assessment center format provides a capacity for meeting a wide array of assessment challenges.

In addition to multiple evaluation advantages, a profusion of nonevaluation advantages would also appear to assure the future viability of assessment centers for companies. As highlighted in Chapter 6, assessors learn a common language which forces them to reflect constructively on values of the organization. In addition to receiving practical training in evaluation and leadership, assessors learn much about how to provide accurate feedback data, as discussed in Chapter 8. In general, interactions among assessors and assessees in an assessment center context provide an effective learning experience focused on the individual's responsibilities and opportunities within the organization.

CONCLUDING STATEMENT

Enough is known about how and why assessment works to encourage optimism about the likelihood of developing and maintaining effective assessment centers for a variety of purposes. In previous chapters, the assessment center method was described as a sophisticated rating procedure designed to minimize rater bias or other potential errors of measurement. In this chapter, some of the psychological forces harnessed by the assessment center method were discussed. In addition, an attempt was made to clarify why assessment centers should work at least as adequately as has been demonstrated. Over the decades, improvements in assessment techniques and procedures have been developed which correspond optimally·with what assessors are capable of doing most and least effectively.

REFERENCES

Bray, D. W., & Grant, D. L. The assessment center in the measurement of potential for business management. *Psychological Monographs*, 1966, *80* (17, Whole No. 625).

Carmichael, L. *Basic psychology: A study of the modern healthy mind.* New York: Random House, 1957.

Cohen, B. M., Moses, J. L., & Byham, W. C. *The validity of assessment centers: A literature review.* Pittsburgh: Development Dimensions Press, 1974.

Cronbach, L. J. *Essentials of psychological testing.* (3rd ed.) New York: Harper & Row, 1970.

Holmes, D. S. The assessment program and the interplanetary simulation: An introduction. *JSAS, Catalog of Selected Documents in Psychology*, 1975a, *5*, 348 (Ms. No. 1138).

Holmes, D. S. Concepts underlying the assessment program and the interplanetary simulation. *JSAS, Catalog of Selected Documents in Psychology*, 1975b, *5*, 348 (Ms. No. 1139).

Holt, R. R. Yet another look at statistical prediction: Or, is clinical psychology worthwhile? *American Psychologist*, 1970, *25*, 337-349.

Huck, J. R. Assessment centers: A review of the external and internal validities. *Personnel Psychology*, 1973, *26*, 191-212.

CHAPTER 8

FEEDBACK OF ASSESSMENT CENTER RESULTS
Leonard W. Slivinski
and
Robert P. Bourgeois

INTRODUCTION

The importance of feedback in the assessment process cannot be minimized. The reports given to either the individual or management (or both) reflect the real cost of assessment.

Strategies for feedback vary as do the types of reports presented and the nature of the information provided. What is important is that the feedback process provides the user-recipient of assessment data sufficient information to evaluate intelligently the information gleaned by this method. As noted in this chapter, feedback mechanisms historically were seen as an afterthought—an appendage to the center itself. What appears to be needed is a concerted effort to train the users of assessment data on how to receive and use this information.

As with the training of assessors, special training for those providing feedback is needed, particularly when information is given to an individual in a counseling/career development sense. Behavior modeling techniques afford an ideal method of such training and several organizations are presently using this method in assessor feedback training.

Len Slivinski and Bob Bourgeois have written a most interesting chapter. They have attempted to sample feedback practices in a number of different organizations and have contrasted several different strategies. These are, of course, not the only ways of providing feedback but are seen as fairly representative. In examining AT&T, General Electric, Ford, Miracle Mart, Ontario Hydro, and the Public Service Commission of Canada, a number of different management climates in two different countries are presented. These climates reflect how feedback is conducted as well as how the information is used.

* * *

FEEDBACK: PURPOSE, PRACTICES, POLICIES, ISSUES

The purpose of this chapter is to discuss the various methods, practices, and procedures used in feedback by various organizations which have adopted the assessment center approach.

The first section outlines the purpose of each of the assessment center programs in terms of either identification of managerial potential and/or identification of developmental needs. The purpose of assessment necessarily influences the type of feedback given. This section provides the necessary background information on the nature of the various assessment center programs within a number of organizations. These are not all of the organizations using this method, but provide a cross section of different feedback applications. The organizations discussed are: AT&T, General Electric, Ford, Miracle Mart, Ontario Hydro, and the Public Service Commission of Canada.

The subsequent sections discuss various issues connected with feedback—its purpose, format, uses to be made of assessment information, the length of time the information is seen as being valid, etc.

General Description and Purpose of Programs

1. *American Telephone & Telegraph*[1]

    a)   *First-Level Management Programs*

    American Telephone & Telegraph has two first-level management assessment programs, one intended for the immediate identification of candidates having managerial ability, the other being more developmentally oriented.

    i.   *The Personnel Assessment Program (PAP)*

    PAP was the first industrial applied use of the assessment center method. It is a two-day assessment procedure designed to take a thorough look at nonmanagement employees who are being considered for promotion into first-level management positions in the near future. PAP rates the employee's current promotability and feeds this rating back to line management. Employees usually seen in PAP average eight to 12 years of service.

    ii. *The Early Identification Program (EIP)*

    The Early Identification Program looks at young nonmanagement employees early in their careers at a one-day assessment center. Those individuals assessed as having high potential are placed on special development programs. The program is designed to evaluate a large number of short-service nonmanagement employees (one to three years) with the goal of

---

[1]Personal communication with J. Moses.

accelerating the placement and development of those candidates showing potential for further advancement.

Assessors make an overall evaluation of the supervisory potential for each candidate as high, moderate, or low. Utilizing all data available through the evaluation process, the assessment director prepares a special summary report. This contains comments on performance, major occupational interests, and developmental recommendations.

All employees rated high at the EIP assessment are potential development candidates. Development opportunities are also made available to some employees rated moderate if line supervisors choose to do so.

b)   *Management Assessment Program (MAP)*

MAP is designed to obtain estimates of the promotability to higher levels of management of present first-, or in some companies second-level managers. It is a more rigorous assessment than either the PAP or the EIP Programs mentioned above.

It is both geared toward the *selection* and *identification* of middle management candidates, but the emphasis is somewhat *developmental* as well.

2.   *General Electric Company*[2]

Middle Management Program: "Talent Development Program"

The objectives or purposes of this middle management program cover both the *selection* aspect and the *developmental* or *career* planning aspects.[3] The career development and planning approach represents a systematic step-by-step attempt to guide the candidate's thinking about his or her strengths and weaknesses and to enable the candidate to look at career development over the next two years in a realistic light. The next major objective of the Talent Development Program is to provide feedback to the individual's immediate manager regarding the strengths and deficiencies as shown at the assessment center. One of the by-products of the assessment program is the identification of developmental actions which the manager could take to further develop the candidate for higher level management positions.

---

[2]Personal communication with W. D. Storey and B. Baker.
[3]W. D. Storey, *How to Develop a Career Plan: Basic Theory and Methodology for Self-Directed Career Planning,* Proceedings of the Third Annual Frontiers in Education Conference, Purdue University, 1973, pp. 226-230.

3. *Ford*[4]

    a) *First-Level Management Program: "Foreman Assessment Center"*
        The Foreman Assessment Center program of the Ford Classes
        Division is used for the *identification* of participants having potential
        to become foremen within the organization at some time. It also has
        a developmental approach built into it.

    b) *Middle Management Program: "Management Career Planning
        Center"*
        The purpose of this assessment center is essentially geared toward
        identifying the candidate's strengths and weaknesses in light of
        attaining the middle management level. It is a *development and
        career planning center* as opposed to immediate promotion of
        candidates to the middle management level. However, promotions
        may be considered or reviewed for some of the participants going
        through the program, depending upon assessed potential.

4. *Miracle Mart*[5]
    Middle Management Assessment Center Program
    Miracle Mart in Canada has a five-day assessment program. The main
    purpose of the program is to aid decision making in three areas:
    promotions, transfer, and development. Another objective of the program
    is to give the participants the tools to permit them to evaluate their
    strengths and weaknesses as managers.

    The participants are usually store managers or group managers, buyers
    or warehouse managers, who have been identified by their supervisors as
    having the ability to handle greater administrative responsibility.

5. *Ontario Hydro*[6]
    Middle Level Management Program
    The emphasis of the program is equally placed on *selection* and
    development.

    Immediately after the assessment center and before observer reports are
    available, all the participants take part in a day and one-half training
    session. This session is aimed at helping the candidates to better
    understand the experience they have just participated in, to enable them
    to understand their own performance, to become aware of alternative
    ways of performing the managerial job, and to prepare for their
    participation in a feedback session.

    ---

    [4]Personal communication with T. Jeswald.
    [5]Internal document (Miracle Mart).
    [6]Personal communication with Ralph Nicholson.

6. *Public Service Commission, Canadian Federal Government*

   a)   *First-Level Management Program*

This assessment program is designed for the Department of Customs and Excise in order to help in the identification of candidates with managerial potential. The information is also used to place individuals on job assignments to aid in this development. Following assessment, a report is written on each candidate. The report gives a general description of the candidate's behavior in the assessment exercises and presents ratings on each of the qualities or dimensions assessed with specific behavioral examples to explain the ratings given. The report also contains a description of the candidate's strengths and weaknesses and outlines possible developmental recommendations which can be implemented by the candidate to prepare for first-level management. Finally, there is a rating of the candidate's managerial potential.

Candidates assessed as having first-level management potential are selected for the Internal Management Development Program and participate in rotational work assignments within the department. These assignments are geared toward the rapid development of the candidate for first-level management positions.

   b)   *Career Assignment Program.*

The primary objective of the Career Assignment Program (CAP) is to provide a means by which the Public Service of Canada can maintain a continuing supply of personnel assessed as having broad experience, proven performance, and potential for executive positions.

At the end of the three-day assessment center, an overall assessment report is written on each candidate. This report contains a general description of the candidate's overall performance at the assessment center, a rating and behavioral description of the candidate's performance in relation to each of the characteristics assessed, a summary of the individual's strengths and weaknesses, and developmental recommendations. Applicants who are successful in the selection process are admitted to the Career Assignment Program, attend a three-month in-residence management training program, and participate in rotational assignments in government departments, agencies, or private industry.

How Feedback is Conducted

1. *American Telephone & Telegraph*
   a) *First-Level Management Programs*
      i.   *Personnel Assessment Program (PAP)*
           About two weeks after the candidate has been through the center, feedback is given in a face-to-face interview situation. The feedback session usually takes one to two hours to conduct. During the interview, the employee may ask any questions regarding the assessment experience. The assessee's opinions are also discussed and he/she may ask any questions about the evaluation procedure in general. Every attempt is made to have the feedback constitute a positive experience for all employees.

           One member of the assessment center staff may be permanently assigned to feedback; or a member of the assessment center staff may stop assessing for one week and conduct feedbacks. Consequently, there is usually one additional staff member on a rotating basis who is doing feedback.

           It is felt at AT&T that the candidate's immediate supervisor should never perform the feedback interview.

           In most cases, the participant's immediate supervisor is also present at the feedback session. Feedback is done in a private office away from work. The candidate has the choice of deciding whether or not to have the immediate supervisor present at feedback. It has been found typically that between 80% and 90% of the participants elect to have the boss present. The candidates also have the choice of whether they want to receive feedback. Almost all the participants usually state that they do.

           The overall philosophy of feedback is that the candidate is treated as an adult and the feedback interviewer's responsibility is to answer questions regarding the candidate's performance at the assessment center but not to emphasize career development. The candidate can take notes but cannot tape record any of the information presented at the session. The assessment center process is reviewed and the candidate can read through the report which was written by the assessors but gets no copy of it. Most of the variables discussed are "skill areas" and are not susceptible to much development.

           Some of the assessors, however, will have mentioned in the report the candidate's range of interests and will offer developmental recommendations pertaining to some of the dimensions, such as oral and written communication skills. But the primary emphasis in feedback is on providing the candidate with a very clear idea of how his or her performance in assessment was seen by the staff. Following the feedback session, the assessment interviewer prepares a short report describing who was present at the feedback session as well as outlining the participant's reactions to the information presented. This file is returned to the assessment center.

ii.   *Early Identification Program (EIP)*
In EIP, feedback is sometimes not the responsibility of the assessment center. Feedback is handled by specially trained individuals in the candidate's home department, usually the personnel representative of the department. This person is in this assignment for a fairly long period of time and gets as much training as an assessor would (approximately one week) and then obtains three or four days of special feedback training on how to deal with different kinds of participants and also how to do developmental counseling. The feedback session covers the information available from the assessment center data as well as information available from other sources, such as biographical data, interest data, interview data, and career development data. The feedback format is very similar to that outlined above for the PAP program. The person's immediate supervisor usually attends the feedback session.

For high-potential candidates, there is a joint goal-setting review between the candidate's immediate supervisor, the feedback person, and the participant. The candidate's immediate supervisor prepares a developmental plan for the individual with the help of the program coordinator or the person doing feedback.

For the low-potential and moderate-potential individuals, the feedback session is more of a counseling kind of interview. The feedback interviewer may encourage the candidate to rethink his wish to become a manager. The feedback interviewer might also suggest that other kinds of nonsupervisory management positions may be available. For example, if the individual is interested in equipment, he or she may attend a special engineering assessment center; if the individual is interested in selling, he or she could attend a sales assessment center.

b)   *Management Assessment Program (MAP)*

The feedback procedures in MAP are similar in format but more detailed than in the case of the previous programs discussed. The feedback is done by an assessor and the candidate's immediate supervisor is invited to attend the feedback session. The feedback interviewer presents the data and answers any questions which the candidate may have. Following the feedback session, the summary report goes to management and there is usually a follow-up on the candidates. The feedback interview also has a personal counseling element to it, discussing with the participant how he or she can maximize career aspirations and abilities over the next 20 or 30 years within the organization. During the feedback interview, the candidate obtains a verbal report of the information present in the written report, which is fed back to management two or three levels removed from the candidate.

2. *General Electric*

a)   *Talent Development Program*

Feedback at General Electric is not a one-shot affair for the candidate; rather, it is a continuing process while the candidate is at the assessment center and after he or she returns to work.

During the assessment center, the candidate receives feedback from the interviewer conducting the *in-basket feedback* session. The purpose of this interview is to give the candidate an idea of how higher level managers handle these kinds of problems. While at the center again, the candidate also receives *feedback from peers*. This peer feedback is done in groups of six and involves a half-day session in which participants write assets and deficiencies narratives on each of the five other people. This is preparation for the career development and planning exercise worked on during the actual assessment center. This must be completed by Friday evening of each assessment week. Also, again during the assessment center, the candidates view audio recordings of their performance in the small group exercises; they study the interactions, the contributions of each of the members, and the assets and liabilities of the participants involved.

While at the center, the candidate receives feedback from the assessment center staff on Friday afternoon of each assessment week. Each participant meets with two staff members who have constructed a report of assessment and development of the participant. This interview lasts for approximately one and one-half hours. During the feedback, the final assessment report is covered and the two staff members talk to the participant about assets and deficiencies or weak points and strong points demonstrated during the week.

The feedback session thus is an occasion to confirm the individual's self-evaluation or check on the areas of disagreement between his or her self-evaluation and the assessment center evaluation. Participants are encouraged to ask questions concerning their performance at the center. The staff then discusses developmental plans with each participant and informs the participant of their developmental recommendations and the reasons for them. This serves as the point of closure for the staff members and a wrap-up session for the participant. The flavor of the feedback session is fairly directive in the assessment part of the feedback session. However, in the developmental plans and recommendations session, the approach is more problem centered with joint problem solving being the approach used.

3. *Ford*
   a) *The Foreman Assessment Center: First-Level Management*
   The feedback discussion is confined to the content of the report and is mainly an information-receiving session for the participant. The participant may read a brief written report but returns it immediately after the feedback session. Numerical ratings are discussed with the participant. The participant may invite the plant training specialist or the foreman to the feedback session. The feedback is given by an assessor who is generally a line manager at the candidate's plant. The approach tends to be quite directive in most cases and the feedback session would occur approximately two weeks after assessment.

   b) *Management Career Planning Center (Middle Management)*
   The feedback discussion is mainly confined to the report on assessment center performance. However, other appraisal information is at hand if the participant wishes to discuss it. The participant reads a brief written report on his or her performance during the feedback interview but must return it after the feedback session. The report is rather general and little is contained in it in terms of specific test scores, but a detailed file of performance in each exercise is available. Numerical rating scores are not discussed. The feedback interview is conducted by personnel planning coordinators and the training people. The feedback is rather directive and is basically an information receiving session for the participant. Feedback has been held as long as six weeks after assessment.

4. *Miracle Mart: Middle Management Assessment Center*
    Feedback to candidates is performed by the assessment center adminis-
    trator, usually three to four weeks after the participant has gone through
    the assessment center. The assessment center feedback interviewer
    discusses with the participant how he or she was seen both by peers and by
    the assessor staff. The result of the feedback session is a "made-to-
    measure" training program involving the assessment center administrator,
    the candidate, and a management development committee. The objective
    of this training program is to expand the potential of the candidate for a
    middle management position. The feedback approach used by Miracle
    Mart requires the candidate's fullest participation, thereby maximizing the
    chances of a very positive use of the results in terms of development.
    Before coming in for the assessment center feedback interview, the
    candidate usually does a self-diagnosis of strengths and weaknesses, which
    is tied in at the feedback interview with the perception of the staff.

5. *Ontario Hydro*
    The report prepared by the observers is sent to the senior manager of the
    unit. The feedback to the candidate from the report is carried out by a line
    manager through the assistance of personnel officers and other profes-
    sionals. The exact way the feedback is carried out varies from work
    location to work location. It ranges from telling the participant all that is
    contained in the report to just covering a small portion of the information.
    Not uncommonly, the participant sees the report and feedback is a
    discussion of a common written document.
    The assessment center report is in three portions. Under each category,
    there is a column for the assessment of the supervisor, which is made prior
    to the participant going to the assessment center. The middle column is for
    the report of the observers during the exercises; the third column is
    normally used to write in the reaction of both the supervisor and the
    participant to the observers' report. It is important at Ontario Hydro that
    the nature and the content of the assessment center report be well
    understood and accepted by the participant. The feedback is also aimed at
    joint development of learning objectives. Part of the feedback session is
    developmental in the sense that the supervisor and the participant must
    decide on what the developmental plans will be for the particular
    candidate being considered. After assessment, there must be a report
    submitted annually reviewing what has been accomplished toward these
    objectives. In most locations, the review of accomplishment is a joint
    matter and consequently the feedback is a *continuing process.*

6. *Public Service Commission, Canadian Federal Government*
    a)   *First-Level Management Program*

The aim of feedback is to provide the assessee with an opportunity to compare the self-evaluation of his or her performance with the interpretation of the assessment staff and to discuss performance and future career plans with a psychologist. Further, the feedback session provides the individual with the necessary amount of information in a growth-oriented context that makes the information as acceptable and valuable as possible. The assessment center feedback session is typically carried out by a member of the professional assessment staff as well as by a member of the department at a senior level, each interviewer playing a specific role within the feedback session.

The assessment interviewer is chiefly concerned with the actual feedback of assessment center results to the candidate, obtaining the assessee's feelings and impressions concerning the assessment center, and comparing the assessee's identification of his developmental needs with the training and development recommendations made by the assessor in the overall assessment report (OAR).

The departmental interviewer is chiefly concerned with discussing the implications of the OAR with the assessee in terms of career plans within the department, investigating the possible implementation of the assessors' training and development recommendations, and explaining the selection process to the candidate.

The assessment interviewer provides the assessee with the *retrospect* of the assessment center technique, including its goals and general rationale, historical development, and characteristics measured.

The assessee is given a list of the dimensions used in the evaluation and each one is explained.

Before going on to the actual feedback of information, the interviewer attempts to get the assessee to verbalize feelings about the assessment center technique in general, perceived performance, and anticipated results. The main objective here is to afford the interviewer the opportunity to get a feel for the assessee, to evaluate motivation, strivings, attitudes toward the interview, and the assessment center generally.

The feedback session is of a problem-solving nature and not a simple reporting of results. The interviewer begins by explaining the scaling procedure to the assessee and gives the rating on each dimension with supporting evidence explaining that these results represent the view of the assessors. Although the initial reporting is done in terms of the assessment center dimensions, an attempt is made to integrate these results more meaningfully by interpreting the assessee's performance under four secondary qualities (i.e., cognitive effectiveness, interpersonal relations, personal characteristics, and administrative management skills).

Regardless of the performance of the candidate, every attempt is made to stress strengths and to keep the discussion on a descriptive-integrative rather than evaluative level. Following the actual reporting of results, the interviewer asks the assessee to summarize the assessment center performance. This allows the psychologist to assess the candidate's emotional reaction to the feedback session. Signs of disappointment may indicate a misunderstanding either of the information or its significance. If anything has been misunderstood, a re-explanation is necessary.

The interviewer then asks the assessee to identify developmental needs. If the assessee's identification of developmental needs is similar to that of the assessors, there is no problem. If they are not similar, it opens the door for discussion. The recommendations of the assessors are then interpreted to the candidate.

The departmental interviewer then discusses the possible implementation of the candidate's training and developmental needs, clarifies the selection process as well as various points concerning the administrative trainee program, and explains departmental policies concerning the use of assessment center information and confidentiality of reports.

b)   *Senior Executive Assessment Program*
Feedback to the Candidate
Each candidate receives assessment center performance feedback approximately two weeks after going through the center.
The major steps of the feedback process are:
i.   *Retrospect of the Assessment Center Technique*
The participant is given background information on the assessment center technique, general rationale, and dimensions measured—in short, all information pertaining to the assessment center.

The dimensions are grouped under three general headings: cognitive effectiveness (such as intelligence and creativity), more personal characteristics (such as oral communication and motivation), and administrative management skills (such as judgment and planning and organization of work).
ii.   *Assessee's Feelings About the Assessment Center*
The psychologist asks the assessee to express feelings about the assessment center in general, and the assessee's performance

and perceived opportunity to manifest the necessary abilities. The advantage of getting the assessee's participation and involvement early in the session is that it is easier to maintain the session as a joint effort. Also, once the assessee outlines objectives, it becomes possible to relate the experience at the assessment center to those objectives.

Another advantage is that this gives the psychologist an opportunity to get a feel for the interviewee.

iii. *Feedback of Results*
The psychologist presents the assessment center data to the assessee in light of the fact that this information is to be used for CAP selection. The session is one of a problem-solving nature, not only a simple reporting of results when dealing with the developmental recommendations of the assessors.

iv. *Getting the Assessee to Summarize*
One of the aims of feedback is to provide the assessee with an accurate understanding of the assessment center information. Perhaps the best indicator of this understanding is a reading by the psychologist of the assessee's emotional reaction to the feedback session. It is also important to note whether the assessee has cognitively understood the information conveyed.

v. *Asking the Assessee to Identify Developmental Needs*
Getting the assessee to identify developmental needs permits a check of whether the feedback information is understood. Also, if the assessee identifies developmental needs independently, the individual is more likely to accept those from assessors, if they are similar. If they are not similar, it opens the door for discussion.

vi. *Discussing the Personality, Interest, Administrative Judgment, and Sentence Completion Blank Data*
Prior to the assessment center, all candidates complete a personality test and an interest test. During the assessment center, the candidate completes a sentence completion blank and an administrative judgment test. These tests are not used for selection purposes, but only for personal counseling. An attempt is made to present the information available from these tests in the light of possible application for career planning. In this section, the developmental needs are discussed and the selection aspect is deemphasized.

vii. *Career Development*
One of the objectives of the assessment center is to help the assessee generate career development plans. Prior to feedback

interview, the assessee has had time to work with a set of career planning worksheets. This process generates a discussion of the assessee's developmental and training needs at the feedback session.

How Assessment Information Is Used

1. *American Telephone & Telegraph*
    a) *First-Level Management Programs (PAP)*
       At AT&T, the assessors' written report of assessment center performance is usually sent to the district-level manager of each participant. The middle manager then makes a local decision regarding the promotability of the candidate and will judge whether he or she should participate in a special training program. In many cases, the district-level manager can communicate with the assessors if further information is required.
    b) *Management Assessment Program*
       Basically the same procedure as above is followed. The written assessment report goes back to management. It is a general report concerning the candidate's performance during the assessment center. Specific scores on dimensions or on tests are not given. Rather, the one and one-half page report deals with managerial strengths and weaknesses and the assessors' overall judgment of the candidate's potential. Recommendations for placement are also made.
       The report is retained in the confidential files of a manager two or three levels removed from the candidate.

2. *General Electric: Talent Development Program*
   The policy guidelines adopted by General Electric are geared toward the systematic follow-up of the candidate's development after he leaves the assessment center.
   Three or four weeks after the participant has left the center, the overall assessment report is sent to the manpower manager at the division organization. The manpower manager again discusses the content of the report with the candidate and gives the candidate a copy of the report.
   Following this meeting with the participant, the manpower manager then meets with the participant's manager and provides a copy of the candidate's assessment center report. Both managers then discuss additional developmental recommendations which the candidate's supervisor should implement. The participant and the manager then make commitments to each other in terms of the points discussed.

The custody of the reports remains with the organization and manpower manager, the participant's immediate manager, as well as the assessment center office. It is considered valid for up to three years. If assessment center information is requested from a candidate's prospective employer, the information is provided by the appropriate manpower manager or by the assessment center.

The assessment center report does not become part of the personnel folder on the candidate.

3. *Ford*
    a) *Foreman Assessment Center*
        No one outside of the assessor group has access to the report after the formal feedback. The personal files in the plant only contain pass-fail information. The assessment report is considered valid for one and one-half or two years.
    b) *Management Career Planning Center (Middle Management)*
        After the candidate has had individual feedback, the report is seen by the participant's supervisor, division training supervisor, and the personnel planning coordinator. Also, when promotions are considered, a top manager may review the report. All assessment center files on all division management and professional personnel are kept by the personnel planning coordinator.

4. *Miracle Mart*
    Miracle Mart's assessment program is geared essentially toward the identification of developmental needs rather than toward selection. It is in fact policy at Miracle Mart that participation in the program does not guarantee one's immediate or future selection for a management position and that candidates who have participated in a center are considered with other qualified candidates.

5. *Public Service Commission*
    a) *First-Level Management Program*
        The assessment center information in this particular program is used to identify managerial potential and to diagnose training needs. The assessment center reports are sent to a central management selection board composed of departmental managers who make the final selection of administrative trainees on the basis of past job performance and assessment center reports. Approximately one month after this process, the candidates meet with a departmental representative from the manpower planning unit and an assessment center staff member.

The candidate's assessment center results are discussed both in selection and developmental terms. Assessment center reports are then returned to the central confidential files at the assessment center, no copies being left at the department. The assessment center information is considered valid for up to two years from the date of testing.

b)   *Senior Executive Assessment Program*

The policy guidelines adopted by the Public Service of Canada are geared to maintaining the confidentiality of assessment center results.

After the assessment center feedback interview, the nominee signs a release letter, indicating whether or not he or she still wishes to be considered for CAP.

If not, the report is returned to assessment staff confidential files. If so, the report is made available to the nominee's departmental selection committee for use in the CAP selection process. Other information from the department (i.e., information contained in the assessee's personal file, performance evaluations, etc.) is also used in the final selection of CAP participants by management.

To ensure that CAP participants are of a consistently high caliber, a Selection Review Board was established to review candidates finally recommended for CAP by departmental selection committees. The Selection Review Board (composed of four deputy ministers) makes a final decision based on departmental information and assessment center information and notifies the deputy minister of the department concerned. The deputy minister then notifies the nominees of their status. All assessment center reports are thereafter kept in the assessment staff's confidential files and the aggregate data is used for research purposes.

The overall assessment report is considered valid for up to two years. No copies of the report are kept at the department or in the candidate's personnel file. Candidates may return for additional feedback sessions regarding their assessment center performance.

The Current State of the Feedback Art: A Summary

While the feedback procedures generally adopted by most of the organizations emphasize both the selection and the developmental aspects of the assessment center data, most organizations are becoming more and more developmental in their emphasis; General Electric, by far, is the most advanced in the area of career planning. The use of the assessment center data in most of the organizations is geared toward formal job training or job rotations as well as management courses which can be followed by individuals.

The delay in communicating assessment center information to candidates is approximately two weeks. Usually specific scores or ratings are not fed back to the candidate. This is the approach followed by AT&T and General Electric. The rating on potential as viewed by the assessors is usually fed back and the results are interpreted in terms of broad ability areas. The developmental recommendations from the report and the occupational interests are normally fed back to participants. Consequently, the approach is highly verbal in terms of the exchange of information and no written reports are available to the participant.

Feedback can be done by a staff leader with the supervisor present or not present, a member of the assessment center staff, an assessor, or someone from the personnel department. The duration of the interview will vary from one hour to three hours in most programs.

Assessment center reports are usually retained in confidential files, a number of levels removed from the level of the candidate, and the assessment center report or information is considered valid for two or three years maximum.

Historically, it seems that feedback procedures usually have been developed as an afterthought by most organizations, with little consideration being given to follow-ups in terms of effectiveness of the feedback procedures used, however, the Public Service of Canada systematically follows up on the effectiveness of its feedback system.

There appears to be a growing emphasis on using assessment center feedback in career and manpower planning.

Although little systematic effort in this sense has been achieved by most organizations, with the exception of General Electric, the trend seems to be in this direction.

CHAPTER 9

ATTITUDES TOWARD ASSESSMENT CENTER PROGRAMS
William E. Dodd

INTRODUCTION

Dr. William Dodd, of the IBM Corporation, has done an excellent job of summarizing much of the current research on the viewpoints of various groups of people who are involved with the assessment method. While the chapter concentrates on perceptions of the assessment center process by participants, much interesting data are also provided from the point of view of the managers to whom the participants report and managers in general throughout the companies that have utilized the assessment center procedure.

One of the most important facts to come out of this chapter is the finding that participant satisfaction is related to effective developmental action on the part of the immediate supervisor. Dodd finds that supervisory response in terms of training and development suggestions has the same positive effect on employee attitudes as promoting the individual. Most experienced assessment center administrators would agree with this finding. It reinforces the need for effective follow-up action relative to any assessment program.

Probably the most striking feature of the article is the consistency of the positive findings reported, not only in various organizations in the United States but in organizations throughout the world.

Since Dr. Dodd collected the data for his article, a number of other organizations have published or distributed summaries of attitude survey research relative to assessment centers. These include the U.S. Civil Service Commission, Steinberg's Limited, S. C. Johnson & Son, Inc., Blue Cross of

Illinois, and some general survey results encompassing a number of organizations using assessment centers conducted by Development Dimensions, Inc. The results of all these surveys reinforce and support the data.

* * *

In considering the assessment center technique, one is usually convinced by the original AT&T studies and subsequent reports of the validity of the assessment center. It does have much potential for use in an organization for producing the information which will be valuable in the development and/or selection of managers. But, what about accommodating a formal program of this kind to an organization which may previously have used very informal methods for selecting and developing management candidates? How will people react to the idea of being sent to an assessment center for the purpose of formally reviewing their qualifications for higher level positions? How will they react to the exercises and demands made upon them in the assessment center process? Will they see it as valid? Will the situation be too stressful for them? How will they react to being told about their performance in the assessment center? How will they feel about the use planned to be made of the results? What will they perceive the effect to be on their careers, on their morale and motivation to perform? In other words, will this technique be acceptable to those people whose careers it will affect? Finally, will management itself see it as a valuable tool in terms of the use which can be made of the information and the experience to be derived from acting as an observer in the program?

Because many organizations which have considered the assessment center process have entertained such questions and have sought to answer them, we are fortunate to have data from sources* which give us some answers. These data have come from surveys conducted with participants and with management

---

*Bourgeois, R. P., Slivinski, L. W., & Grant, K. W. Assessees' reactions to CAP assessment center 73-2. *Managerial Assessment and Research Division, Career Assignment Program*, Public Service Commission of Canada, December 1973.

Casserly, M. C., Slivinski, L. W., & Bourgeois, R. P. The assessment center counselling session: The candidates' reaction. *Managerial Assessment and Research Division, Career Assignment Program*, Public Service Commission of Canada.

Di Costanzo, F., & Andretta, T. The supervisory assessment center in the Internal Revenue Service. *Training and Development Journal*, September 1970.

personnel. In some cases, these questionnaires were administered directly following the assessment experience. In some cases, they were repeated after a feedback session had taken place, and in some cases the questionnaires were administered after several years had gone by since the assessment experience. The timing of when these questionnaires were administered is sometimes importantly informative in interpreting the results; when that is the case, we shall point it out.

PRE-ASSESSMENT:
ATTITUDES TOWARD THE SELECTION PROCESS AND
INFORMATION PROVIDED ABOUT THE PROGRAM

Although the variety of assessment centers that exist today differ on the dimension of self-selection versus management selection, most assessment center operators feel that it should be presented to the potential participant as voluntary. In the Michigan Bell program, where a participant may have heard about the program either from printed material, his supervisor, co-workers or some other sources, survey responses from about 300 former participants in the Michigan Bell assessment center indicated that most (57%) had heard about the program from their supervisor. About 17% had heard of the program from printed material and an additional 19% had heard about it primarily from co-workers. With respect to the perception of whether their attendance at the program was voluntary or not, 88% overall felt that it was completely voluntary.

Gershon, A. The personnel assessment program Part I—Opinions of participants. *Personnel Research Studies*, Field Engineering Division, IBM Corporation, May 1971.

Kraut, A. I. Management assessment and international organizations. *Industrial Relations*, 1973, *12*, 172-182.

Penzer, W. N. Participant reactions to a one day personnel assessment program. *Personnel Research Studies*, Data Processing Division, IBM Corporation, 1968.

Personnel Relations Department. Employee survey results, early identification program. Michigan Bell Telephone Company, March 1972.

Personnel Research. MAP evaluation survey. Michigan Bell Telephone Company, May 1973.

Tighe, R., & Dodd, W. E. Unpublished study of participants' and managers' attitudes towards assessment centers. Office Products Division, IBM Corporation, September 1972.

Wolfson, A. The participants' opinions; study of opinion responses of 36 assessment participants after having received feedback. Corporate Headquarters, IBM Corporation, 1974.

It was interesting, however, that while only 3% of the 57 high-performing former assessment participants reported feeling that they had been pressured to attend, 16% of the 113 low-performing former assessment participants registered that feeling. In the same organization, in an assessment center designed to select first-level managers for second-level management, 75% of 88 former manager participants indicated that they had heard about the program from their supervisor and, in this case, 32% felt that they had been pressured to attend the program. The authors of the report interpret this pressure as reflecting a feeling on the part of survey respondents that future advancement opportunities might be jeopardized by refusing to attend.

In the assessment center designed for inputs to the Career Assignment Program of the Public Service Commission of Canada, 50% of 60 former participants in the program indicated that they had wanted very much to go to this assessment center. Only 15%, however, agreed that they felt pressured into attending the assessment center. Parts of IBM have used or have experimented with assessment centers. In one division of IBM, which used the assessment center as inputs to selection for a special management development program, a group of former participants recalled whether or not they had been told in advance of coming to the assessment center that participation was voluntary. Twenty-nine percent of about 300 respondents indicated that they were not told it was voluntary. In another division of IBM, which has used the assessment center as inputs to first-level management promotion decisions, 12% of about 700 former participants agreed that they felt pressured into attending the program but, 59% agreed that they wanted very much to attend. In another part of the IBM organization, in a survey conducted among 36 participants of a pilot program following their feedback interviews, 22% felt pressure to attend, but 70% said that they very much wanted to attend the program.

It appears, then, that anywhere from 9% up to 32% of former assessment participants at Michigan Bell, the Public Service Commission of Canada, and parts of IBM did not feel the program they attended was strictly on a voluntary basis. It is not clear from the research why it is important for the participant to feel that he has gone to the program voluntarily. One suspects that there are few management development activities which organizations would classify as voluntary, but when a program such as the assessment center does carry the option of electing not to attend, it is obvious that a full discussion of the alternatives to not attending is mandatory.

It was indicated that most assessment participants in the Michigan Bell organization found out about the program from their supervisors. Another aspect of information about the program frequently important to programs that have been around a while in the organization is how much "inside" information the participant brings to the program, how much he or she perceives other participants bringing with them, and, finally, how important the participant believes such information is to doing well in the program.

In a survey of the Public Service Commission of Canada's management assessment program, 93% of 61 respondents disagreed that they had "inside" information about the assessment center exercises prior to attending the program. Only 62% of 63 respondents, however, disagreed that others had inside information about the exercises. In a division of IBM which had been using the program for a number of years, 74% disagreed that they had inside information about exercises while only 14% disagreed that other participants had inside knowledge about exercises. Among these respondents, which numbered approximately 700, only 37% believed that such knowledge would help a participant perform better to a great or very great extent. Thirty-four percent was the comparable figure for the Public Service Commission of Canada study.

In another IBM division, which had been running the program for a number of years, 20% of approximately 300 respondents indicated that they believed others had received advance information or clues on how to perform that might have given them an undue advantage.

It is clear, then, that long-standing programs need to be concerned with the dissemination of information about exercises which can be perceived to give some participants an unfair advantage. One way to offset this, which probably doesn't work too well over the long run, is to implore participants not to discuss the content of the program. Another, and more controllable technique, is to start all the participants off with approximately the same amount of information by giving them a thorough orientation as to what will happen in the assessment center program in which they are about to participate. Such an orientation given by the staff leader in the Michigan Bell program is apparently responded to very favorably by former assessment participants. Eighty-seven percent of approximately 300 respondents indicated that the staff leader's remarks were helpful in preparing them for the day's activities.

ASSESSMENT EXERCISES AND PERFORMANCE IN THE ASSESSMENT CENTER

In following up on the almost 100 former participants in their Early Identification Assessment program, Michigan Bell asked about the components of the program—how enjoyable they were to participate in, how difficult or easy they were, and how valuable they were seen to the participants in terms of informing them of their strengths and weaknesses. Their program consists of an oral presentation, a group discussion, and an in-basket and written exercise. Participants who were considered by staff ratings to be high or medium performers in the program agreed that the group discussion was the most enjoyable task, followed by the oral presentation, the in-basket, and the written exercise. Former participants who were rated low performers in the program, however, found the in-basket and written exercise to be the most enjoyable, followed by the group discussion and the oral presentation. Regardless of performance in the program, the most difficult task was seen as the oral presentation. The easiest task was seen as the group discussion by former high performers and the written exercise was seen as the easiest by medium or low performers. All agreed that the written exercise was the least valuable for self-insights. High performers felt that the oral presentation was most valuable, medium performers felt that the in-basket was most valuable, and low performers felt that the group discussion was most valuable.

It is no surprise that, in a program designed to highlight individual skill differences, attitudes toward various components of the program are greatly modified by the overall skill level in the program itself.

Other organizations have asked about attitudes toward the various components of the assessment center along the lines of their face validity for measuring what the programs purport to measure. The Public Service Commission of Canada asked about the effectiveness of the parts of the assessment program in measuring important qualities required of a senior executive. The parts of the program they asked about were the in-basket, simulation exercises, and exercises assessing intelligence and creativity. Prior to receiving their feedback on performance, 85% of the respondents indicated that they thought the simulation exercises were very effective or effective. Eighty-three percent thought so after the feedback exercises. As for the in-basket, 84% believed it to be very effective or effective in measuring important qualities prior to their feedback. Subsequent to feedback, 93% believed that it was measuring important qualities very effectively or effectively. With respect to intelligence and creativity, which were measured by paper-and-pencil tests, the feedback of performance on these was evidently quite important in changing attitudes toward their perceived effectiveness. For example, before feedback, 47% believed that intelligence was very effectively or effectively measured. After feedback, 82% believed it was very effectively or effectively measured. As for creativity, the comparable figures were 45% prior to feedback and 76% after feedback. Here again, it appears that performance in these exercises may mitigate considerably the attitudes toward them. Learning about performance on intelligence and creativity tests certainly seemed to have a positive effect in how effectively the participants believed these qualities were measured. This suggests that to the extent that there is heavy emphasis on paper-and-pencil tests in the assessment center, feedback becomes very important for the face validity attitudes of participants.

Overall evaluations of the face validity assessment programs were investigated by various organizations. In the Public Service Commission of Canada, 52% of 60 respondents believed that the program measured important qualities necessary for success as a senior executive. That was before they received their feedback on performance. Afterwards, 69% believed that the program was measuring these qualities to a very great or great extent. In one division of IBM, where the program had been used to select people for a special management development program, 88% of those who had been selected indicated that they believed the program to be measuring many of the important qualities required of effective managers. Sixty-three percent of those who had not been selected to attend the program said "yes" to the same question. These data were derived after several years had elapsed and the effect of their selection to the program had been allowed to take place. It is not surprising that there is a difference in how these two groups perceived the face validity of the program; that 63% of the group most negatively affected by this selection still believed the program was valid is an important attitudinal endorsement of the program.

In a division of IBM which used assessment, approximately 30% of 700 former assessment participants indicated that the process measured characteristics important to management to a great or very great extent. Fifty-five percent believed that it measured these qualities to a moderate extent, and 15% believed that it did not measure these qualities very much or at all. Among another IBM group of 36 participants, following feedback of results, 42% indicated that they believed the assessment program measured important qualities necessary for success as a manager to a very great or great extent, only 8% thought that it did so to little or no extent. Reporting on reactions to an Internal Revenue Service assessment program, DiCostanzo and Andretta (1970) reported that 58% of participants believed the assessment center was a good method for demonstrating supervisory potential and 28% thought it was not. Immediate unfavorable reactions to face validity, reported by Kraut (1973), in several foreign IBM programs and one in the United States range from zero to four percent.

Thus, in the area of attitudes toward the face validity of the program, it is clear that performance, feedback on performance, and use of the data all can have substantial effects on attitudes toward the validity of the program. Negative attitudes, however, under any conditions, tend to run very low, even after intervening years and use of data.

Another attitudinal dimension for which we have some data from former participants is in the area of behavior fidelity—that is, do participants see themselves behaving and reacting in an assessment in a way that they would in a "real life" situation? In the Canadian Public Service Commission, prior to receiving their feedback, 28% of the participants indicated that their reactions were different than they would be in real life situations and 59% said that they were not different. After feedback, 37% believed that their reactions were different and 54% believed that their reactions were not different than they would be in real life situations. After several years intervening between assessment and attitudinal measures, 41% of respondents in a division of IBM reported that they believed their reactions were different from real life and 47% believed that they were not different from real life. Thus, if these data are representative, we can believe that feedback and intervening time both tend to place the assessment behavior in a light which makes it appear unreal. It is possible that some of this reaction can be due to the fact that the situations themselves are somewhat unusual.

Another aspect of attitudes toward performance in the assessment center is whether or not the program is seen to overwhelm the participants to the extent that they believe their performance to be generally poor. In one IBM division, 81% of former assessment participants in the study said that they believed they did as well or better than most good IBM managers would do in such a program. In another division, the comparable figure was 91%. Even with 81% believing that they did well, in the one division there was an apparent relationship with actual performance in the program. Among Canadian Public Service Commission former participants, 78% indicated that they believed their performance was as good or better than most. In these three studies, there appeared to be a consistent tendency for most participants to evaluate their own assessment performance favorably—for some, probably more favorably than it was observed to be by others.

There is no data on hand reflecting participants' feelings about stress during the program itself. However, the Canadian Public Service Commission and two studies in IBM asked if outside influences such as the family or the job might have produced any undue stress or handicap adversely affecting assessment performance. In two of these studies, about 14% of the respondents indicated that their performance was adversely affected because of stress from the job or the home at the time they were assessed. In the other study not one of 36 respondents reported stress due to external circumstances having any effect on performance. It is suggested that stress due to any source, including the program atmosphere itself, should be studied directly.

Other aspects of the ambience at the assessment center include the facilities, location, and administration of the center. The Public Service Commission of Canada achieved very favorable ratings along these dimensions with close to 90% or more of their respondents satisfied with these aspects of the program. Often assessment centers occur in the context of a larger program such as management development. This was the case in one IBM division in which 700 former assessment participants reflected back several years on their attendance at the program. In Table 9-1, it can be seen that somehow ratings of the week as a whole added up to better than the ratings of either the assessment portion of that week or the development portion of the week.

Even more favorable results were obtained in another IBM division with respect to assessment versus development (88% vs. 42% very good or good) immediately after feedback for 36 participants.

In still another IBM division, in which an experimental program was set in the context of a vestibule training program for new employees, 60 participants

Table 9-1

Rating of:	Very poor	Poor	Fair	Good	Very good
Week as a whole	0%	2%	15%	43%	40%
Assessment portion	1	5	21	48	25
Development portion	1	5	20	43	32

were asked to indicate whether the assessment portion detracted from or enhanced their overall training program. Thirty-five percent believed that it definitely enhanced the overall program, 35% believed that it neither enhanced nor detracted, and 30% felt that it definitely detracted from the overall program. It should be pointed out that there was no performance feedback in this assessment program and an indefinite statement was made about the possible use of the data in the future.

It appears, then, that assessment activities themselves compared quite favorably to more traditional developmental activities. In the context of vestibule entry job training without clear purpose or feedback, attitudes are not especially positive.

POST-ASSESSMENT USE OF DATA

The Feedback Process

Although they did not all start out that way, most assessment centers today provide feedback to the participant in a personal interview on how he or she performed in the program. Former participants in Michigan Bell's Early Identification Program believed that they understood the feedback very well. Eighty-four percent indicated as much for the overall rating and 80% believed that they understood the ratings on leadership, decision making, etc. very well. In Michigan Bell's management assessment program for first-level managers, 82% of 247 respondents indicated that they had a complete understanding of ratings such as personal ability, administrative ability, etc. At the Public Service Commission of Canada's Career Assignment Program assessment center, 87% of 70 respondents indicated that they found the interpretation of their performance in the feedback session extremely or very clear and understandable. Programs where specific ratings are not furnished may run into some difficulties with attitudes toward feedback. In one division of IBM in which 100% of the group were given feedback, although not given specific performance ratings, 21% indicated that they did not receive feedback.

What about perceived accuracy of evaluated performance? Sixty-six percent of Michigan Bell's nonmanagement former participants felt the staff had accurately evaluated their performance, 30% felt that it had not been accurately evaluated. The Public Service Commission of Canada asked about accuracy with respect to identifying strengths and weaknesses as well as accuracy in identifying potential to become a senior executive. Sixty-two percent of former participants felt that the identifying of strengths and weaknesses was extremely accurate or very accurate. Only five percent considered it not accurate at all. With respect to accuracy in identifying potential, 61% believed it was very accurate or extremely accurate and only 10% believed it was not accurate at all. When 700 former participants in an IBM program looked back upon the accuracy of the program ratings, 50% indicated that the ratings were very accurate or extremely accurate, with 11% indicating some degree of inaccuracy. Following feedback, 83% of 36 IBM participants agreed that feedback reflected actual performance. Only two participants disagreed. Another dimension in the feedback is the utility of the information. In the Michigan Bell nonmanagement program, 86% indicated that they thought the information provided to them regarding their strengths and weaknesses would be helpful. Thirty-seven percent of about 700 former IBM participants indicated that the feedback interview was valuable for understanding and using results, while only 19% indicated that the feedback interview was not very valuable or not at all valuable for those purposes.

Many assessment programs now provide developmental recommendations to participants as part of the feedback. In the Career Assignment Program assessment center of the Canadian Public Service Commission, 29% of former participants felt that the training and development recommendations of the assessors were very helpful or extremely helpful. Seventeen percent considered them to be not helpful at all.

It is apparent that specificity in feedback may play a dominant role in attitudes toward this aspect of the program. Satisfaction with the feedback seems generally high when a full explanation of the rating scales is made. When this does not happen, a significant number may feel that they have not even received feedback. In the Canadian Public Service Commission program, where the feedback was specific, only seven percent of their respondents believed that it was "too specific," 25% believed that it was "more or less specific," 62% believed that it was "both specific and general," three percent thought that it was "more or less general," and three percent thought that it was "too general." Eighty-six percent of these people liked the method of presenting results.

Attitudes Toward Use of Results

A strong test of the attitudes of former assessment participants is asking them about their beliefs with respect to the use of data when it happens that such use could have an effect on their own careers. Kraut (1973) has reported favorable attitudes from United States and foreign IBM affiliates which range from 64% to 100% favorable on the question: "To what extent do you believe assessment information could be used to help in selection of employees for promotion to first-line management?" In a retrospective look at the assessment program which had been used to select them for a special management development program, 91% of former assessment participants in an IBM program who had been selected to attend the program believed that the assessment information should be used to make such a selection; of those who had not been selected, 64% believed that the program should be used to make such a selection and 26% believed that it should not be used. Again, the differences are strong, but the balance of favorability is with the use of the information even for those whose careers could be seen as negatively affected by it.

In the Career Assignment Program assessment center of the Canadian Public Service Commission, 53% of the former participant respondents indicated that the information should be used to help in the selection and promotion of individuals to first-line management to a moderate extent and, as in IBM, 25% believed that it should not be used for this purpose very much or at all. In response to a similar question with respect to the use of information to promote individuals to middle management positions or above, 90% of the Canadian sample believed that it should be used to some, to a great, or to a very great extent for this purpose. Ten percent believed that it should not be used at all. These data were derived following the feedback session.

Former participants in Michigan Bell's Management Assessment Program were asked if the program, in their estimation, would be successful in meeting the objectives of uniformly measuring the special managerial qualities required for second-level supervisory positions. Sixty-nine percent of this group said "yes," five percent said "yes with reservations," 19% said "no." Among Michigan Bell employees who had participated in the Early Identification Assessment, 84% indicated that the program was of value for the purpose of assessing management potential in employees with relatively short service and thus helping these people to formulate career plans.

It appears, then, that generally favorable responses with respect to the use of assessment information for selection purposes can be expected even when those uses could negatively affect the careers of those people responding, but that most former participants favor moderation in selection use of the data.

Another common use of the information derived from assessment centers is for highlighting developmental needs. We have already touched on some aspects of this with respect to the feedback process. However, there are some general attitudes toward this aspect of information use from former participants and from some of their managers which is of interest. Among foreign IBM affiliates, Kraut (1973) reports 64% to 94% favorable on the question: "How do you rate the program's value in giving you additional information for your self development?" The Canadian Public Service Commission reports 76% who indicate that the information helped in personal self-development to a moderate, great, or very great extent prior to feedback, and 88% subsequent to feedback.

Eighty-six percent of Michigan Bell's former management assessment participants indicated that they thought the information provided to them regarding their strengths and weaknesses would be helpful. In Michigan Bell's Early Identification Program, only the high performers embark upon a developmental program. Sixty-eight percent of these highs indicated that they had embarked on such a program. Of these, 78% indicated that they were involved in activities on the job that they had not been participating in prior to the assessment and 67% indicated that their supervisor was enthusiastic about helping them in their development. In one IBM division in which the information is used as inputs to selection decisions, it is also used to give managers more information on developing subordinates who have participated in the program. Many of these participants (40%) felt very or extremely motivated to improve themselves when they left the program. However, only 27% of their managers believed that the program was good for this purpose and 21% believed that it was poor or very poor for the purpose of motivating a subordinate to start a developmental program. The managers did not rate the usefulness of the recommendations for developing subordinates very highly either. Sixty-two percent believed that the information was valuable to some extent, 17% to a great extent, and four percent to a very great extent. Thirty-five percent of these managers rated the program good or very good for establishing a self-improvement program.

It is one thing for recent assessment participants to endorse the technique for projected use in selection or development systems which may have an effect on their careers and quite another to have former participants reflect upon the program retrospectively in the context of their performance and satisfaction at their present point in their careers. We have seen how use of assessment for selection tends to mitigate the endorsement of nonselected participants. Do former participants who have not benefited from the accelerating effects of the program blame the assessment center? Are they satisfied in their present jobs? To what extent do managers of former participants perceive "demotivation" to perform their work? In one IBM division using the program for selection to a special management development program, identical percentages (78%) of selected and nonselected former participants (who ranged in elapsed time since assessment from one to five years) indicated that they did not know of anyone whose career had been adversely affected by the assessment program. Eleven percent and 10%, respectively, said that they had known such persons. On the assumption that nonselected former participants would more likely include themselves as "victims" if they felt their careers had been adversely affected, it is an important finding that these two groups were so similar on this issue when they differed on other endorsements of the program.

Another IBM division had used the assessment center as partial input to selection to first-level management for a number of years and surveyed former participants who had been assessed from two to four years prior. The author analyzed these data with the AID* computer program. The schematized results are presented in Figs. 9-1 and 9-2. In Fig. 9-1 the "dependent" variable was a 7-point scale ranging from "I am completely satisfied" to "I am completely

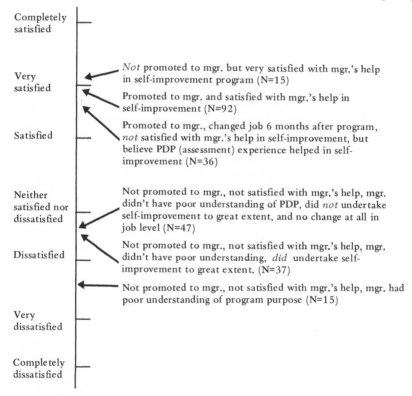

Fig. 9-1. Contributors to Overall Feelings about Present Employment Situation.

---

*This program makes successive dichotomous splits of a sample using independent variables to "predict" the dependent variable so as to maximize differences among the split groups.

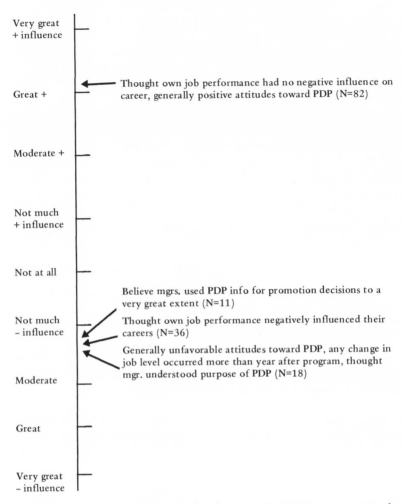

Fig. 9-2. Contributors to Perceived Influence of PDP (Assessment) Performance on Career.

dissatisfied" in answer to the question: "Considering everything, how would you rate your overall feelings about your employment situation at the present time?" Thirty different possible "predictors" or correlates of this dependent variable entered the program, including a question on whether the respondent believed that his or her career had been positively or negatively influenced by his or her assessment performance, whether a promotion had been received or not, and attitudes toward the manager's role in using the data. Figure 9-1 depicts the extreme groups on present satisfaction and how they are defined by the major correlates of this variable. Two dimensions emerge very clearly. Being promoted results in greater present satisfaction and the manager's help in the participant's improvement program also is a positive influence on present satisfaction. The most satisfied group of all (15 participants) had not even been promoted but were very satisfied with their manager's help in development. The most dissatisfied group (also N=15) had not been promoted, were not satisfied with their manager's help in development, and in addition thought the managers had a poor understanding of the program. Conspicuously absent in this result is the perception of influence of assessment performance on present overall satisfaction two to four years after assessment.

A similar analysis was done, this time using perceived influence of assessment performance as the "dependent" variable. Again, using extreme groups defined by the main correlates, Fig. 9-2 shows that a large group of 82 former participants believed that the assessment had a great positive influence on their careers. Understandably, they were found to have generally positive attitudes toward various aspects of the assessment program and, importantly, harbored no thoughts that their own job performance negatively influenced their careers. Toward the negative end of this scale are three smaller groups, the largest of which (N=36) thought their own job performance *did* negatively influence their careers. It is tempting to interpret this result as an aspect of the construct validity for assessment performance. Here from the survey responses of former participants, we have a correlation between the perceived influence of their assessment performance and their job performance on their present careers. The other two smaller extreme negative groups of N=11 and N=18 are distinguished respectively by a belief that assessment information may have been overused and by generally unfavorable attitudes toward the program coupled with delayed job level changes and a feeling that the managers *did* understand the purpose of the program.

The IBM data suggest that, retrospectively, former participants do not tend to attribute any present dissatisfaction to performance in the program or feel that people get hurt by the program. On the contrary, the weight of attitudes favors the positive influence of the program or the influence of their own job performance on their career movement.

In Table 9-2 we have attempted to summarize the ranges of attitudinal data which are available among major common themes. The data of Table 9-2 not only reflect a variety of studies and organizations but also elapsed time between assessment and attitudinal measurement. Also the wording of the questions and the response scales differ for data summarized under the same topic. As we have indicated, some of those findings appear to be influenced significantly by such moderators as elapsed time since assessment, benefiting or not from data use, and presence or absence of good feedback.

Table 9-2 Summarized Attitudes Toward Assessment Centers

	Favorable Range		Unfavorable Range	
	Low	*High*	*Low*	*High*
Adequacy/helpfulness of information provided about center	84%	87%	10%	11%
Others have inside info	14%	63%	5%	53%
Desire to attend	50%	70%	5%	10%
Pressure to attend or voluntary	52%	88%	9%	32%
Content Relevance/face validity	30%	93%	0%	28%
Compared to development/ or other connected activity	35%	86%	5%	30%
Performance vs. others	78%	91%	0%	30%
Behavior fidelity	49%	59%	28%	41%
Stress from external sources	60%	80%	0%	14%
Feedback Accuracy	50%	83%	5%	30%
Understanding	80%	87%	0%	19%
Diagnostic value	29%	86%	10%	19%
Use of data: For selection	18%	100%	19%	46%
For development	64%	94%	19%	24%
Overall endorsements Would repeat	73%	88%	5%	16%
Would recommend to friend	74%	100%	0%	14%

In spite of the cautions which must be exercised in reviewing the data summarized in Table 9-2, there are several results which stand out. On the positive side, the organizations which had some reason to ask about it generally found a high range of favorable responses about the information provided concerning the assessment center. Also, participants generally report that they performed as well or better than others even when they may not have. Understanding the feedback information was generally favorable for members of organizations who asked. However, we have seen that this assumes that detailed information is actually given in feedback. When it is in general terms, even the perception that feedback was given may be absent. Happily, some of the most positive attitudes of all are for overall endorsements in terms of willingness to do it again or recommending it to a good friend.

On the unfavorable side of the ledger, "behavior fidelity" comes under the most pressure. For anyone who has worked with assessment centers, this is a familiar complaint. "What you saw you accurately evaluated, but that was not the real me!" This has been a difficult issue to handle in feeding back results. There are some theoretical issues raised by this perceptual or attitudinal problem. First of all, this problem is not so large that it destroys the validity of the program. Therefore, the person we do see in the assessment center, real or not, tends to be the one about whom we can make fairly accurate predictions. Also, supervisory managers tend to agree with the assessment report. In an IBM survey of about 480 managers of former assessment participants, 58% agreed with the assessment report of strengths and weaknesses on their subordinates to a great or very great extent. Thirty-eight percent agreed to some extent and only four percent agreed to little or no extent.

In some other research done by the author in the early identification of management potential, results indicated that assessment center performance was unique from other opportunities to observe the management potential of short-service employees in that "interpersonal effectiveness in groups" was a dimension of behavior not normally available in such early observational opportunities as job training or on-the-job performance. It is possible that some of the behavior fidelity problems reported by participants reflect unfamiliarity with their own behavior in group interactive situations because they have not often encountered such situations in their early careers.

An apparently more manageable problem and one evidently influenced by the age of the assessment center is the perception that others have advanced information on program content. Few practitioners with whom I've discussed the issue believe that advance information has any strong effect on real performance, so the problem is likely to be more perceptual and, as indicated, could be influenced by the degree of orientation information dispensed at the program's opening.

As for attitudes toward using the data for selection, this is influenced by whether the participant benefited or not from actual selection use of information, whether some selection use other than the current one is proposed, and whether the respondent is allowed to consider partial or moderate use as one of the attitude alternatives. Except in some of Kraut's foreign samples, whose attitudes were tapped following pilot programs and who were much more certain about use of the information, American assessment participants generally do not favor absolute use of the data for selection. Recognizing this, it may be well to clarify just what influences assessment data will have in an organization, indicating how job performance, training, appropriate experiences, job openings, and availability of candidates all bear upon promotion decisions.

MANAGEMENT ATTITUDES TOWARD ASSESSMENT

Much of the attitude data on assessment centers are from the participants' or former participants' points of view. The attitudes of management, which utilizes assessment output and authorizes the programs, of course, are also very critical to the continuation of the program. In surveying managers of assessment participants, in a division of IBM which has used the program for a number of years, the investigators were able to break out 180 managers who had participated as assessors in one or more programs from 309 managers who had not had that experience. Table 9-3 provides some selected questions from the survey on which managers who were former assessors differ somewhat in their attitudes toward the utility of the assessment program. Although the differences are not large, the direction consistently shows former assessors somewhat more favorable than other managers. On two direct questions about the effect of assessor experience, the level of favorability of former assessors tends to corroborate what many have believed about assessor experience—namely, that it has a positive influence on judging skills in identifying potential and improves the estimation of the worth of the assessment program.

We believe that attitudes toward assessment centers in general are quite positive. In some cases, as in self-perceived performance levels, results are more positive than they have any right to be. More importantly, the attitude survey is an effective means for management's getting at the reactions to the program and to the use of information. By its very nature, the assessment center as an evaluative, behavior-revealing process can easily be viewed in a negative light by vocal participants. A systematic way of getting at the reactions of all participants may be crucially important in offsetting the influence of a few vocal critics. As an ongoing procedure, it can help the practitioner track administrative and procedural changes in his program to make sure that it continues to improve in participant and management acceptability.

Table 9-3 Attitudes of Former Assessors (N=180) and Other Managers (N=309) Toward Aspects of Assessment Center Programs

Does assessment measure qualities necessary for management?				
Not at All	Not Very Much	Moderate Extent	Great Extent	To a Very Great Extent
Former assessors	0%	5%	57%	35%	3%
Other managers	0	10	61	25	4

Have you seen any change in subordinate's job performance since (assessment)?				
Great Deterio- ration	Slight Deterio- ration	No Change	Great Im- prove- ment	Very Great Improve- ment
Former assessors	0%	5%	51%	41%	2%
Other managers	1	5	61	33	0

To what extent would you urge promotable employees to attend (an assessment center)?				
Not at All	Little Extent	Some Extent	Great Extent	To a Very Great Extent
Former assessors	2%	5%	14%	43%	37%
Other managers	4	3	22	42	29

To what extent is the (assessment center) useful as a management tool?				
Former assessors	1%	7%	39%	34%	20%
Other managers	1	8	46	34	11

Has (assessor) experience facilitated your judging the long-term potential of your own subordinates?				
Former assessors	3%	11%	39%	34%	13%

Has (assessor) experience improved your estimation of the worth of the (assessment) program?				
Former assessors	1%	2%	23%	35%	39%

While there has been some exchange of question formats for assessment attitudes across organizations, it would be highly productive for people working in the field, especially with new organizations entering all the time, to have a standard questionnaire format. The questionnaire we suggest for this purpose is shown in Table 9-4.

Table 9-4   Suggested Survey Questions for Measuring Attitudes Toward Assessment Centers

Please indicate your agreement or disagreement with each of the following statements about the assessment center:	Strongly Agree	Agree	Neither Agree nor Disagree	Disagree	Strongly Disagree
☐ I had adequate information to understand what the assessment center was all about before I agreed to attend it.	1	2	3	4	5
☐ I wanted very much to attend the assessment center.	1	2	3	4	5
☐ I felt that I could easily have refused to attend the assessment center without fear of undesirable consequences.	1	2	3	4	5
☐ I was given enough information about exercise content and objectives to offset any advantage others may have had because of "advance" or "inside" information.	1	2	3	4	5
☐ The_____ exercise measures important qualities required of (managers).	1	2	3	4	5

Table 9-4 (continued)

	Strongly Agree	Agree	Neither Agree nor Disagree	Disagree	Strongly Disagree
☐ Overall the assessment center measures important qualities required of _____ (managers).	1	2	3	4	5
☐ The assessment program schedule was executed efficiently.	1	2	3	4	5
☐ Adequate materials were on hand to carry out the program.	1	2	3	4	5
☐ Adequate information was provided about the facility and the schedule of events.	1	2	3	4	5
☐ I feel my performance in the program was equal to or better than what could reasonably be expected of persons in my position in the organization.	1	2	3	4	5
☐ My behavior in the assessment exercises was not greatly different from what it would be in comparable "real life" situations.	1	2	3	4	5
☐ I have had previous experience on the job or elsewhere in ("in-basket" situations) (making formal presentations) (influencing others in group situations).	1	2	3	4	5

Table 9-4 (continued)

	Strongly Agree	Agree	Neither Agree nor Disagree	Disagree	Strongly Disagree
☐ My performance in the program was not greatly impaired by any feelings of stress or tension on my part.	1	2	3	4	5
☐ I understood clearly the information which was fed back to me regarding my performance in the program.	1	2	3	4	5
☐ The observations of my performance in the program were accurate.	1	2	3	4	5
☐ The information which was fed back to me regarding my performance in the program was valuable for my personal development.	1	2	3	4	5
☐ The developmental recommendations I received were worthwhile.	1	2	3	4	5
☐ Information from assessment centers like the one I attended should be used for _____ _____	1	2	3	4	5
☐ I would attend another assessment center similar to the one I've already attended if given an opportunity.	1	2	3	4	5

Table 9-4 (continued)

	Strongly Agree	Agree	Neither Agree nor Disagree	Disagree	Strongly Disagree
☐ I would recommend to a good friend at about the same level in the organization that he or she volunteer (or accept an invitation) to attend an assessment center program.	1	2	3	4	5
☐ My career has probably benefited from my attendance at the assessment center.	1	2	3	4	5

The intended respondents would be former participants. The questionnaire covers most of the content mentioned in this chapter, including an attempt to revise some of the ways that we have asked questions, we hope, for the better. For example, we ask about tension as it affects performance in the program, not restricting such felt tension to external sources as had been done up to now. Another feature of the questionnaire is that it has a common response scale (agree/disagree) to all questions. This will allow easily for the inclusion of additional questions which can be interpreted in comparison with the extent of agreement with other issues. (In a first-time survey, interpretive comparisons may be very scarce.) In addition, all the statements are positively worded to enhance interpretive comparisons among issues. We have indicated by dashes or parentheses that the statement type can be applied to a series of similar program aspects such as exercises or uses of the results.

CHAPTER 10

ASSESSMENT AND MANAGEMENT SELECTION

Thomas E. Standing

INTRODUCTION

As pointed out in this chapter, management selection is the major reason
behind the assessment center movement. Clearly, the majority of centers
operate to select potentially qualified candidates for further advancement.
There are fundamentally two types of selection systems which are
operating. In one, a specific target assignment is identified and individuals
are chosen to fill these jobs as a function of successful performance in the
center. An alternative system examines the individual in more general
terms by assessing individual strengths and weaknesses.

It does become clear that there are great similarities, as Dr. Standing
notes, in the assessment processes used, the kinds of behaviors identified,
and the nature of the assessment dimensions rated in widely differing
organizational settings. These similarities cannot be attributable simply to
imitation of the AT&T method. Rather, it reflects a point of view that the
characteristics of successful managers are similar regardless of the
organizational setting in which managers function.

To Dr. Standing's list of major behaviors identified in an assessment
process, we would add an administrative factor. Most centers rely, as
pointed out in Chapter 5, on an in-basket which helps provide much
information on this domain.

We would conclude, then, that the factors related to management
success include communications skills, administrative and interpersonal
effectiveness. All of these skills are measured in the typical center.

The cost-benefit nature of assessment decisions is also discussed. A few organizations, such as IBM, have shown the relationship between assessment performance for failure as well as success. For the most part, the actual cost of assessing an individual is an insignificant figure when related to the potential contribution of successful assessees. The indirect benefits include the management development training offered by being an assessor and increased awareness and communications within the organization, themes which will emerge in later chapters.

* * *

In many ways, management selection is the *raison d'être* of the assessment center method. Had this approach not made sense for such an objective, the assessment center would not be what it is today. Exactly what the assessment center is today is dealt with in great detail by many other chapters in this book. In essence then, this chapter is concerned less with a detailed analysis of the content of an assessment center program than with the logic and meaning of the method as a tool for improving the quality of an organization's workforce at the management level.

This chapter attempts to provide an explicit statement of the rationale behind the use of the assessment center method. This rationale is implicit throughout the other parts of this book. However, one can easily become fascinated by various aspects of the process itself with the danger that one may inadvertently lose sight of the output of the process and consequently fail to ask what the output means to the organization employing the process. Such circumstances are the stuff of which fads are made. Many valuable techniques have failed to contribute their full potential in the personnel management field due to their faddish and inappropriate application. There must be a fit between any particular technique and the organization in which it is applied.

Those techniques which are bought off the shelf because of their glittering packages or a desire to be "with it" suffer from a high mortality rate. The organizational body will soon reject practices that are foreign to it. A clearer conceptualization of what it means to select managers via the assessment center method will lead to more selective and appropriate usage. In order to help develop such a conceptual basis, this chapter will elaborate upon the historical and organizational context within which this technique has been applied, the meaning of management potential as defined by this method, and some possible approaches to refining the technique's application to the problem of selection decisions.

HISTORICAL PERSPECTIVE

It is important to note that assessment centers would exist today even if there were no such entity as AT&T. However, only a very small group of people would probably be aware of it. These people would be psychologists who were interested in the study of personality. They would be conducting assessment centers, but with different purposes in mind. These psychologists would be heirs to the pioneering efforts of Henry Murray and his colleagues at Harvard University and would be using multiple observers and multiple methods to elicit and measure individual differences. Using the behavior made manifest by the assessment center process, these researchers would be attempting to determine "what goes with what" in healthy, effective people as the basis for constructing personality theory. (Dr. Donald W. MacKinnon has in fact pursued such a course at the Institute for Personality Assessment and Research at Berkeley.)

But the assessment center method today is not an esoteric technique being applied only to problems of personality theory. Rather, it is a vital, pragmatic tool of business enterprises interested in filling positions of influence and responsibility with competent, effective people. Such is the case because the assessment center technique is eminently suited to the critical needs of managerial selection. These critical needs relate to the susceptibility of pertinent individual applicant differences to direct observation and measurement. The assessment center method makes these differences manifest.

AT&T's original application of the assessment center was closer to the personality research than to the personnel selection tradition. "The Management Progress Study . . . is a study of growth and development during the adult years" (Bray, Campbell, & Grant, 1974). As such, it was necessary to measure and track relevant personal characteristics through the initial stages of a manager's career. A baseline description of the new hires was required. To this end, the assessment center, which has served as a model for the rest of industry, was designed.

The initiators of the Management Progress Study were not oblivious to the question of improved management selection through the use of assessment center judgments. However, the developmental questions were paramount. Consequently, assessment results were not made available to managers for use in personnel decisions.

But the Management Progress Study exposed the assessment center method to the view of operating managers in the Bell System. At Michigan Bell, these managers saw the selection implications in the procedure and asked that it be adapted for operational use. Consequently, in 1958, the first industrial application of the assessment center method appeared, explicitly for management selection.

ORGANIZATIONAL CONTEXT

Michigan Bell was interested in improving its selection of first-line supervisors in the Plant Department. Candidates for these positions came from craft jobs through the recommendation of their supervisors. These men were already seen as competent employees. However, when faced with a decision regarding which of several knowledgeable craftsmen should be given the responsibility of directing and coordinating the work of other craftsmen, management at Michigan Bell wanted more information. They wanted to avoid the classic consequences of promoting their best craftsmen—losing a good craftsman and gaining a poor supervisor. The Personnel Assessment Program met this need. It provided a standardized, logical basis for making such a selection decision.

The logic of the method has been spoken of elsewhere in this book and will be mentioned only briefly at this point. To a large extent, it centers around the simulation aspect of the assessment center process. The structured exercises of the assessment program attempt to establish circumstances which are approximations to those involved in the job to be filled. In this manner, it becomes possible to observe relevant features of an individual's behavior which are otherwise unavailable for systematic, controlled evaluation. This feature of assessment centers makes it well suited to the problem of supervisory/ management selection. The craftsmen in Michigan Bell's Plant Department had demonstrated their performance effectiveness primarily in the role of individual contributors. They had actually done the work themselves. Their mechanical and technical skills were the prime determinants of effectiveness. In a supervisory role, the task requirements shift to the problem of getting work done through others. Evaluating how well an individual could accomplish this was done through the simulations offered in the assessment center.

Bray et al. (1974) have succinctly explained why it is that assessment centers make sense. These authors dichotomized the requirements of management into two basic categories. One category relates to the technical aspects of a job, to the procedural and informational foundation of effective performance. The second category encompasses various features of a managerial skill nature, including communications, motivation, influence, and leadership. Each position in a managerial hierarchy represents some blend of these two components— technical skill and managerial skill. This simple, but not simplistic, differentiation highlights the essential goal of assessment center measurement, which is an evaluation of managerial skills through a standardized, controlled process. Specific technical competencies are left behind as a candidate enters the assessment and the assessors are required to concentrate upon the more universal aspects of effective management performance—working with and through other people.

The behavioral indicators of management skill were unavailable for systematic observation within the craftsman population. But this skill was an area of obvious relevance for the selection of new supervisors from the craftsman ranks. Since the assessment center's simulations and exercises elicited behavior from the management skill domain, significant information could be provided for use in the selection decision. Thus, the Personnel Assessment Program has become a staple part of supervisory selection decisions in 18 Bell System companies with over 100,000 candidates assessed between 1958 and 1975.

In 1962, The Standard Oil Company of Ohio (Sohio) became the second business enterprise to apply the assessment center as a means of measuring individual differences in managerial skills. Sohio's program was a direct extension of AT&T's assessment process in most of its essential features. There were differences, however, and one of the major ones relates to the intended use of the assessment results.

The Personnel Assessment Program (PAP) was adapted specifically to aid in selecting first-level supervisors. While this program requires assessors to judge some 18 different characteristics, these ratings are intermediate information processing steps toward a summary judgment of promotability to the supervisory level. A "go/no-go" decision will be made by line management about each candidate and the PAP committee approximates that decision most directly in its final rating of "each candidate as being more than acceptable, acceptable, questionable or not acceptable in terms of his ability to handle a first level management assignment" (Moses, 1972a). The organizational context of the Sohio program is reflected in its label—Formal Assessment of Corporate Talent (FACT). The use of assessment results has a broad, corporate focus which is reflective of the fact that, as a capital-intensive business, there are a large number of relatively unique positions, each occupied by very few incumbents (often only one). Assessees come to the program not as craftsmen being considered for a well-defined promotion, but as specialists and lower level managers whose capabilities can be better utilized in the future if systematically described on a corporately meaningful basis. Consequently, in the Sohio program, "the purpose is to establish reliable and valid judgments about the extent to which each assessee possesses each of several personal characteristics believed to be relevant, in varying degrees, to success in a multiplicity of management assignments" (Finkle, 1976). The emphasis remains on management skills, but the organizational realities are such that the separate characteristic ratings, as opposed to a summary judgment of promotability, present the assessment results in the format most appropriate to future selection decisions.

The Sohio application, therefore, represented a broadening of assessment usage beyond the AT&T application. While retaining a selection character, certain aspects of placement have also emerged. There is no immediate single purpose for which the evaluations have been developed. Rather, there is a catalog of relevant judgments available at such time as a management position needs to be filled.

The evolution of the assessment center method since the early 1960s has seen its application at both higher and lower levels of the organizational hierarchy and in governmental agencies and nonprofit organizations as well as business settings. In each of these applications, the question of the target job(s) for which assessment is being done has been answered implicitly or explicitly. Generally speaking, the higher the organizational level of the assessees, the less likely it is that a particular job or job level has been (or can be) specified. Within each organizational context, however, the assessment center and who attends it can be seen as an operational definition of the most difficult and critical selection decisions which occur within the organization.

Other chapters (see especially Chapter 3) have catalogued the most prominent uses of the assessment center method. However, for the sake of highlighting the flexibility of the approach as a selection technique, a few of the distinctive applications will be mentioned here.

By far the single greatest application in many organizations has been to the selection of first-level managers using a variant of AT&T's Personnel Assessment Program. These management positions are usually in manufacturing supervision or field sales management. Bender (1973) reported that, of 38 assessment center applications by 32 companies and governmental agencies included in his survey, 24 examine the suitability of candidates for first-level management positions. The extent of the desire for more and better information regarding candidates for initial levels of supervision is indicated by the existence of a "pre-packaged" assessment program intended for multiorganizational use (McConnell & Parker, 1972) in the evaluation of first-level supervisory management ability. A recent study (Worbois, 1975) has reported current validation data supporting the notion that such a generalized program can be usefully imported into a company. The study also illustrates the kind of corporate commitment (in time and manpower) and professional verification required for such a transplant to be accomplished in a sound, supportable manner.

A recently developed assessment program at the Ford Motor Company illustrates the potential pitfalls of an uncritical acceptance of such generalized programs. The Ford program is designed to aid in the selection of first-line supervisors, as was true of the program investigated by Worbois. However, the extensive job analysis conducted at Ford led to three simulation exercises, none of which involves group activity.* With its heavy use of group simulations, the "typical" program might have been largely inappropriate for the job requirements of the Ford supervisor.

Several examples can be given of the extension of assessment center methodology to levels before management and nonsupervisory management. Thoresen and Jaffee (1973) used the technique to identify individuals who

---

*Personal communication, John Murray, November 1975.

would work effectively as members of autonomous work teams in a chemical plant. Bray and Campbell (1968) have reported on an assessment process for selecting communications sales personnel. Potential to perform effectively in low-level technology engineering positions has also been evaluated by this method (Moses, 1972b).

The Thoresen and Jaffee procedure, besides being directed at a level below management, assessed applicants for employment rather than current company employees. The use of assessment center results for initial employee selection has also been used to help identify promising college graduates (Moses & Wall, 1974).

Each of these applications below the management level can be seen as illustrating the classical flow of assessment program development from job analysis, to the definition of relevant characteristics, to the creation of simulations and exercises designed to elicit behavior relevant to the judgment of the characteristics. The jobs listed above as being targets for assessment center selection methods contained elements of interpersonal contact and influence ("management" in a very broad sense), with the exception of the engineering position. Consequently, assessment centers designed for the identification of potential to perform these jobs have contained leaderless group exercises (with the exception of the engineering and Ford selection efforts). However, without exception, these assessment center programs have contained simulation exercises in order to produce samples, as opposed to signs, of relevant capabilities (Wernimont & Campbell, 1968).

Another class of assessment efforts implemented below the management level is the Early Identification Assessment (EIA). Again, AT&T has led the way in developing this type of application of the assessment center method. While the goal of this process has much in common with an earlier effort at Standard Oil of New Jersey (Exxon) (Laurent, 1962), EIA as currently conceived differs substantially. Its two main distinctions are that it employs the assessment center technique (Jersey Standard used psychometric methods exclusively) and is designed for use with relatively short service, non-exempt employees. EIA does build on the belief, as the Jersey Standard effort did, that it is possible to observe and measure skills and characteristics related to supervisory and management ability quite early in an individual's career. Having done so, the organization is then in a position to better use such talents in a data-based manpower planning process through accelerated advancement and development placement (Moses, 1973).

Assessment center programs whose participants are at or above the first level of management can be characterized in terms of the diversity of job assignment selection decisions to which the assessment judgments are to be applied. It is unusual that assessees in such higher level programs are being evaluated in terms of promotability to a tightly defined job level, much less to a target job. In Bender's survey (1973), 16 centers evaluated candidates for middle management positions and three focused upon upper management. Because of the pyramidal shape of business organizations, assessees for such programs will tend to come from a multiplicity of functions and/or divisions within the corporation. Again, the communality in diverse future job assignments, which makes the standardized assessment procedure useful, stems from the concept of management skill. These heterogeneous jobs may be embedded in various technologies, functions, and organizational structures, but each requires the ability to work with and through others toward the attainment of organizational objectives.

DEFINING MANAGEMENT POTENTIAL

It would be worthwhile at this point to elaborate upon the concept of management skill by examining its operational definition—i.e., the specific characteristics measured in actual assessment centers. Table 10-1 presents the rated variables from six different assessment efforts. Examination of the lists indicates that only two aspects of performance are included in all programs—oral communications and interpersonal influence (variously labeled "leadership," "impact," "persuasiveness"). Several dimensions—decision making, planning, organizing, drive energy, personal likability/acceptability, stress tolerance—are included in four of the six programs. Obviously, assessment centers define management skill to a significant extent as working with and through others.

Another way of better understanding the individual differences that are being measured by the assessment center method is to search for underlying factors in the judged characteristics. Three factor analyses are readily accessible in the literature. From the Management Progress Study, Bray et al. (1974) have reported that seven general areas can be described as accounting for the interrelationships among the 25 assessment variable judgments. These seven factors and the committee judgments most related to them are:

1. Administrative skills: planning and organizing, decision-making
2. Interpersonal skills: personal impact, oral communications skills, human relations skills, behavior flexibility
3. Intellectual ability: scholastic aptitude, range of interests
4. Stability of performance: tolerance of uncertainty, resistance to stress
5. Work motivation: primacy of work, inner work standards
6. Career orientation: need for advancement, need for security (inverse relationship), ability to delay gratification (inverse relationship)
7. Dependence on others: need for superior approval, need for peer approval, goal flexibility

Table 10-1   Personal Characteristics Evaluated in Six Different Assessment Center Programs

AT&T Personnel Assessment Pgm. (Moses, 1973)	AT&T Management Progress Study (continued)	IBM (Wollowich & McNamara, 1969)
Energy	Written communications skills	Self-confidence
Resistance to stress	Human relations skills	Written communications
Inner work standards	Personal impact—	-Administrative ability
Self-objectivity	forcefulness	Interpersonal contact
Forcefulness	Personal impact—	Energy level
Likability	likableness	-Decision
Range of interest	Behavior flexibility	Resistance to stress
Scholastic aptitude		Planning and organizing
Awareness of social	SOHIO	Persuasiveness
environment	(Thompson, 1970)	Aggressiveness
Behavior flexibility		Risk taking
Leadership	Amount of participation	Oral communications
Need for superior approval	Oral communication	
Need for peer approval	Personal acceptability	AMA
Organizing and planning	Impact	(Worbois, 1975)
Decision making	Quality of participation	
Oral communications skill	Personal breadth	Company orientation
Written communications	Orientation to detail	Controlling
skill	Self-direction	Creativity
	Relationship with authority	-Decision making
AT&T	Originality	Flexibility
Management Progress Study	Understanding of people	Functional ability
(Bray et al., 1974)	Drive	Initiative
		Leadership
Perception of threshold		Oral communications
social cues		Organizing
Scholastic aptitude		Planning
Range of interests		Written communications
Inner work standards		
Primacy of work		IRS
Need advancement		(DiCostanzo & Andretta,
Need security		1970)
Ability to delay		
gratification		-Decision making
Resistance to stress		Decisiveness
Tolerance of uncertainty		Flexibility
Need approval of superiors		Leadership
Need approval of peers		Oral communications
Goal flexibility		Organization and planning
Energy		Perception and analytic
Self-objectivity		ability
Social objectivity		Persuasiveness
Bell System value		Sensitivity to people
orientation		Stress tolerance
Realism of expectations		
Organizing and planning		
Decision making		
Creativity		
Oral communications skills		

Thomson (1969) factor-analyzed 13 committee ratings from Sohio's FACT program and identified five underlying factors:

1. Group task effectiveness: impact, amount of participation, oral communications, quality of participation, potential, self-direction
2. Need for structure: orientation to detail, originality, self-direction, relationship with authority
3. Interpersonal effectiveness: personal acceptability, understanding of people
4. Quality of independent thinking: personal breadth, potential, quality of participation, originality, self-direction, understanding of people, relationship with authority
5. Work-oriented motivation: drive

An analysis of IBM's assessment ratings has been reported by Hinrichs (1969). Since the factor analysis is based upon only 47 assessees from one function within this company (marketing), the results must be seen as only a tentative indication of the underlying sources of individual difference in IBM's assessment program. The three interpreted factors were labeled as follows:

1. Activity: persuasiveness, aggressiveness, energy level, interpersonal contact, oral communications, self-confidence
2. Administration: decision-making, planning and organization, written communications, administrative ability
3. Stress resistance: risk taking, resistance to stress

The two characteristics common to all six programs listed in Table 10-1—oral communications and interpersonal influence—contribute to a single factor in each of the three factor analyses. In each analysis, this was the single factor accounting for the greatest variance in the assessment committee rating. Thus, it appears that if one were to ask what is measured by the assessment center method in the most simple and general sense, the answer would have to describe in some fashion the ability to express thoughts to others and to influence others in their course of action.

Such an answer would of course be an oversimplification in the context of any particular assessment center program. There is a great deal of reliable variance unaccounted for by this single basis for differentiating among assessment center participants. Other systematic discriminations are also being made. Nevertheless, the communications/influence construct is the preeminent basis for judgment.

SELECTION DECISION MAKING
BASED UPON ASSESSMENT CENTER RESULTS

Donald W. MacKinnon (1975), in a review of the current status of assessment center applications, also examined the redundancy in assessment judgments as indicated by factor analytic studies. He concluded that "meaningful distinctions are being made which may be clinically if not statistically justified" (p. 16). This statement goes to the heart of what may be the greatest weakness in assessment center applications to date. The reference to "clinical" justification alludes to the richness of individual assessee description afforded by the technique. A unique profile of relative strengths and weaknesses, within the individual as well as between the individual and other candidates for managerial advancement, is generated by the assessment process. Especially in higher level programs, it is this profile which promises the greatest possible improvement in selection accuracy and in manpower utilization. These benefits, however, will not be achieved at a maximum level as long as professional contribution is limited to the assessment process per se.

The assessment process results in a report for each participant. This report, usually narrative in nature, records the integrated judgments of the assessment committee in terms of separate characteristics or dimensions and a summary evaluation. However, this report is *not* the reason an organization establishes its assessment center. That purpose most often relates to selection and promotion decisions. Therefore, a critical issue in applying the assessment center method must be the manner in which the data contained in the report are integrated into the decision process of the "hiring" manager.

Examination of the assessment center literature reveals the almost universal statement that assessment center results are written into a narrative report which is provided to management one or more levels above the assessee. If any additional reference is made to the actual selection decision process, it is usually in terms of the importance of considering additional information (e.g., education, job history, current job performance). That other factors are considered in actual practice is attested to by studies which examine the subsequent promotional history of assessees (Kraut & Scott, 1972; Moses, 1973; Moses & Boehm, 1975). Even individuals judged "less than acceptable" for promotion to specific first-level management positions still receive such promotions. This type of overall rating is the most straightforward translation of assessment center results into selection-related terms. There is little subtlety in a summary judgment of "less than acceptable." The appropriate use of the clinically justified distinctions referred to by MacKinnon becomes even more problematic when dealing with judgments from higher level assessment centers. Since these programs usually lack a single target job, the most pertinent assessor judgments are transmitted by the characteristic ratings rather than by the overall or summary evaluation of promotability/potential.

Ultimately, a total selection decision system should be developed for considering and weighing the many factors, in addition to assessment results, which are relevant to any particular selection decision. More immediately, there are steps that can be taken to increase the probability that assessment judgments are blended into the process at the appropriate point and in an increasingly sophisticated and judicious manner. A first step is an analysis of who sees assessment reports and when. It does the individual or the company little good if assessment reports are reviewed by higher management immediately upon their completion and then are filed away. Along the same lines, maximum benefit is not possible if there is no mechanism for providing assessment results to managers outside of the department or division in which the assessee worked at the time of assessment.

One approach to overcoming these possible limitations is that employed by Sohio. By company policy, vacancies in management are communicated to a central staff unit, which prepares a candidate list for the opening. This list is compiled by a search of computer records based upon specific qualifications with regard to technical training, work experience, current job performance, and job level. The candidate list also indicates to the requesting manager those individuals who have attended the company's FACT program. The narrative assessment report is then provided at the manager's request. This procedure provides some assurance that managers will be continually reminded of the availability of talent within the company but outside of the immediate work area.

A second step which deals with improving the use of assessment results in selection decisions relates to the reaction of the manager when viewing the written report of assessment performance. While it is undeniable that assessment centers are generally well accepted by managers, wide variation is possible in individual managers' familiarity with the significance of the process and its output. Some method should exist for orienting managers who will logically be in a position to receive such reports. No doubt the best way to acquaint a manager with the meaning of assessment judgments is to provide experience as an assessor. However, with the exception of the Sohio program, which employs three new management assessors with each session, such "learning by doing" opportunities are severely limited. Nonetheless, every organization employing the assessment center method should devise ways of educating the users of assessment information in such matters as the following: Who is eligible to attend the assessment center? What methods are used? What is the nature of the assessment committee? How are assessment characteristics defined? What is the nature of the rating scale used in terms of alternative scale values and normative base? The answers to these and other questions will provide the necessary structure for comprehending more fully the information contained in an assessment center report.

Given this type of orientation, a manager faced with a selection decision should be able to understand more fully the relative capabilities of those individuals under consideration. However, there is one final refinement in the application of this understanding which is, potentially, the single most beneficial step in improving assessment-based decision making. This refinement relates to a clearer and more specific definition of the requirements of the particular job opening. It also relates to the linkage between specific job requirements and specific assessment judgments.

With the exception of nonmanagement applications (e.g., sales, technical engineering), no assessment center operates to select people for just *one* definable job. Even first-level supervisory/management assessment programs really have a range of target jobs which, while sharing the management skill requirement to some degree, differ in terms of the exact degree of that component as well as the other components measured in a specific assessment program. In higher level programs the heterogeneity of possible promotions is usually even more apparent.

Variations in job requirements argue for increased efforts in management job analysis. The work of John Hemphill has often been cited for its promise in this area (Campbell, Dunnette, Lawler, & Weick, 1970). A recent research report by Tornow and Pinto (1976) has begun to advance Hemphill's Executive Position Description Questionnaire from promise into reality. A 208-item adaptation of Hemphill's questionnaire was completed by 433 managers from various levels, functions, and technologies within a diversified corporation. Factor analysis of the items indicated 13 interpretable dimensions. These 13 dimensions were then used to cluster management positions according to the similarity of position requirement profiles.

The availability of a device for analyzing management jobs into their constituent elements suggests the possibility of using assessment results in a more selective fashion. By relating separate assessment characteristics to specific job requirements, assessment reports that are tailored to the needs of the open position can be provided to a manager. This would eliminate the need for sifting through entire reports in search of the most salient features and, even more importantly, would eliminate the possibility that the selection decision would be influenced by characteristics of tangential significance to the particular job.

A model is available in the literature which encompasses the features necessary to arrive at a tailored assessment report. This is the concept of "synthetic validity" (Guion, 1965b). Within this model, a job is broken down into elements that are common to some, but not all, other jobs. Valid predictors are then identified for separate job elements. This allows one to "synthesize" a valid prediction scheme for new or different jobs through the use of a job analysis which identifies significant performance elements within the job that are tied back to individual differences predictive of performance in those elements.

Within the assessment center context, the process would entail a determination of the relationship of each assessment characteristic to each job element. Then, at the point where a selection decision is required, only those personal characteristics that are most strongly related to the significant elements in the job need be reported to the hiring manager.

CONCLUSIONS

Other writers (MacKinnon, 1975) have remarked about the essential similarity among assessment centers. Regardless of variations in organizational purpose, hierarchical level, and functional responsibility, people around the country (and around the world) are experiencing daily a process of evaluation bearing the hallmarks of the assessment center method. With nearly the same frequency, observations and measurements of behavior are being combined by committees of assessors into scalar statements of similarly defined personal characteristics. Certainly some of this uniformity can be attributed to the influence of AT&T's successful pioneering efforts. However, the fact that this basic model has been effectively incorporated into so many different organizations may say something about the nature of management itself.

There are, undoubtedly, features of organizations that alter the performance requirements of management positions across organizational settings. Nonetheless, these variations may effect differences in job performance primarily as a function of individual differences in technical knowledge and experience. The core of managerial effectiveness may involve abilities to influence, communicate, and administer which are common, regardless of organizational context. The utility of the assessment center method stems from its ability to tap individual differences in these core abilities. If this view is accurate, then management assessment centers are essentially similar across organizations because management jobs are likewise essentially similar. Mintzberg (1975) has recently argued for the view that management jobs are more alike than different.

The assessment of management candidates is not an inexpensive activity. A cost of $500-600 per assessee is often cited. This normally covers the "out-of-pocket" expenses for such items as transportation to the assessment location and motel costs. Other costs not included in this figure are salaries of all participants (administrative staff, assessors, and assessees) and costs of preparing, maintaining, and using reports. A great deal of variety exists in how (or whether) such costs are tracked and accounted for in individual companies.

As is usual with personnel programs, the benefits of an assessment center are less easily quantified than the costs. However, a few of the likely outcomes related to management selection can be cited in the interest of providing a frame of reference for a cost-benefit type of analysis.

The major potential benefit is increased performance effectiveness in those management positions filled with the assistance of assessment center information. If we assume (for the sake of illustration) that 50% of the organization's managers currently at the program's target level(s) are highly effective in their work, and assume further that assessment results correlate with indices of management effectiveness at the .40 level (see Chapter 14 regarding validation findings), then a selection ratio of 20% (i.e, five candidates for each position filled) would result in approximately 75% highly effective managers at the target level(s). In other words, there would be a 50% improvement in the number of highly effective managers.

While this statistical argument sheds some light on the benefits from an assessment program for management selection, the more powerful argument is the less scientific one which centers around a manager's multiplier effect. The performance of a manager normally affects a great number of people and their ability to do their jobs well. The financial and psychological consequences of ineffective managerial performance are profound. Subordinates, peers, superiors, customers—all are liable to be adversely affected. Therefore, any procedure that increases the likelihood that management positions are occupied by people competent to handle the responsibilities probably pays for itself several times each year through the positive actions taken and the negative actions avoided by managers promoted by that procedure.

Since assessment programs simulate the behavioral requirements of jobs which assessees do not yet occupy, the chances of people being promoted to their level of incompetence should be reduced.

Other indirect benefits include freer movement of qualified people across organizational boundaries, quicker identification and utilization of managerial talent, and increased belief in the fairness of the organization's selection and promotion decisions. Potential positive outcomes in terms of development, both individual (assessee and assessor) and organizational, are treated in detail in other sections of this book.

Management selection has always been an amorphous area, replete with fads, personal biases, and covert processes. If only because of its open, intelligible approach, the assessment center method presents a refreshing alternative. Given its significant research tradition, the management assessment center promises to continue to provide a foundation upon which to build a better understanding not only of management selection, but of management behavior in general.

REFERENCES

Bender, J. M. What is "typical" of assessment centers? *Personnel*, 1973, *50*(4), 50-57.

Bray, D. W. & Campbell, R. J. Selection of salesmen by means of an assessment center. *Journal of Applied Psychology*, 1968, *52*, 36-41.

Bray, D. W., Campbell, R. J., & Grant, D. L. *Formative years in business: A long-term AT&T study of managerial lives.* New York: Wiley Interscience, 1974.

Campbell,, J. P., Dunnette, M. D., Lawler, E. E., III, & Weick, K. E. *Managerial behavior, performance and effectiveness.* New York: McGraw-Hill, 1970.

Di Costanzo, F., & Andretta, J. Implementation of an assessment center in a federal agency. *ASTD Journal*, September 1970.

Finkle, R. B. Managerial assessment centers. In M. Dunnette (Ed.), *Handbook of industrial psychology.* New York: Rand McNally, 1976.

Guion, R. M. *Personnel testing.* New York: McGraw-Hill, 1965a.

Guion, R. M. Synthetic validity in a small company: A demonstration. *Personnel Psychology*, 1965b, *18*, 49-63.

Hinrichs, J. R. Comparison of "real life" assessments of management potential with situation exercises, paper-and-pencil ability tests, and personality inventories. *Journal of Applied Psychology*, 1969, *53*, 425-432.

Kraut, A. I., & Scott, G. J. Validity of an operational management assessment program. *Journal of Applied Psychology*, 1972, *56*, 124-129.

Laurent, H. Early identification of managers. *Management Records*, May 1962, 33-38.

MacKinon, D. W. An overview of assessment centers. *Technical Report No. 1.* Center for Creative Leadership, Greensboro, N.C., May 1975.

McConnell, J. H., & Parker, T. An assessment center program for multi-organizational use. *Training and Development Journal*, 1972, *26*(3), 6-14.

Mintzberg, H. The manager's job: Folklore and fact. *Harvard Business Review*, 1975, *53*(4), 49-61.

Moses, J. L. Assessment center performance and management progress. *Studies in Personnel Psychology*, 1972a, *4*(1), 7-12.

Moses, J. L. *The engineering selection program.* Personnel Research, American Telephone & Telegraph Company, October 1972b.

Moses, J. L. The development of an assessment center for the early identification of supervisory potential. *Personnel Psychology*, 1973, *26*, 569-580.

Moses, J. L., & Boehm, V. R. Relationship of assessment center performance to management progress of women. *Journal of Applied Psychology*, 1975, *60*, 527-529.

Moses, J. L., & Wall, S. J. *Management hire assessment validation study.* Personnel Research, American Telephone & Telegraph Company, May 1974.

Thomson, H. A. Internal and external validation of an industrial assessment center program. Unpublished doctoral dissertation, Case Western Reserve University, 1969.

Thoresen, J. D., & Jaffee, C. L. A unique assessment center application with some unexpected by-products. *Human Resource Management*, 1973, *12*(1), 3-7.

Tornow, W. W., & Pinto, P. R. The development of a managerial job taxonomy: A system for describing, classifying, and evaluating executive positions. *Journal of Applied Psychology*, 1976.

Wernimont, P. F., & Campbell, J. P. Signs, samples, and criteria. *Journal of Applied Psychology*, 1968, *52*, 372-376.

Wollowich, H. B., & McNamara, W. J. Relationship of the components of an assessment center to management success. *Journal of Applied Psychology*, 1969, *53*, 348-352.

Worbois, G. M. Validation of externally developed assessment procedures for identification of supervisory potential. *Personnel Psychology*, 1975, *28*, 77-91.

CHAPTER 11

ASSESSMENT AND MANAGEMENT DEVELOPMENT

Virginia R. Boehm
and
David F. Hoyle

INTRODUCTION

In this chapter, Virginia Boehm and David Hoyle differentiate among three purposes of the assessment center method—selection, identification, and diagnosis. They point out that traditionally selection has been the focus of assessment centers, but that assessment centers are becoming more developmental in orientation both within the AT&T system, of which the authors are a part, and in programs in general. They point out that development is extremely compatible with assessment and provides a needed preliminary step in developing a combined assessment/ development program.

The authors concentrate on the use of the assessment center method for "identification" of individuals with high potential who can be "fast-tracked" into supervisory or other positions. They use as illustrations some innovative AT&T early identification programs and their recent middle management women's assessment program. Several theoretical patterns of development aid the reader in understanding this important use of assessment.

Diagnostic centers are also discussed. This is defined as the use of assessment to identify the strengths and weaknesses of individuals so that the individual and organization can concentrate on building on strengths and overcoming weaknesses. They point out a need for this kind of assessment, particularly when an organization finds itself with people already at a level of the organization where there is no further opportunity for any use of assessment other than diagnosis.

The authors feel that perhaps new technology is needed to perform diagnostic assessment. As the authors point out, to have an effective selection or identification program, only the final go or no-go decision must have a high degree of reliability. In a diagnostic program reliability must be achieved at each dimension being assessed. This may be done by having more exercises, therefore more redundancy of observation for each dimension. It is not unusual for a diagnostic assessment center to have as many as nine very complicated exercises as opposed to a typical identification center with three or four exercises.

The issue of whether people can be changed, and therefore the need for diagnostic assessment centers, is raised as well. Certainly, the act of diagnosis is a necessary precursor to effective training if it can be obtained. We are not positive that we can bring about real changes in such dimensions as judgment, decisiveness, and managerial flexibility. Certainly if we can, the only way we could do it would be to identify very specifically what these things mean, who needs it, and then concentrate a heavy developmental program on the specific dimension(s). A program requires an intensive allocation of resources both at the diagnostic as well as the developmental ends of the equation. This clearly appears to be the exception, rather than the rule.

* * *

The principal use of the assessment center method, since its inception as an operational program in the late 1950s, has been the selection of supervisors and managers. This use of assessment has made a valuable contribution to selecting more capable managers. Numerous studies over the years have shown that assessment center results do permit organizations to make better selection decisions.

Development in the organization is usually viewed as a separate and distinct function from identification and selection. While it is not a new concept, "development" is an overused word and is not well defined. Development is traditionally an informal process which consists of a person handling a variety of assignments along an established route of advancement (e.g., salesman, sales manager, division sales manager, and director of sales). To some, development is training and course work designed to impart knowledge and information needed for successful job performance. To others, it is the process of moving through prescribed chairs to gain knowledge and job experience. More recently, development has been described as formal career pathing aimed at providing needed background and experience on a systematic basis. Self-development or personal efforts to acquire knowledge, background, and skills also fall within the realm of development.

However it is defined, development of people is seldom part of the management reward system and infrequently encompasses the entire organization.

The role of assessment in the developmental process has been limited primarily to determining promotability of people considered ready for promotion—people already considered "developed" for the next job.

In recent years, the role of the assessment center as a selection device within this framework has been questioned. Is the assessment process related more clearly to identification and development than its past would indicate? Are we making optimal use of this concept in meeting the changing needs of organizations and individuals? Given ever-changing conditions and organizational commitments, should selection continue to be the major focus of assessment centers? The answers to these questions are only beginning to emerge as traditional concepts of management development are undergoing change.

One reason for this change is the impact that rapid technological change has had on the business community. Also, the social climate within which business operates is rapidly shifting, and these changes affect the organization.

Organizational climates are changing, too, in response to social changes and to changes in the technology of management. Growing use of team management and task forces combine with frequent reorganizations to disrupt the traditional routes of advancement.

Closely related to these changes are changes in the expectations of people regarding their work and the role it should play in their lives. A generation reared in a climate of abundance seeks more intrinsic satisfaction from work. Business is responding to this need through the evolution of more participative management structures, job enrichment, and other means.

These changes have a clear impact on management development strategies. Traditional management development was intended to equip an individual to meet the organization's needs and fulfill a role the organization defined. Today, the purpose of the developmental enterprise is shifting, with a new focus on matching the needs and aspirations of the individual with organizational needs and goals. Both the organization and the individual are considered malleable. While employees are still expected to be willing to modify their goals to mesh better with those of the organization, organizations are also expected to respond to the needs of their employees. The organization is no longer the sole instigator of the development process and the definer of the process' goals, but rather a partner in an enterprise where joint positive outcomes are defined and worked toward.

This altered concept of the goal of development reflects an abrupt shift in attitudes toward authority. Numerous studies during the last two decades have noted marked decreases in the extent to which traditional attitudes toward authority are held by the American people. Development, in the traditional sense, where the young manager strove to "grow into" higher level jobs within the organization following the guidance of a sponsor or organizational tradition, is not what many young people today seek, even when the young manager is from the traditional (i.e., white male) pool of potential management talent.

And, increasingly, today's managerial prospect is female and/or a minority group member. The traditional concept of development frequently becomes, in such instances, even less applicable.

Traditional development assumes that the organization and the individual being developed have a similar value system—that they agree on what constitutes success and on the principle that hard work is the primary means for achieving it. But, frequently, minorities and women do not agree with the managerial hierarchy on these basics, and for good reason. Realistically, no amount of hard work, ability, and drive would have brought about traditional "success" in the corporate environment for a black or a woman a generation ago. Consequently, the minority males and females of all ethnic groups of an earlier generation had to adapt different ideas of what success was. Frequently, it was these nontraditional ideas, not those of corporate managers, that minority families taught their children and that white mothers passed on to their daughters.

Even when the managerial aspirant who is not a white male has learned and internalized the traditional definition of success and achievement through effort, informal developmental routes within the organization may not be open. Sponsors who serve as role models tend to prefer young people whom they perceive as being like themselves. It is the rare individual who is willing and able to assume the sponsor's role for a young woman or minority group male.

Since traditional ways of development no longer meet today's needs, new procedures are needed. One potentially useful strategy is the joining of assessment and development programs into a unified system.

A LOGICAL RELATIONSHIP—
ASSESSMENT AND DEVELOPMENT

The ultimate goal of assessment center programs is essentially the same as the wide variety of existing development strategies—to maximize individual effectiveness (job performance) and consequently the attainment of organizational success. In the pursuit of this common goal, assessment and development are concerned with the same elements of job performance.

In a broad sense, a person's performance on any job (manager, engineer, accountant, financial analyst, etc.) is a function of two major elements—individual factors and environmental factors. The individual factors can be divided into two significant and distinguishable subcomponents—one is individual ability and the other is personal motivation. In addition to having the same ultimate goal, assessment programs and development strategies both focus on these three major components of job performance—*ability*, *motivation*, and *environment*.

The *ability component* includes a long and sometimes complex series of individual qualities such as aptitudes, specific skills and abilities, proficiencies, and special knowledge. For want of more definitive categories, a spectrum of personality characteristics, health, and physical attributes are also included in this component. Assessment center programs do exist and can be built to identify and measure many of these individual qualities. Development strategies are designed either formally or informally to build or more effectively utilize these qualities.

The *motivation component* includes another unique group of personal qualities: work and life-oriented interests, goals, aspirations, attitudes, and a number of psychological needs. The needs for security, recognition, achievement, and status are important parts of this component. Here, again, assessment programs have been used to identify and evaluate these qualities. In addition, development strategy is sometimes aimed at influencing, directing, or modifying these motivational qualities.

The *environmental component* encompasses the existing conditions which surround the individual and are largely beyond his or her control but do influence performance. These conditions include organizational philosophy, programs, policies, practices, and opportunities. Peers, subordinates, superiors, working conditions, family, and friends are also part of the person's environment. Assessment and development programs are in themselves part of the environmental component.

When using an assessment center for identification or selection purposes, the organization is providing the opportunity (environment) for an individual to demonstrate abilities relevant to successful job performance. When assessment is used as a diagnostic tool, the organization is providing opportunity to identify certain weaknesses that, when overcome, will enhance individual performance.

A person's effectiveness (job performance), then, is determined by a long series of individual abilities, personal motivations, and existing environmental conditions. These factors are interrelated and the relationships are frequently complex. Since the ultimate goal of both assessment and development are the same (to maximize effectiveness) and both are related to and are part of the major determinants of effectiveness, a natural and complementary relationship exists between the assessment center method and various development strategies. In fact, recent experience strongly suggests that this complementary relationship is essential to the maximum utility of both assessment centers and development programs.

This is evidenced by the movement away from using assessment strictly as a selection tool and its increasing use for identification and diagnosis. These more recent assessment center applications almost demand subsequent individual development activities, thus providing objectivity, structure, and purpose to both formal and informal development efforts.

MAJOR COMPONENTS OF THE
ASSESSMENT-DEVELOPMENT SYSTEM

Recognizing the logical relationship between the assessment center concept and the function of development is only the first step in establishing an integrated system. The major components of such a system and their interrelationships are shown in the flowchart presented in Fig. 11-1.

First, organizational needs must be clearly defined and quantified through an analysis of staffing requirements by both functional area (sales, manufacturing, finance, etc.) and occupational group (managers, engineers, salesmen, etc.). Job descriptions based on objective evaluations are also needed, since the abilities or qualities measured in assessment and focused upon in subsequent development efforts must be relevant to the job. For example, the abilities, knowledge, and experience required to be a financial analyst are quite different from those required to be a manager in the financial area.

Once different job categories have been defined, projections should be made of needed numbers within prescribed time frames. Projections should consider the effects of organizational growth, changing technology, and employee turnover (retirements, resignations, etc.). Time frames should encompass short-term (0 to one year), intermediate (one to five years), and long-term (five plus years) considerations. The staffing analysis is complete when projected vacancies by job category are matched against available people with the required abilities, background, and experience to perform successfully.

In today's business environment, organizations, small and large, cannot ignore affirmative action. The need for and availability of minorities and women should be incorporated into the staffing analysis by function and occupational group. Changing technology, organizational structure, and economic conditions should also be considered in determining differences in manpower supply and demand especially in the intermediate or long term.

Short-term staffing analyses are easier to complete because factors determining supply and demand are less variable. Intermediate and long-term analyses are difficult to construct due to more variable and unknown conditions. But, in all cases, the organization will be further ahead by constructing the best blueprint possible on which to base its assessment and development system. In the long run, a realistic manpower analysis tied to relevant assessment center and development programs will lead to better manpower utilization, higher individual effectiveness, and greater organizational success.

A major step in establishing an integrated assessment-development system is the choice of an assessment center program. The choice will be strongly

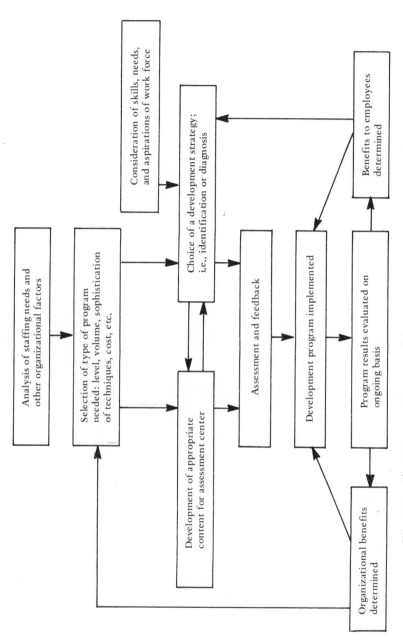

Fig. 11-1. The Major Components of the Assessment/Development System

influenced by the results of the staffing analysis, and the availability of assessment techniques to measure potential in occupational areas where deficiences are indicated.

Assessment center programs have been used for years to measure potential for various levels of management. Some assessment centers are aimed at determining potential for first-level supervisory assignments, while others are designed to measure potential for middle and executive-level management. Supervisory assessment centers are less elaborate and less costly than middle or higher level management programs. Sophistication and cost can be directly related to organizational consequences of making a poor decision on who should be developed and eventually selected for a particular management job.

Another major consideration in devising an assessment-development system and one frequently ignored or overlooked, is the individual needs of those people who will be called upon to fill future vacancies. Seldom are individuals consulted when their potential and careers are determined. Usually, potential is determined subjectively for the next immediate opening, and a career emerges informally with little input from the individual.

As pointed out earlier, the social climate in which businesses operate and the motivations of people regarding work are changing. Individual needs of people must be considered along with organizational needs. The individual should actively participate in any process or procedure designed to identify and develop potential for a given position. A system which puts the individual on an equal footing with the organization is required to establish a match between organization and individual needs.

The choice of developmental strategy is a major link in a total system of assessment and development. Development strategy is tied to and shaped by the primary aim of the assessment center program—i.e., identification or diagnosis. The differences between the identification and diagnostic development strategies are discussed in more detail in the next section of this chapter.

Regardless of the primary aim of the assessment center, development strategy cannot be left to chance. The time and effort of knowledgeable people must be devoted to formally establishing the who, how, where, and when of development. This provides a framework for development which needs to be translated into workable methods and procedures, introduced to the organization, accepted by the people involved, and carried out as an integral part of day-to-day operations.

The use of assessment centers as a basis for development has a number of advantages over less formal and subjective procedures. These advantages benefit both the organization and the individuals who participate. The benefits can be condensed into "selling points" to facilitate obtaining necessary acceptance:

Benefits to the Organization:
1) A valid estimate of individual potential not influenced by the job environment, supervisory evaluations, or functional and occupational differences
2) An objective procedure which measures all participants on relevant abilities or qualities using equivalent standards
3) The opportunity to learn about individual motivation (needs, expectations, goals, and interests) using standard procedures outside the work environment
4) The opportunity to identify specific strengths and weaknesses in assessed qualities for each participant and use this information for career guidance and development
5) A pool of high potential people who, with appropriate development, will be ready to fill future vacancies in the management ranks with a high probability of success

Benefits to the Individual:
1) Equal opportunity to demonstrate potential for advancement independent of current job functions, responsibilities, and performance
2) Better understanding of what a manager does and the qualities needed to be a successful manager
3) Opportunity to express career interests, goals, and aspirations under conditions designed to effectively use the information
4) Opportunity to learn through feedback about individual strengths, weaknesses, and overall potential for self-development purposes
5) Opportunity to make better informed decisions on personal career plans and life goals

When the assessment center is used effectively, these benefits provide a sound foundation for career development, placement, and constructive manpower utilization, regardless of the developmental strategy selected.

All management-oriented assessment center programs can be tied to particular development strategies. Sometimes development strategy will vary with the level of assessment. Supervisory assessment centers, for example, may perform an identification function and subsequent development activities will be experience oriented. Executive-level centers, on the other hand, may function as a diagnostic tool with subsequent development activities aimed at strengthening individual deficiencies.

Diagnostic applications have largely been limited to the executive levels of management for self-development purposes. Recent progress in the field of behavior modeling could well bring more emphasis on this application from a development standpoint.

In an identification system, the scope of development can take a variety of forms. The aim of development might be providing a high-potential individual with the opportunity to move ahead one organizational level within the immediate organization. This requires a careful analysis by both the boss and the individual of all the factors—skills, knowledge, experience, and abilities—needed to perform successfully at the target level, followed by the joint development of a career plan. A number of individual abilities and qualities are determined in the assessment process, but some must be determined from present job performance, experience, background, and education. Given the same overall potential, people will differ on a variety of dimensions which will affect their readiness to advance. Development might encompass formal or informal training, job assignments, formal schooling, etc. Certain personal qualities, not measured in assessment (e.g., integrity, reliability, etc.), plus personal motivation need to be considered in planning for development. Present job content and performance as they relate to the target position must also be considered.

The analysis and discussion between boss and individual should result in a mutually agreed-upon formal development plan. The plan will incorporate assessment center results and input from the post-assessment analysis and discussion. The plan should be in writing and should include developmental time frames and an estimated target date when the individual will be considered ready for advancement.

Target dates for advancement consideration should be consistent with the organization's staffing requirements. The assistance of a career planning and development specialist can be invaluable to the individual and the boss in formulating an effective plan.

The scope of development may extend beyond the immediate organizational group and call for lateral moves to other areas of the business prior to advancement. A career plan and development strategy may go beyond the next organizational level. Development plans which go beyond the next organizational level and include other areas of the business call for the assistance and coordination of a personnel specialist with influence at higher management levels and across organizational groups.

The individual, line management, and the personnel organization have certain responsibilities in making the system work. The individual has the responsibility of participating in the creation of the development plan. He or she must agree with the plan, recognize organizational needs, and demonstrate commitment to the plan. Line supervision must also participate in creation of the plan and must be prepared to implement and carry it to conclusion. Both the individual and line management must be flexible and ready to adapt development plans to changing needs and conditions. The personnel organization is responsible for constructing the framework for development; developing procedures, methods, and guidelines; assisting in the design and implementation of individual development plans; and coordinating the entire identification and development system throughout the organization. They also are responsible for integrating the system with the manpower needs of the organization. Responsibilities should be clearly defined and well understood by all of those involved in post-assessment development strategy.

The overall administration of the assessment-development system is usually the responsibility of the personnel organization. In addition to control over the assessment process, this involves the monitoring and control of development programs, the defining of derived outcomes and the measurement of the overall effectiveness of the system in meeting staffing requirements and employee needs.

The importance of effective evaluation and monitoring cannot be overemphasized. Without effective administration, the potential benefits of an assessment-development system will remain largely unrealized. Both competent personnel and a high organizational priority are needed to assure a successful effort.

IDENTIFICATION AND DIAGNOSIS—
TWO MAJOR DEVELOPMENT STRATEGIES

As was mentioned above, two different types of development programs can be derived from assessment results—programs designed for identification and those centering around diagnosis. The major differences between these approaches are outlined below:

Differences	Identification Strategy	Diagnostic Strategy
Population	Primarily high potential people	All interested assessees
Focal point of feedback	Overall rating with some attention to individual variables	Individual variables; overall rating perhaps not given
Developmental concentration	Technical and job administration skills	Weaknesses in management skill areas
Organizational involvement	High; centralized monitoring and control functions	Low; reliance on self-development and possible immediate supervisory involvement
Goal of development	Upward advancement within organization based on systematic career plan	Individual's increased satisfaction and improved job performance

An identification program is intended to provide a means for selecting potential managers early in their careers. Rather than assessing candidates for immediate promotion (as is usually the case in assessment for selection), an identification-oriented assessment is done considerably before that time. Individuals seen as having high potential are given the opportunity to receive the kinds of assignments and training that will build the job experience and technical skills needed for promotions as rapidly as possible.

Diagnostically oriented development programs, on the other hand, focus on the development of weak areas identified in assessment. Unlike the identification programs, diagnostically oriented ones do not necessarily have upward mobility of the individual as their eventual goal.

The philosophies behind the two kinds of programs are sharply divergent. An identification program usually assumes that only high-potential individuals are to be developed, and that the development efforts should focus on other skills, the managerial ones already being present to an adequate extent. On the other hand, diagnostic programs assume that most motivated people can develop some of their weak areas. Such programs focus on those who are seen as needing development and being able to benefit from it, rather than only on people with obviously high potential.

The two types of programs reflect a fundamental question—should development focus on strengths or weaknesses? The development-of-strengths strategy assumes that most weak areas are either undevelopable or else so difficult and time consuming to develop that the payoff to the organization is small. The development-of-weaknesses strategy focuses more on individual than organizational needs and assumes that personal growth and increased self-esteem will result from the development of weak areas.

Whichever strategy is utilized, the tools available to the developer are the same—job assignments, training (either formal or informal), off-the-job activities, and just plain time and experience. However, the use made of these tools will depend on the strategy chosen.

For example, one strategy calls for placing a person in an assignment that meshes with strengths, as identified in assessment, in order to provide the individual with the opportunity to learn technical and job administration skills needed for advancement. On the other hand, the development-of-weaknesses strategy would place the individual in an assignment where an opportunity exists to develop a weak area in the managerial skills area. Similar differences exist in the type of training that would be considered developmental, and in the criterion that would be used to evaluate the program's effectiveness.

There are also differences between the two kinds of programs in the extent of the organization's involvement in the development process. Since upward mobility within the organization is usually the prime goal of identification programs, the organization is usually heavily involved in every phase of the process, and monitors it closely. Diagnostically oriented programs, on the other hand, are frequently viewed as primarily self-developmental in nature. The individual (and usually the individual's management) is given the assessment results and perhaps some suggestions concerning their use. But, beyond that point, actual development activities are seen as primarily the individual's responsibility. There may be little or no formal organizational follow-up.

Both kinds of programs possess advantages. Identification programs are easier to devise and more apt to succeed for a higher proportion of people because the group being dealt with is pre-selected. The benefits of such programs to the organization are fairly obvious, and the cost is comparatively easy to justify. On the other hand, diagnostic programs can be boosters of employee morale in that they are seen as providing opportunity for all, and can help in affirmative action efforts. The benefits to the organization are less immediate, but perhaps equally important long range. The choice will usually depend on the amount of resources that can be committed to development efforts and on the types of problems confronting the organization.

Some programs attempt to combine the two orientations—to identify the high-potential portion of the assessed population and to provide diagnostically oriented aid to the others. Such a program makes the highly dubious assumption that the same assessment techniques are appropriate for both purposes.

In fact, most current assessment technology lends itself more readily to the identification-type program. Assessment is demonstrably more valid than paper-and-pencil tests alone and more comprehensive in the amount of behavior observed. The use of simulations also gives the process a high degree of face validity for both assessees and the organization. But, the process is not error free and the overall rating, the most reliable and valid assessment outcome, is used in an identification program while a diagnostic program utilizes the somewhat less accurate predictions made from individual variables. Also, assessment does not measure all traits known to be necessary for managerial success, so even the most successful diagnostic program is likely to be incomplete. Considerable modification of existing assessment techniques would probably be required to maximize the diagnostic value of the information obtained through assessment. Consequently, most of the operational programs outlined in the following section are aimed more at identification than diagnosis.

OVERVIEW OF OPERATIONAL
ASSESSMENT-DEVELOPMENT PROGRAMS

While the combination of assessment and development is still quite new, recent years have seen the construction of a number of assessment-development programs that are currently operational.

In 1971, AT&T began shifting the emphasis of its assessment center programs from pure selection to identification and development. In the late 1960s, a growing demand for competent supervisors, the declining experience level of candidates for promotion, and an increasing focus on affirmative action foreshadowed this change in emphasis.

The Early Identification Program (EIP) was introduced to Bell System companies in 1971 as a three-step process—assessment, feedback, and development. The program is aimed at identification of first-level supervisory potential in nonmanagement employees and presumes a period of formal development after assessment for those seen with high potential. Short-service employees (one to three years) are the target population, but longer service employees nominated by their supervisors or nominating themselves are also eligible.

The supervisory assessment center, the identification step in EIP, is a one-day process. A summary report on assessed strengths and weaknesses, overall potential, and career interests is prepared on each participant for feedback to the organization and the individual.

Following assessment, a personal feedback is given to each participant with the supervisor in attendance. During feedback, the high-potential employee is told that he or she has the opportunity to embark on a formal development plan aimed at eventual promotion to first-level management. The employee is told that high potential is no guarantee of promotion and that job performance during the development period is considered. Career interests and goals, organizational opportunities and qualifications are discussed, and the individual is asked to consider these prior to formulation of a career development plan.

Following feedback, the individual and the supervisor meet to formulate the career development plan. The formal plan, tailored to advance the career of an individual along a specific route to a stated goal within a prescribed period of time, is written by the supervisor with input and assistance from the individual and a departmental coordinator. "Development," as used here, refers to a systematic series of activities (e.g., assignments, on-the-job coaching, training courses, educational courses, etc.) designed specifically to move an employee from his or her current job to the point where the employee is ready and able to perform successfully as a first-level supervisor. This form of development is goal oriented, limited in scope, and highly structured. The focus is clearly identification rather than diagnosis.

A periodic review of the plan is conducted to make the necessary changes based on individual progress and changing conditions. The goal may be changed, the route altered, or the time periods modified for a variety of reasons originating from either the individual or the organization.

EIP has been expanded since 1971 to include the identification of potential for first-level nonsupervisory technical positions. Assessment center programs have been designed to measure potential for a number of telephone engineering jobs and communications sales jobs. These programs have been tied into the identification phase of EIP, as shown in Fig. 11-2. As the diagram

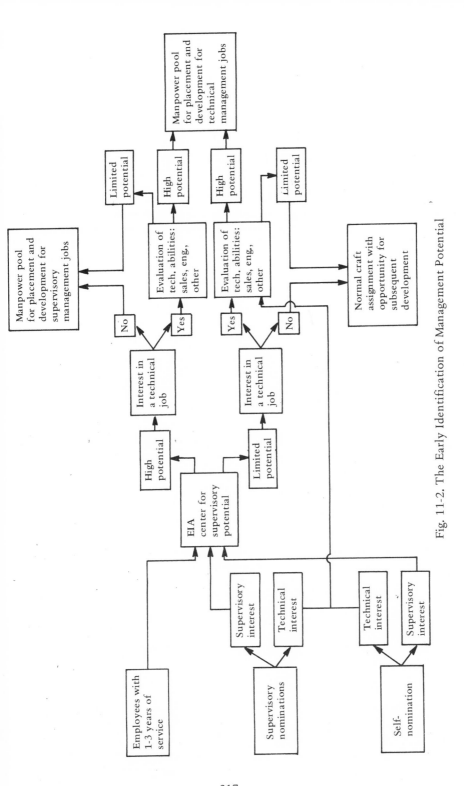

Fig. 11-2. The Early Identification of Management Potential

shows, candidates for the evaluation of technical potential may come via the assessment center for supervisory potential or directly from supervisory nomination or self-nomination. In the supervisory assessment process (EIA), prospective technical candidates are identified on the basis of expressed interests, goals, relevant background, and experience uncovered in the personal interview and biographical questionnaire. Candidates seen as having high potential in the technical evaluation programs are subsequently given the opportunity to be developed for first-level technical positions.

In 1972, the principle of identification through assessment coupled with formal career planning and development was extended to middle management in a special Bell System program. Under terms of an agreement between AT&T and the U.S. Government, college graduate women hired between July 1965 and December 1971, who were currently at the lower levels of management, were offered the opportunity to participate in a middle management (third level) assessment center program. During a 15-month period, close to 1,700 women were assessed.

Over 700 women were identified as having middle management potential. The intent of the agreement was to provide these women with real and meaningful opportunities to advance to middle management (third level) positions in the Bell System companies. To accomplish this purpose, AT&T constructed formal guidelines for the career development of these high-potential women. The guidelines established systematic procedures for career planning, development of management skills, and utilization of potential. Formal written career plans, periodic follow-up by AT&T, and coordination with affirmative action efforts were integral parts of the post-assessment program.

The Guidelines for Manager Development (GMD) introduced to Bell System companies in 1973-74 by AT&T as a first-year development program for newly appointed first-level managers also incorporates the assessment center method for the identification of middle management potential. It is designed to provide a first-year management experience which is challenging and motivating, effectively involves the natural boss, determines career interests and potential to advance, and provides the basis for a year-end career decision. A personnel coordinator works directly with new managers and their bosses, assisting in job design and performance evaluation in addition to conducting orientation and experience meetings.

The new manager's natural boss is the critical link in this program. The boss conducts initial orientation, sets job objectives, conducts periodic performance review meetings, and provides feedback on performance and potential on a systematic and planned basis. The boss receives intensive initial training designed to help build meaningful work modules based on the principles of job design. Each boss is given background in joint target-setting techniques, joint problem-solving methods, and performance-evaluation procedures.

Near the end of the first year, the new manager attends an assessment center to determine potential for advancement beyond first level—i.e., the identification of potential for middle management. The assessment center results are made part of the year-end career decision process, which will determine second-year job assignments and longer range career objectives.

Figure 11-3 illustrates a fully integrated system for the identification and development of management potential. It starts with the Early Identification Program (EIP), incorporates the Guidelines for Manager Development (GMD), and ends with formal career development of high-potential people for middle management. This sytem can only operate within the framework of objective staffing analysis, identification of manpower needs, and effective manpower planning at the supervisory and management levels.

The Bell System (AT&T) does not stand alone in combining the use of the assessment center with developmental programs.

Since the late 1960s, a number of industrial organizations have included assessment centers as part of formal management development (IBM, Public Service Commission of Canada, Ford Motor, General Motors, Ontario Hydro in Canada, Wickes, and Bendix). Some of these programs are aimed at the identification and development of executive-level potential. Post-assessment development programs are usually comprehensive and demanding, involving some form of career planning, formal management training, programmed job assignments over a period of years, and extensive follow-up and evaluation. Although the principal aim is identification, some programs incorporate diagnostic procedures, programmed self-development, and personal counseling.

A number of programs which focus on middle and lower levels of ` management are designed along the same lines but are usually less comprehensive and sophisticated. Frequently, these programs deal with building skills, providing a basic foundation of knowledge, and working with various elements of personal motivation and individual growth.

Assessment centers also have found their way to the college campus. Several colleges and universities (e.g., Pace, Baylor and Eastern Michigan) have incorporated assessment centers into graduate programs for business. The major focus of these applications is diagnosis, self-development, and counseling. Research has also established that assessment center performance can predict successful completion of a graduate program in business.

A very unique application of the assessment center approach has taken place at Alverno College in Milwaukee. Here, assessment is used as the basis for a competence-based learning program. A student advances toward a degree on the basis of assessed competence rather than the accumulation of course credits. Assessment teams, selected from the faculty, advanced students, alumnae, and professionals evaluate the proficiency of each student. Results are also used for advising and counseling.

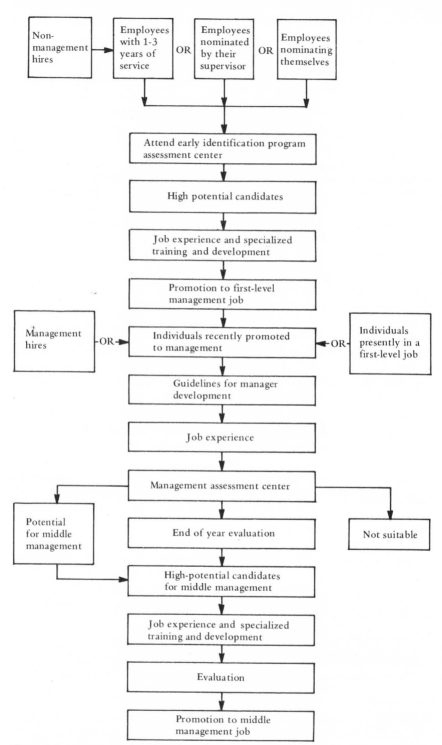

Fig. 11-3. A System for the Identification and Development of Management Potential

The growing popularity of assessment-development systems is a reflection of the potential direct benefits they can supply to individuals and organizations.

FRINGE BENEFITS OF
ASSESSMENT-DEVELOPMENT SYSTEMS

Beyond the many direct advantages already discussed, there are a number of important fringe benefits in combining the assessment center method with development strategy. Serving on an assessment center staff as an assessor is a developmental experience in itself. Line managers who use assessment center results, participate in formulating individual development programs, and are responsible for implementing them are also exposed to a developmental experience. These experiences benefit the organization in a variety of ways.

At the assessment center, the assessor gains more than the participant in terms of direct development by means of formal training given to the staff and continuous participation in the assessment process. An assessor usually leaves this assignment with improved interviewing and observational skills. There is ample opportunity for increased appreciation of group dynamics, leadership styles, and new insights into behavior. Repeated working with various case problems and simulations leads to stronger management skills and a broader repertory of problem-solving techniques. It also leads to more definitive standards for evaluating performance and a more precise vocabulary for describing behavior back on the job.

Based on the self-reports of former assessors, there are many on-the-job uses made of these improved skills. One that is frequently mentioned is improvement in both the accuracy and success of appraisal interviewing. Assessors often say after returning from an assessment staff assignment that they look at performance and evaluate its effectiveness in a very different light. Some organizations, such as the General Electric Company, feel so strongly about the benefits of assessor training that they increased the ratio of assessors to participants in order to expose more managers to the experience.

Other organizations consider developmental benefits in staff selection and use the assignment as a development step for high-potential managers. Training and experience as an assessor offers a unique opportunity for managers to focus on observing and evaluating behavior without the normal interruptions associated with business. The evaluation procedures learned as an assessor through training and repeated application are stamped into memory. In addition to the developmental aspects, exposure as an assessor increases familiarity with the program, assuring more effective use of assessment results.

Through feedback of assessment results, construction of individual development programs, and the administration of these programs, line managers are also exposed to developmental experiences. Managers become more familiar with the major elements of successful job performance—i.e., abilities, motivation, and environment. They are better able to put these elements in perspective, and relate them to present job performance and potential. Performance and potential of a subordinate may be seen as low by a manager. The assessment center results may indicate high potential in assessed abilities, and it may be recommended that the individual be developed for advancement. The manager then must look at nonassessed abilities, motivation, or environment for a possible explanation of low performance and potential. This results in a more objective appraisal of the individual and, through the joint construction of a development program, allows the manager to deal more realistically with the elements of performance. Through this process, the manager develops a better knowledge and greater understanding of the relationship between the determinants of job performance and actual job performance. In this way, he or she is better able to deal with subordinates as individuals.

The fringe benefits which accrue to assessors and line managers also benefit the organization. One result is better performance appraisal in all areas of the business. Frequently, the entire performance appraisal system can be tied to and made part of the assessment and development process. At a minimum, this combined process can bring increased objectivity and broader dimensions to existing appraisal systems. The net result is more creditable and open advancement procedures which will be more realistic, effective, and fair.

PROBLEMS AND UNRESOLVED ISSUES

While the combination of assessment and development programs is becoming increasingly common and has many benefits, both direct and indirect, a variety of problems and unresolved issues remain.

The issue of to what extent the qualities commonly evaluated in assessment can be developed has not been satisfactorily resolved. There is some agreement that skills evaluated, particularly communication skills, can be developed by a motivated individual. More personal qualities such as behavior flexibility and willingness to tolerate uncertainty are extremely difficult to change, if change is in fact possible.

But, there are other commonly assessed variables, such as leadership and decision-making ability, where opinions as to developability vary widely. The reliability of assessment results over time points to the conclusion that, in fact, most people's ratings on these qualities do not change appreciably. But, on the other hand, little systematic development of them has usually been attempted.

Also, regardless of the possibility of change, there are some other assessment variables, such as the importance of work in relation to other aspects of the individual's life and the person's need to gain position and status where a question can be raised concerning the wisdom of the organization's attempting to bring about change. Not only is there a question of "is development possible?"—there is also one concerning whether it is necessarily advisable.

Part of the "what is developable" problem results from a related one—what to tell people who do poorly in assessment. The possibility of assessment error can be pointed out, but the question "How can I improve myself?" is a very natural one for a poorly performing assessee to ask.

Not going beyond the limited amount of concrete developmental advice that can be given with some confidence while still helping the assessee maintain self-esteem is a difficult task. Growth and development are always possible, but sometimes very unlikely.

The assessee's manager may also want to know how to bring about change in an individual's performance and may feel that if the assessment center cannot come up with answers that the manager considers satisfactory, the money spent on assessment is wasted. This may be especially true when the manager wants to improve the managerial abilities of a minority or female assessee to meet an affirmative action objective.

The question of management's use of assessment results becomes much more complex when assessment is viewed as part of an assessment and development system. An identification-type program does not require much of a change from the use of assessment results as a selection device. Assessment merely occurs at an earlier time. However, when assessment is intended to serve diagnostic purposes, those who use the results need considerably more information. The variables rated must be carefully explained, and information given concerning their relevance to job situations.

Assessment is expensive. Some managers will want to overuse the results, discounting other information about the individual and the possibility of assessment error. Others will tend to discount the value of the obtained information, particularly when it is at odds with previously formed opinions. By opting for diagnostic assessment, the assessment center takes on the responsibility of educating management in the proper use of the results presented.

Given the knowledge gaps that still exist in the area of development, this is a heavy responsibility. Assessment and development programs must very plainly spell out what they claim to do, how, and for whom. Unsubstantiated claims, or even vague promises, designed to sell a particular program will backfire in the long run.

Development is a convenient word in that both the humanistically oriented and bottom-line oriented manager can agree that it's a good idea; but the two are speaking about very different kinds of activities. Development costs money, and the question of the extent to which an organization can, and should, accommodate personal goals should be squarely faced when an assessment and development program is devised.

Until the extent of available knowledge about development increases substantially, an identification-based development effort with clearly specified, if limited, goals is probably preferable to a more ambitious diagnostic undertaking. Development, as an outgrowth of assessment, is still very new. Because there is a demand, there is a tendency for programs to run substantially ahead of knowledge in the area.

While there are substantial problems and unanswered questions about the purpose and feasibility of development, the combination of assessment and development efforts for both identification and diagnostic purposes is likely to continue to grow.

Hopefully, the differences in method and purpose between identification and diagnostic programs will be more clearly delineated. Because of the shape of the usual corporate pyramid, it is likely that programs at or near the point of entry into management will tend to be identification-type programs. The need to deal with large numbers of people makes diagnostic programs unfeasible, and a probable surplus of people who can potentially fill entry-level management positions makes such programs unnecessary. Furthermore, not all employees wish to be managers and the degree of motivation needed if a diagnostically oriented program is to have any chance of success may not be present.

At or near the middle management level, where commitment to a managerial career is likely to be strong and the numbers of people much smaller, diagnostically oriented development programs are more likely to be sought. In order to devise such programs, considerable basic research relating adult learning concepts to specific assessment variables will be called for. Questions concerning the likelihood of developing different areas of managerial competence must be confronted.

The need to use assessment results to determine particular developmental needs will probably bring about changes in the assessment process itself. The assessor's role may become much more that of a counselor and less of an evaluator. Use of videotape playback to assessees and discussion of observed behavior at the time it occurs may place the evaluative function primarily in the hands of the manager being assessed. Some simulations commonly used in assessment, particularly in-baskets, are currently used as training devices by some organizations. Why not diagnostic use as well? For example, a carefully constructed in-basket might define which areas give a person particular decision-making problems. Does a manager make better personnel decisions than sales decisions? Group problems might be used to answer similar questions in the interpersonal skills area.

The demands of the development component of an assessment and development system are likely to play an increasing role in determining the future direction of assessment research and applications. Assessment primarily for selection purposes may become the exception rather than the rule, if emphasis on development continues to grow in response to organizational and individual needs.

CHAPTER 12

ASSESSMENT AND ORGANIZATIONAL DEVELOPMENT *
Albert Alon

INTRODUCTION

To many individuals, the notion of assessment and organizational development are antithetical. Assessment, with its focus on the individual, implicitly assumes that most of the characteristics measured are stable and predictable. Organizational development's focus on the organization encourages a dynamic force for change. Often, practitioners of each discipline tend to view their activities as different lights at the end of different tunnels.

From a more global perspective, there are a number of ways to enhance organizational effectiveness. One strategy is to direct efforts on the individual as the building block for effectiveness. Proponents of selection practices would encourage the proper selection of people as the necessary input. Assessment centers are very popular in this context. Others focus on the individual through training and development. As seen in the last chapter, this approach also has considerable assessment appeal.

Another strategy sees the organization itself as the building block for change. Efforts at job design and organizational diagnosis represent this approach. In this context assessment centers emerge as an effective tool for organizational intervention.

In this chapter, Albert Alon demonstrates that it is possible to translate concepts from different disciplines as a vehicle for enhancing organizational effectiveness. Drawing upon his personal experiences at Steinberg's Limited, he shows how one can integrate both individual and organizational needs as a systematic force for change and growth.

* * *

---

*This article was prepared while the author was associated with Steinberg's Limited, Toronto, Canada.

This chapter deals with the developmental impact of the assessment center method on an organization. It shares positive spin-off effects of that method on a user organization with readers who may be contemplating the feasibility of employing it as a selection/development strategy in their own company. Furthermore, it illustrates how the introduction of the method into an organization offers an excellent opportunity for integrating both organizational and individual needs for growth.

From the former perspective, the assessment center method provides an organization with a planned strategy of change for upgrading the skills of its management population to meet its growth needs. From the latter perspective, assessment provides the individual with diagnostic insights which can serve as stepping stones for mapping out a meaningful plan of development for increasing his or her personal competence as a manager.

Beginning with a brief discussion of some concepts and ideas related to organizational development, this chapter describes the implementation of a planned learning process aimed at capturing vital developmental aspects of the assessment center concept and channeling them back into the live work situation of the line manager.

ASSESSMENT AND ORGANIZATION DEVELOPMENT (OD)

Current management literature attests to innumerable definitions of organizational development (OD). No single one can adequately encompass the broad spectrum of ideas and concepts that organizational development typically includes. However, for our purposes here, a meaningful definition may be found in one that regards OD as a "process of planned change geared to increasing an organization's effectiveness."

Emerging OD theories include a variety of strategies for initiating change and improvement in an organization that enable it to adapt and cope with the environment. First, there must be a recognized need for change—an awareness that the organization or any part of it is "hurting." Second, the problems must be real in the sense that they represent legitimate barriers identified by the people affected by them. Hence, the concept of "diagnosed need" comes into play as a major strategy of organizational development.

Other strategies of OD consist of "team building" and "linking up" the different subsystems within an organization to achieve an effective unity of purpose and action. While plans are formulated which aim at coordinating and integrating efforts, they sometimes ignore individual capabilities and the need for a "here and now" assessment of people's strengths and weaknesses. In this vein, the assessment center method can be engaged as a planned strategy for change in that it both generates and utilizes vital data about individual behavior, focusing on how it may be employed, in turn, to increase organizational effectiveness.

The aim of the peer-learning process described in this chapter is to capture positive spin-off effects of the assessment center method and, by design ("planned change"), use them as a lever for individual growth and development throughout the organization. The conceptual frame of reference for many of the activities associated with OD emerges from the behavioral sciences. These provide organizations with a theoretical as well as a pragmatic springboard for formulating an approach toward survival and growth. The prime focus of OD centers around the interface between the individual and the organization and the delicate meshing of their respective needs for attaining that growth.

POSITIVE SPIN-OFFS OF THE
ASSESSMENT CENTER METHOD

At this point, it would be appropriate to begin sharing with the reader some vital spin-offs of the assessment center method on the Steinberg's Limited organization of Montreal, Quebec, Canada. We shall then proceed to describe the implementation of a planned peer-learning process in this organization which aimed at capturing vital developmental aspects of the assessment center method and channeling them back into the live work situation of the line manager.

Steinberg's Limited is a large, retail organization operating in Eastern Canada. Employing about 28,000 employees, it boasts an annual sales volume of $1,200,000,000 (1973-74), derived chiefly (but not exclusively) from its supermarket operations in two major trading areas, Montreal, Quebec, and Toronto, Ontario. Throughout its 60-year history (since 1917), it has consistently earned the reputation of a pioneering and innovative organization which has a considerable list of "firsts" attributed to its name.

With a rapidly growing enterprise expanding at the rate of 15-20% yearly, the administrative helm at Steinberg's Limited was traditionally receptive to some of the latest developments in the personnel and human resources field. In the late '50s, some of its top executives were exposed to the early "T" group sessions at Bethel, Maine. In the mid '60s, more than 1,000 of its middle and top managers had gone through the Blake and Mouton Managerial Grid. Using a "fanning out" method of instructing its own cadres of experts and animators, these in turn began to disseminate the concepts of Theory X and Y and participative management throughout the managerial ranks. 1969 had seen the company institute its first job enrichment program (Myers, 1970, pp. 87-95) in the Quebec Food division in Montreal, with which this author was directly involved. Historically, the Steinberg organization has invested considerable funds and energies in the field of human resources development and OD, in the belief that they manifest a major key to continued success of the organization in the years to come.

For several years now, the Quebec Division of the Steinberg Corporation (Montreal, Quebec, Canada) has been employing the assessment center method in the identification of future store managers (second-level management) for their supermarket division. The Ontario Food Division of Steinberg's (Miracle Food Mart) has also adopted the method as a major selection/development strategy during the past two years. The Quebec Division is composed of about 150 retail food stores divided geographically into three operational areas (units). Each unit (see Fig. 12-1) is divided into four subregions, respectively, numbering about 10 to 15 supermarkets. Each of these subregions is supervised by a zone

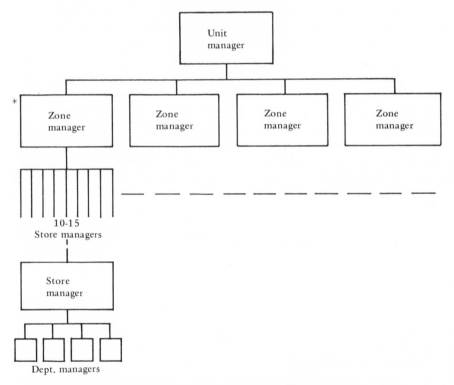

Fig. 12-1. Unit Management Team

---

*For greater simplification, the diagram illustrates the progressive breakdown of one zone only. Note also the subsequent management structure of a single store—i.e., the store manager (second-level supervision) and the four department managers (first-level) reporting to him! The same applies to all subregions (zones) in a given unit.

manager who, prior to the introduction of the assessment center method, traditionally registered the greatest single voice in selecting eligible candidates for promotion to store management from the department manager (first-level) ranks.

These selection decisions, while not entirely judgmental (the hard data sales and profit figures attained by a potential candidate were certainly part of that decision), were often formulated on the basis of comments such as: "He's a good man," or "He's a hard worker," or "He's a dependable guy, I know he'll do the job for us." Coupled with some peer negotiations at the zone manager level as to where the candidate could best be placed, these judgments were then passed up the line to head office from where the final (formal) decision would be announced.

It was not uncommon to find that certain managerial candidates who had been transferred from one region to another were "just not working out." What had been deemed "high potential" through traditionally informal evaluation techniques in one region was found to be considerably "lacking" and "weak" in a second. Alas, we were faced with a significant frequency problem concerning what constituted a "good manager"!

By contrast, one positive residue of the assessment center method has been the continuous alignment of perspectives among all levels of management regarding a model supermarket store manager. At Steinberg's, this has become an ongoing process, for as change takes place rapidly about us, so do we continue to review and reappraise our managerial criteria in order to keep up with changing demands of the marketplace and society as a whole. The constant dialogue and exchange of views between those responsible for the assessment center program and the operating managers served as a lever for unfreezing hitherto accepted views of the definition of a model manager.

Serving as an assessor, for example, has definitely improved the observation skills and selection accuracy of the zone manager group in identifying new management candidates. As a number of zone managers have stated: "In making our rounds in the stores we are now able to observe and evaluate our store managers more critically." This reference is to the predetermined set of assessment center criteria which they personally helped develop and which have evolved as their new common yardstick for evaluating both the strengths and weaknesses of their line managers.

As discussed in previous chapters, a typical assessment center will evaluate an individual against a predetermined (diagnosed) list of management criteria being sought, such as leadership, planning, judgment, decision making, etc. Through a series of behavior-anchored narratives, assessors must submit empirical evidence of what it is that an assessment center participant says or does that qualifies his or her actions as a manager.

With a center itself, a major output of a three-day center is the global evaluation. This evaluation contains an in-depth analysis of a participant's strengths and weaknesses. This global evaluation describes the individual participant as an "organic whole" rather than merely bifurcating the person into a series of separate dimensions such as leadership, flexibility, problem analysis, etc. It is this global evaluation that later serves as a prime basis for formulating (jointly with the participant) a personal development program for increasing his or her managerial competence.

Coming back to the Steinberg experience, the overall global evaluation became the lever that helped to bolster a growing awareness throughout the Quebec Division (and other parts of the corporation) of the need for encouraging management development inputs at all levels. It was this "tool changes the user" effect that positively influenced the need in the organization for developing planned career programs with those participants who had attended an assessment center.

In reflecting on the positive spin-off effects that were emerging out of our experience with the assessment center method, the question arose: "What was taking place here?" It soon became evident that all those people who had participated in an assessment center had been caught up in what had become one of the most profound behavior change processes ever experienced in the Steinberg organization.

This was especially true for the group of 12 zone managers who were involved from the beginning in determining the criteria to be used in selecting new management candidates. Acting as assessors on a rotating basis, they had been trained in observing and evaluating people in the laboratory situation. They were the ones who were now responsible as a group for submitting the global evaluation of a center participant to top management. It was the members of this peer group that began to accept (it must be said, skeptically at the beginning) promotion recommendations from each other for individuals selected as prospective management candidates from their respective regions.[1]

This constant interaction between assessors from 12 different regions who did not ordinarily come into close contact with one another, was lending a healthy cross-fertilization of ideas throughout the division regarding a "model manager." This was to serve the organization well as it continued to shape a more highly professional approach toward the selection and development of its future management personnel.

Looking back at these results, some further questions came to the fore: "How could we duplicate the vital experience of the zone manager group and transfer it to other levels throughout the organization?" "How could we make the shift from the laboratory to the everyday live work situation and integrate some of the main ingredients of the assessment center process into the daily work milieu of the line manager?"

---

[1] At a typical assessment center the "no-go-boss" rule was rigidly applied. In other words the assessor team (in a given three-day center) would only be composed of those zone managers who were *not* the superiors of any one participating candidate.

Reconsider for a moment the element of planned change used in our definition of OD at the beginning of the chapter. We seemed to be at the threshold of designing a vital learning experience for line managers that would ultimately enhance their individual growth and development and that of the organization as well.

DEVELOPING THE PEER-LEARNING PROCESS

Capitalizing on the above experiences, we designed a "Peer-Learning Process" (see Fig. 12-2) to transfer the benefits already incurred at the zone manager level to the next level of management—namely, the store manager group. The main objectives of this process included:

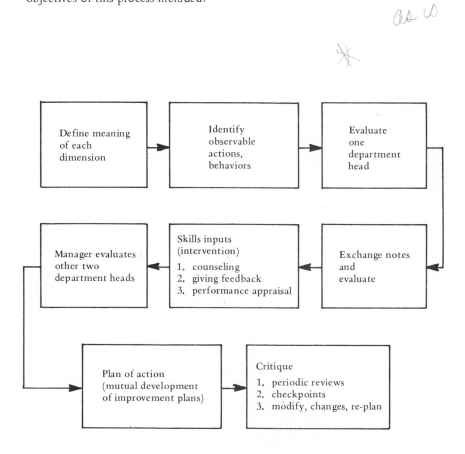

Fig. 12-2. Peer-Learning Process

1.   integrating the vital aspects of the assessment center method—i.e., observation, analysis, and evaluation according to a predefined set of managerial dimensions, directly into the daily work activity of the line manager;

2.   affording line managers an opportunity to improve their observation and evaluation skills; and

3.   developing a common yardstick among existing managers regarding the caliber of promotable candidates being sought for the future.

Following a discussion with one zone manager who was "hurting" in the area of performance appraisal, a pilot project was initiated to take the group of store managers (the "learner" group) reporting to him through a series of sequential learning steps aimed at imparting an understanding of evaluation criteria. The ultimate aim of the peer-learning process was to develop (with the learners) a set of behavior-anchored dimensions around which significant observable actions could be identified and subsequently used in evaluating future managerial candidates from among the ranks of first-level (department) managers. The process would help store managers identify and evaluate what it is that a person says or does on the job that manifests effective managerial behavior or, conversely, an absence of it.

Following the diagram illustrated in the peer-learning process (see Fig. 12-2), first steps centered around identifying and defining those dimensions deemed essential for effective managerial success. The objective here was to seek out a common, meaningful definition of terms such as leadership, planning, judgment, etc. to replace what were hitherto considered to be vague "headings" left to the imagination of every line manager to interpret for himself.

The group of store managers in this exercise was taken through a series of pre-work meetings and tasks designed to formulate and define each of the dimensions that was selected to comprise the overall model manager profile sought by the organization. (See Table 12-1 for a sample of a pre-work task.)

Periodic meetings were held on a planned basis to pool the descriptive paragraphs brought forth by the group of store managers until a meaningful, working definition was forged for each dimension to the agreement, and there was understanding of all concerned.

For example, with "teamwork" having been identified as a desirable dimension, the emerging definition read as follows: "Effectiveness in integrating the individual skills and efforts of employees into an organized pattern of activities geared to attaining organizational goals."

These jointly evolved definitions eventually served as common yardsticks for line managers when evaluating their subordinates, both on the job and in an assessment center as well. Through a constant exchange and consensus of ideas, this (original) group of managers had developed "ownership" of the definitions,

Table 12-1 Task Sample

Task 1 — Definition of Criteria

One basic step in the process of evaluating others is to know and understand what it is we are looking for when observing employees at work.

With this in mind, please define in your own words what each of the following list of managerial criteria means to you.

Use the attached sheets to record your definitions and come prepared to discuss them at the next zone meeting on _____ .

Our intent is to firm up each definition so that we can understand and use it as a common frame of reference when evaluating subordinates.

Managerial Criteria

Interpersonal Skills	*Administrative Ability*	*Personal Qualities*
Impression	Planning, Organization,	Motivation
Persuasion	and Controlling	Initiative
Sensitivity	Judgment	Work standards
Flexibility	Problem analysis	Stress tolerance
(Adaptability)	Use of delegation	Company commitment
Authority	Concern for staff	Creativity
(Leadership)	development	Range of interest
Formal oral pre-	Concern for customer	Self-objectivity
sentation skills	relations	Intelligence
Written communi-	Sensitivity to unions	
cations skills	Management style	
	(Grid)	
	Decision-making	

---

even of the dimensions themselves. They slowly began to adopt them into their regular performance appraisal activities with their subordinates as time went on.

The second step in the peer-learning process involved identifying observable actions and behaviors relative to the different dimensions in the managerial profile. This required spelling out in simple and precise language (above all, language meaningful to the learners themselves), typical examples of observable actions and on-the-job behaviors that could enable managers to see a subordinate in action relative to each particular dimension.

If we were to follow the aforementioned definition of teamwork, then this second step in the process entailed identifying what it is that a person says or does or how he or she acts that demonstrates his or her ability in "integrating the individual skills and efforts of employees into an organized pattern of activities," etc. (as per our original descriptive definition).

The learners continued to meet together and pooled their respective submissions among themselves, discussing, cross-checking with each other, and revamping their inputs as required. Several runs were made before they reached consensus on a feasible working document that they could use in evaluating their subordinates on the job.

Following suit once again with our definition of teamwork, here are some examples of the observable on-the-job behaviors they had identified for this dimension.

1. Calls periodic meetings of staff to discuss business opportunities and/or barriers.
2. Develops and initiates department goals and plans of action on a team-wide basis.
3. Encourages group evaluation of results (critique) during the course of regular departmental meetings.
4. Posts objectives and results charts throughout the department to keep employees informed of their achievements.

In order to firm up observable actions like the ones above, an additional task was developed to test the degree to which the evolving instrument actually helped the learners evaluate their subordinates on the job. This now brings us to the third step in our peer-learning process. (See Fig. 12-2, Box 3).

A task was designed whereby each learner manager was asked to return to work and evaluate at random one of the department heads (see Fig. 12-1) with (what was at that early stage) the crude data available—the pooled submissions of the conferees' definitions of criteria and identifiable, observable actions. Through the evaluation of the one department head, the task also called for the following information:

1. confirmation of those actions readily observable on the job;
2. identification of any previously listed actions (as per the group submissions) that were too difficult to observe on the job (these were eventually eliminated from the list); and
3. addition and pooling of any new behaviors to the list that may have been derived through the learner observing the subordinate at work.

Once the members of the learner group had shared their respective observations through a continuous cross-exchange of notes and data (see Fig. 12-2, Box 4), these were consolidated at a later date and edited into what was soon to emerge as a meaningful working document, which they could use as a common yardstick for evaluating managerial potential among their staff.

It should be noted at this point that while we have been illustrating in progression from the evolution of a single dimension—i.e., "teamwork"—the learner group was involved in defining and identifying observable behaviors for the full range of criteria included in the organization's model manager profile (Table 12-1). This included dimensions such as leadership, planning, decision making, judgment, sensitivity toward people, and many others.[2]

What follows, subsequently, is an example of the completed writeup (again) relative to the "teamwork" dimension and how it appears in its final form in the evaluation document. (See Table 12-2.[3]) Note the simple, yet effective "measurement indices" to the right of the document, which are used to indicate the relative degree to which particular behaviors are actually observed on the job (if at all).

It is a given that a potential manager candidate be constantly evaluated for his or her sales and growth results too! These certainly represent the vital success indicators of any business and serve as a precise (but not exclusive) measure of overall organizational ability as well. Hence, when developing dimensions related to more readily measurable technical skills or operational aspects of the business such as merchandising, sales, profit, etc., the measurement indices used were more of a quantitative nature—i.e., "number of displays in evidence," or "quarterly sales achieved," or profit percentage gained, etc.

Even though the document was intended to crystallize precise terms of reference and measurement of managerial dimensions and observable behaviors, the educational process itself through which the learner group was taken was more significant to them.

The process also included helping them acquire specific skills in the area of performance appraisal. In doing so, it served as a tool for increasing their competence as managers and subsequently their self-assurance in the area of evaluating subordinates. The synergistic effects of the learning process had helped to partly unfreeze traditionally threatening attitudes toward learning they may have manifested in the past.

Once the definitions and observable actions of the various dimensions were firmed up (over a time spread of six to eight months), an emergent need for skills training was expressed on the part of the managers involved in the peer learning process. Taking them through the steps described so far had sensitized them to the need for acquiring added skills in the area of performance feedback and goal setting with their employees.

---

[2]What started out as 25 dimensions at the inception of the assessment center method in the organization was later reduced (over a period of two years) to 15. Since then, successful efforts have been made (through factor analysis and frequency study methods) to reduce these even further to about 10 major clusters. Comparative research in this area among user organizations continues to be carried out on an ongoing basis.

[3]An illustration of a second dimension (i.e., "communications") in its final form can be found in the Appendix at the end of this chapter.

Table 12-2 Teamwork

Definition: Effectiveness in integrating the individual skills and efforts of employees into an organized pattern of activities geared to attaining organizational goals.

Comments: The observable actions listed below enable us to see the candidate in action relative to:
- —How he attains operational results through the proper use of team effort and involvement.
- —How he helps employees grow through the medium of peer learning, group problem-solving and team improvement strategies in the live work situation.

Observable Actions
1. Develops and initiates department goals and plans of action on a team basis. (Weekly, Monthly, Quarterly, Never)

2. Encourages and duly considers ideas, suggestions brought forth by employees and informs them of his interest to implement them or not (and reasons why). (Yes, No)

3. Calls periodic meetings of his entire staff to discuss business opportunities and/or operational barriers. (Never, Sometimes, Always)

4. Delegates responsibility with a view toward helping people grow and making proper use of existing skills within his department. (Yes, No)

5. Involves internal departmental resources where and when required. (Never, Sometimes, Always)

6. Develops staff through the planned use of performance appraisal sessions. (Yes, No)

7. Pitches in when emergencies arise and actively lends his support in the face of unanticipated situations. (Yes, No)

8. Participates actively as a responsible member of the store management team in the following areas: (Never [N], Sometimes [S], Always [A])
   □ store meetings   □ interplay between departments
   □ financial results   □ store projects, innovations, etc.

9. Recognizes outstanding achievements of particular team members and highlights same during department meetings. (Yes, No)

10. Encourages team evaluation of results (critique) during the course of departmental meetings. (Weekly, Monthly, Quarterly, Never)

Table 12-2 (continued)

11. Posts objectives/results charts throughout the department to keep employees informed of their achievement. (Yes, No)

12. Number of promotions and demotions during the past year.

☐ In training?

☐ Promotions?

☐ Demotions?

Changes in classification:

☐ Clerk to assistant department head.

☐ Assistant department head to department head.

☐ Department head to store manager.

13. Advises persons of changes affecting them before final decision is taken. (Yes, No)

Unfolding itself here was an excellent opportunity to capitalize on certain expectancies elicited on the part of the learners' "need to know." Since this had been anticipated from the inception of the process, a series of skills intervention sessions were developed in response to the above need (see Fig. 12-2, Box 5).

Equipped with some additional skills inputs, each learner manager would then be ready to adopt a more sophisticated and pragmatic approach to performance evaluation vis-à-vis the department heads (first-line managers) and later the entire staff (see Fig. 12-2, Box 6). Armed with some further concepts (mutual goal setting and critique) and reinforced by the working document he or she helped develop jointly with peers, each learner manager could then embark on a planned program of performance appraisal and goal setting with his or her staff.

Closure to the entire process was envisioned through the subsequent development of an individual plan of action for (with) all subordinates, including improvement steps to be taken, implementation, periodic reviews, determining checkpoints along the way, replanning etc. (For a more detailed description of the approach used, see Kindall & Gatza, 1963.) (See Boxes 7 and 8 in the Peer-Learning Process, Fig. 12-2.)

SUMMARY

The introduction of the assessment center method has had far-reaching positive effects on the Steinberg Organization, particularly on administration's thinking and approach to management selection and development.

The collective experiences shared by the assessor group involved in the learning process from its inception have contributed to what has emerged as one of the most profound behavior change processes that had ever been realized in the Steinberg Organization. This change manifested itself in a gradual unfreezing of widely divergent views of a "model manager" and a corresponding shift toward internalizing an entirely new set of managerial criteria which the organization deemed necessary for its managers of the future.

The OD thrust described in this chapter aimed at optimizing the positive spin-offs of the assessment center method and transferring them further down in the organization through the medium of the peer-learning process.

The peer-learning process was conceived as a planned stragegy for increasing the effectiveness of the line manager "in the complex art of making behavior based, rather than purely impressionistic judgments about people" on the job (Dunnette, 1970). In doing so, the process has partly bridged the gap between vital theory and practice, between the world of ideas and the live work situation.

APPENDIX A

Communication

Definition: The formal/informal transmission of ideas or information orally and/or in writing, executed with maximum effectiveness (i.e., precision, clarity, objectivity).

Comments: The observable actions listed below enable us to see the candidate in action relative to the above criteria in terms of how he:

—Receives and understands communications made by conversation, mail, telephone calls, bulletins, newspapers, etc.

—Transmits information to proper persons concerned—i.e., orders, head office personnel, staff evaluations, etc.

—Expresses his ideas in 1-1 and/or group situations.

Observable Actions

1. Transmits vital information to proper persons concerned.
   (Never, Sometimes, Always)

2. Holds meetings with employees (1-1, 1-all), and encourages them to discuss issues relative to themselves and/or their work.
   (Never, Sometimes, Always)

3. Posts charts and trend sheets showing results of his department relative to:

☐ daily sales   (Yes, No)

☐ weekly productivity   (Yes, No)

☐ monthly profits   (Yes, No)

4. Communicates company policies regularly and effectively.
    (Yes, No)

5. Shares his own operational strategies with his peers in order to
    maximize business opportunities in the entire store.
    (Never, Sometimes, Always)

6. Allocates a strategic corner where employees can see/read proper
    information relative to their work department. (Bulletins, notices,
    company policies, union information, etc.———).
    (Yes, No)

7. Uses company publicity materials (signs, prices, announcements)
    in a proper manner.
    (Yes, No)

8. Leaves clear instructions with his staff on his day(s) off, vacation(s),
    etc.———
    (Yes, No)

9. Reads his mail soon after arriving at the store.
    (Never, Sometimes, Always)

10. Responds in a knowledgeable manner to questions relative to his
    mail.
    (Never, Sometimes, Always)

11. Reads and keeps up to date with industry publications and
    trends.
    (Yes, No)

12. Written communications:

    ☐ Proper use of words, sentence structure, grammar. (Yes, No)

    ☐ Reports are neat and well presented.   (Yes, No)

REFERENCES

Dunnette, M. D. Managerial effectiveness: Its definition and measurement. *Studies in Personnel Psychology*, 1970, 2(2), 6-20.

Kindall, A. F., & Gatza, J. Positive program for performance appraisal. *Harvard Business Review*, November/December 1963.

Myers, M. S. *Every employee a manager*. New York: McGraw-Hill, 1970.

PART THREE

EVALUATION AND BEYOND

CHAPTER 13

MANAGEMENT CONCERNS ABOUT ASSESSMENT CENTERS *

Alan Boche

INTRODUCTION

This chapter examines most of the issues raised by the sponsors of assessment centers. Assessment centers are expensive, not so much in terms of the dollar costs expended per assessee, but rather in terms of the administrative costs of using highly competent managers as assessors when they might be doing other things.

Sponsors of assessment centers have to face some tough questions concerning what is gained by using an assessment center, particularly when an organization feels that it has been somewhat effective in identifying potential in the past.

In this excellent chapter, the author wrestles with many of these concerns. As with every new procedure, there is resistance to change. When a procedure is viewed as removing some of the implicitly held management rights of passage, the procedure may be highly threatening. The importance of proper planning cannot be minimized. You may want to read this chapter and reexamine Chapter 4 to insure that the concerns often raised about assessment centers can be successfully resolved.

* * *

---

*This material draws on the article "Management Assessment in International Organizations," *Industrial Relations*, Vol. 12, No. 2, May 1973, 172-182.

The attraction of an assessment center is obvious to most psychologists. However, they are not always so obvious to executives and others in management. In fact, thoughtful executives learning about assessment centers are likely to ask a number of probing questions. Such questions may be simple or sophisticated, carping or open-minded, hackneyed or ingeniously novel. But they generally deserve serious consideration and well-reasoned answers. This chapter will review some of the most recurrent questions raised by executives about assessment centers.

VALIDITY

One of the most common questions is: "Does it really work?" Fortunately, we can answer this question about the validity of the method with data collected over many years. Evidence collected from throughout the world indicates that the assessment center method is an effective method of supervisory and management selection. Much of this evidence is summarized by Huck in the next chapter. Some long-range studies from Britain (Anstey, 1966, 1971a, 1971b) support his conclusions. In brief, high performance in the assessment center predicts job performance, progress in salary and promotions, and rated potential for higher management.

ACCEPTABILITY

A related concern is how managers and assessees will accept an assessment program. A partial answer is to show the existence of face validity, the degree to which the method looks fair and accurate. Interviews reveal that management observers generally feel the program is valid, the exercises seem reasonable, and they can make evaluations that are meaningful to them.

Face validity extends to the participants themselves. This conclusion is supported by data collected in some affiliates of a large international manufacturing company which uses similar assessment programs (Kraut, 1973). Although the number of people in each of these studies is relatively small, and the questions vary slightly in wording, the major thrust of the evidence is clear. As shown in the first part of Table 13-1, a majority of assessees in each country see the technique as really getting at the abilities important to being a manager.

This face validity on the part of most assessees goes even further. As shown in the second half of Table 13-1, most of them also feel that this data would be useful in making promotional decisions for the selection of first-line managers. These reactions seem to be extremely important for the ultimate acceptability of assessment programs, for a number of the respondents in this

Table 13-1 Assessees' Opinions: Face Validity and Use for Selection

	n	Question 1: "To what extent do you believe the assessment program measures important qualities required of (your company's) managers?				
		To a very great extent	A great extent	A moderate extent	Not very much	Not at all
Austria	(59)	12%	80%[a]	3%	2%	0%
Brazil[b]	(35)	45	46	6	3	0
Germany I	(60)	11	81[a]	3	3	0
Germany II	(70)	[c]	—	—	—	—
Japan	(47)	47	36	17	0	0
Netherlands	(24)	17	75	8	0	0
United Kingdom	(11)	35	55	9	0	0
United States	(46)	4	53	37	4	0

	n	Question 2: "To what extent do you believe assessment information could be used to help in the selection of employees for promotion to first-line management?"				
		Very good for this purpose	Good	Fair	Poor	Very poor
Austria	(59)	7%	57%	30%	5%	2%
Brazil[b]	(35)	37	40	23	0	0
Germany I	(60)	22[d]	51	25	2	0
Germany II	(70)	30[d]	62	7	1	0
Japan	(47)	13	68	17	2	0
Netherlands	(24)	17	75	8	0	0
United Kingdom	(11)	73	27	0	0	0
United States	(46)	22	46	30	0	2

[a]Combines answers to two response alternatives: "a great extent" and "to a sufficient extent."

[b]Question modified to ask ". . . assessment program offers useful data about leadership potential in your company?"

[c]This question not asked in Germany II program.

[d]Slightly different question and response categories: "Do you believe the assessment program can make useful predictions about future success in management?" Yes, very good statement; yes, useful statement; only partly useful (for Germany I)/undecided (for Germany II); no, only a bit relevant; no, nothing.

study were in trial programs and those actually being assessed were among the first to be tested in each country. More research on employee reactions to assessment has been presented by Dodd in Chapter 9.

WHEN ASSESSMENT CAN HELP

Whether an organization can benefit from the introduction of an assessment center depends on its particular circumstances. As with other selection tools, the assessment center is more likely to be useful when a relatively large pool of candidates exists. In fact, the larger the pool, the more likely is a selection device to be of great value, even if the device itself is only moderately effective. The selection method, of course, must be a valid way of measuring the relevant behaviors and must improve on the selection techniques that already exist in the organization.

Assessment centers are especially likely to be helpful when candidates are needed for a job that is quite different from the one they hold, as in a move from nonmanager to manager. In such a case the skills needed in the next job are difficult to observe in the current job. The assessment center can build in exercises which bring out the desired behaviors.

Experience with organizations that have chosen to use assessment centers reveals several conditions affecting their choice. One such condition, very likely to occur in large organizations, is when the key decision makers are not personally familiar with the available pool of talent, particularly the talent within their own organizations. Similarly, a rapid surge in growth creating a need for new managers, which is either unanticipated or difficult to satisfy, also stimulates a need for an assessment center. Other notable stimuli are feelings of dissatisfaction with the existing situation, evidence of management ineffectiveness, or even some dramatic cases of failure. A significant factor is sometimes simply that higher management becomes aware of a better selection technique than whatever is in current use.

In some countries another factor emerges. Management failures may be particularly costly. Legislation in countries such as Brazil and France may actually prohibit the removal of managers from their positions or may make it extremely difficult to fire or reduce the rank of the employees, thus making initial selection decisions critical. One condition that appears to be universal is that companies installing assessment programs are financially successful, can afford to try personnel management innovations, and are interested in constantly enhancing their organization's success.

ORGANIZATIONAL SIDE EFFECTS

How would an assessment program affect the rest of the organization? It is difficult to imagine an assessment center being installed meaningfully without it having a sizable impact on aspects of personnel management other than merely selection. The introduction of such a program raises profound questions about some personnel practices, which may be taken for granted or may not even exist. An obvious example is manpower planning. It is difficult to know how many assessment programs are needed, if any, until one knows how many managerial promotions (or other similar decisions) are to be made in a given period of time. And yet it is surprising how many organizations considering assessment cannot answer such a question.

Since an assessment program yields powerful information about the strengths and weaknesses of assessees, it has high potential utility for improving management development efforts. By forcing attention to participant strengths and weaknesses, an assessment center program encourages career planning, attention to morale considerations, and more intelligent efforts at organizational change and development. The assessment center does not directly do this, but it acts as a stimulant to bring it about. Although it is possible to install a management assessment center without changing other personnel programs, the natural history of many assessment programs indicates that this is not likely to happen. If it did, the yield would be only a small part of the benefit such a program can provide in a total personnel management system.

THIRD PARTY EXPOSURES

Another issue in many organizations is the attitudes of unions toward assessment programs. Assessment center programs have been used successfully in a number of unionized companies and have seemed to cause very little difficulty. Perhaps this is because management selection may not be a matter subject to negotiation. But, more likely, the procedure is, on the face of it, very equitable. In fact, union leaders often are pleased that their members are being objectively and openly considered for promotion. The key point seems to be that the procedure tries to provide a fairer practice than might exist if promotions were based merely on managerial nomination.

National legislation is also a concern in some places. For example, in the United States the desire to provide equal employment opportunities to all minority groups may raise the issues of validity and fairness (as are more often addressed to selection testing). In this respect, the assessment center may be one of the most defensible selection procedures to be imagined. If properly designed, the center focuses specifically on the job behaviors for which a person is being considered and measures these behaviors without prejudice. Validity must be proved, however, and not merely assumed by management. Any organization starting a new assessment center should recognize the requirement it may face to prove its program.

In general, a substantial weight of evidence indicates that the technique is valid. According to Huck (1973a), no differential validity data have been reported for groups that vary on sex, race, and job differences. Some recent research by Huck and Bray (1975) indicates that this method predicts job performance in an equally valid way for members of different minority groups. The same considerations were made in assessment, with equally valid predictions to subsequent performance, for whites and blacks, males and females.

In fact, the American Telephone & Telegraph Company recently entered into a consent decree with the federal government to use assessment centers as a means of judging management potential of women to facilitate their upgrading. This seems to be tacit approval by the government for the use of assessment centers as a tool for affirmative action. The results have been very promising. Of more than 1,000 female supervisors assessed in this way, 42% were judged to have the potential for middle management.[1]

IMPACT ON THE SELECTION SYSTEM

Some specific questions about the potential impact of assessment programs are often raised. For example, when an organization sees this method as having value and installs it, what is the impact on the selection system? One fear is that it may undermine the first-line manager's position. But, generally, a first-level manager nominating a subordinate to an assessment center is in exactly the same position as before—namely, recommending a subordinate to a higher level manager who is asked to choose between several eligible candidates. Typically, the manager's nominees are not automatically promoted. They are considered with the nominees of other managers. Assessment data just provide additional input for the higher level decision maker to use in comparing several candidates.

From another side, different critics may respond, "Doesn't this method serve merely to perpetuate the existing management system, breed conformity, and fail to select the different kinds of talent needed for the future?" This seems to be less true than depending on supervisory nomination alone. According to research by Dodd and Kraut (1970), men nominated to attend assessment centers were more likely to be lower in independence and higher on conformity, as measured by the Gordon Survey of Interpersonal Values, than their peers who were not nominated. But these characteristics were *unrelated* to success in the assessment centers. Still, higher managers may have had valid reasons for not nominating these particular nonconformists.

What techniques can be used to overcome blocks to the nomination of

---

[1] Personal communication, Douglas W. Bray, 1975.

deserving candidates? The most obvious is to invite candidates to nominate themselves to attend the assessment centers. Self-nominations have been used by some companies with great success. Mainly untested, but worth some research effort, is the use of nomination by peers, or promising test scores, or other unorthodox techniques which might foster greater opportunities to talented individuals.

How to select people who will be suitable for the demands of the future is a difficult challenge, although not insurmountable. If we have an idea of the required characteristics, behaviors, and skills, appropriate exercises could be developed. But there is not always a clear consensus as to future demands or how soon they will be demanded. We can get some clues by looking at trends within our own organizations and trends in organization generally, and making educated guesses about the future. In the meantime, it seems reasonable to select people who can function well in today's organization with the expectation that they are the most likely to be adaptable to the demands of tomorrow's organization.

DIMENSIONS MEASURED

Having gotten the right people into the assessment center, we might ask if we are really measuring the right things. Many assessment programs have defined the dimensions to be assessed by an empirical study of the manager's role, through careful job analysis or a critical incident study. But others base their dimensions largely on a review of the research literature and the judgment of executives in the organization as to what makes for an effective manager. Worse, some programs may merely copy programs of other companies. As described in Chapter 4 by Jeswald, the accurate determination of dimensions is all important to the success and validity of a center, and must receive an important place in the planning of any program.

Various programs differ widely in the characteristics they measure, although there is a good deal of overlap. Assessment programs generally measure administrative skills and, to a much greater degree, emergent leadership skills. By contrast, there are some important characteristics rarely captured by current programs. Perhaps it is too much to expect these relatively short programs to tap the skills related to building trust, confidence, and teamwork, but at least we must recognize this limitation.

On the other hand, assessment programs yield some measures that are not otherwise available. A study done by John Hinrichs (1969) in a large technology-based company suggests that the advantage of the assessment program lies in its use of situational exercises intended to display managerial skills. He compared the assessment ratings on 47 managers to ratings independently given by two executives after only a review of the men's personnel files. The two sets of ratings overlapped considerably (r = .47), but the assessment ratings correlated significantly with an outside criterion of relative salary standing (r = .37), whereas the executive ratings were insignificantly correlated with the criterion (r = .10). The two sets of ratings also overlapped considerably on the three major factors tapped by the assessment program except for one. This factor, based on interpersonal activity observed in the situational exercises, is exactly what contributed the greatest amount of unique variance to the criterion, as well as to the overall assessment itself.

RELATIONSHIP OF ASSESSMENT CENTER BEHAVIOR TO JOB BEHAVIOR

We should recognize that some people may act like capable managers if placed in such a role, although they may not have the ascendancy to wrench such a position from peers in group discussion exercises. People generally may act somewhat differently when placed in situations where they are more familiar and confident of the existing conditions and also expect to live with the consequences of their actions.

A related question about measurement is whether people behave naturally in assessment situations. On the one hand, we are told that some people show up poorly in such situations either because they choke up or because the situation is merely artificial. On the other hand, we are also told that some people distort their real personalities to look good. But these adept game players may not be equally good in real life. Again, the evidence on this issue is sparse. Of course, we should assume that most people put into an assessment situation will try to look as good as they can. It may be that the ability to discern and operate on the relevant dimensions of the assessee's role is the major clue as to how one will discern and operate on relevant dimensions if put into a managerial role.

To the extent that the assessment center exercises are properly built, they will be work samples of the managerial role. As such, we would expect that they predict fairly well the performance in the actual managerial role. Research done by Carleton (1970) on Sohio's assessment center program supports this assumption. On a sample of 122 men, he compared assessment center ratings on 13 behavioral characteristics to supervisory ratings of the same behaviors several years later, after the men were promoted to managerial jobs. He found moderately high levels of consistence (.30s and .40s). Apparently, behaviors in assessment centers are comparable to behavior in actual managerial situations. Obviously, more research on this point would be very desirable, but as of now we must stand on the overall validity of the method for most people in most situations.

MORALITY

Validity notwithstanding, doubts about assessment centers have been expressed sometimes at another level—almost morality itself. Some people wonder whether assessment centers, because they are brief and are not restricted to current performance, are a proper basis for making career decisions. To judge the morality of assessment centers, we must examine the consequences of the process as well as the process itself. The consequences have to be compared against the effect of existing promotional systems. This comparison shows that assessment programs are more likely to encourage decision making about promotions to be made openly and objectively, with agreed-upon standards, and based on relevant, systematically gathered data. Further, the explicitness of this method, contrasted with the relative invisibility of existing promotional systems, helps us to evaluate its appropriateness.

Doubts about the morality of assessment programs rest largely on a failure to critically examine current systems of promotional decision making. We must recognize that promotional decisions are continually being made, even in the absence of assessment centers, and usually on a less adequate basis. From what we know so far, the management assessment technique seems to be a morally justified technique.

The advantages of a formal assessment approach are also apparent if we compare it on a psychometric basis to typical promotional systems in most companies. As shown in Table 13-2, the typical system, with heavy reliance on the immediate manager, is overshadowed on several counts. The assessment

Table 13-2 Comparison of Assessment Center Features to a Typical Promotional System

Features	Typical Promotional System	Assessment Center
Number of raters	Immediate manager	Multiple raters
Raters' viewpoint	Subjective is primary	Objective
Raters' formal training in observation	Lower	Higher
Mode of observation	Distracted	Attentive
Skills observed	Current job	Management simulations
Yardstick used	Variable	Common

center technique offers evaluations from multiple raters, who tend to be objective and trained to make judgments of management skills, based on attentive observations of relevant standardized tasks, with all candidates being compared on a common yardstick. These differences are relative, of course, but assessment seems to have the edge.

IMPACT ON CAREERS

Closely related to the morality issue is the question of whether two days' observation is enough to decide a person's entire career. The question is a red herring in two ways. First, we must recognize and admit that many promotional decisions are currently made on much less than two days' observation. The results of a 20-minute speech, a lunch time conversation, or a brief field visit may be the basis for an executive's decision to promote one person over another. The assessment center may represent two days more of observation than existed before.

Secondly, the results are not intended to cast a final die on any person's entire career. Certainly, they affect the next promotional move, but even here the effect of a low rating is not quite a "kiss of death." The promotion rates associated with various assessment ratings in one study of salesmen (Kraut & Scott, 1972) who attended an operational assessment program are shown in Table 13-3. Admittedly, a poor rating slows one down, but the promotion rates for the lowest rated group is still two-thirds of the average of the total group.

The data also answer the fears that such a program must create "crown princes." Overall, only a third of all those assessed had been promoted from one to five years later. Certainly this is not enough for program attendance alone to be a sign of being a "crown prince." The findings also dampen our fears that a high rating in the program will have a "golden boy" effect. A high rating in the program increases one's chances of moving ahead, but does not seem to guarantee it. Promotions seem to be influenced by other things as well and are not necessarily assured by a high assessment rating.

Incidentally, the fear of overly influencing an individual's career with the assessment judgment would be minimized if the published overall assessment rating did not express a person's ultimate career potential. It should express simply how well qualified the person is at the present time to move to the next level job. This judgment is likely to be more accurate, more acceptable, and less abused. The data should also be discarded for any decision-making purpose after two years or so.

Another negative effect of assessment programs is a possible demoralization of those who perform poorly. If this might lead to the loss of trained, competent people, it would be very undesirable. Table 13-3 shows the separation rates of salesmen who get different assessment ratings. The proportion of the

Table 13-3   Promotion and Separation Rates of Sales Non-Management Candidates Assessed from 1965 to 1970

Overall Assessment Rating (of Ultimate Potential)	Distribution of Ratings No.	%	Percent Promoted to First-Line Manager	Percent Later Separated from Company
Executive management	14	3%	86%	0%
Higher management	57	13	60	5
Second-line management	114	26	44	5
First-line management	123	28	33	5
Remain non-management	129	30	24	3
Total	437	100%	35%	4%

$$x^2 = 38.69$$
$$p < .001 \qquad \text{n.s.}$$

Source: Kraut and Scott, 1972.

bottom-rated people does not differ significantly from the top-rated people. If we judge by attrition rates, the program does not seem to demoralize.

IMPACT ON STRESS

Perhaps this criterion of negative impact is too long term. Some critics have raised the issue of short-term negative impacts. In particular they ask if the programs are not too stressful. Certainly, some exercises involve a fair amount of stress, although nothing like that associated with sensitivity training. Attempts are made in most programs to keep stress to an acceptable level. This is done variously by adjusting the difficulty level of exercises, thoroughly informing participants about the program in advance, inviting only those judged to be promotable, making it easier to decline a program invitation, being sensitive and supportive with persons manifesting signs of anxiety, and providing an opportunity to emotionally "come down to earth" gently.

More research needs to be done on the degree and effects of stress. In the meantime, we must recognize that stress is often a fundamental part of the manager's job. Reactions to reasonable amounts of stress are important data in evaluating suitability for management, and most assessment programs rate participants on their resistance to stress.

DEVELOPMENTAL SEGMENTS

Some recent innovations in assessment programs may sharply influence the impact of the assessment center process on participants. Many such programs have added significant development portions to the assessment procedures. A typical development session will add two or three days of training activities to an assessment program with a specific purpose of integrating the two segments. Like other development programs, it may utilize films, discussions, and outside speakers.

Unlike most other development programs, this one will typically include videotape playbacks of the assessment exercises and a personal interview providing feedback on one's assessment performance, during which time specific development alternatives may be considered. Some programs provide systematic feedback and constructive comments from peers. Others include exercises to sharpen individual skills.

Such programs capitalize on the unusually high motivation of the assessees to learn more about the management skills just tested. The assessees want very much to develop their communications and leadership skills, to understand group dynamics, and so on. The developmental portion also permits individuals to decompress from the intensive climate of the preceding days in a supportive climate. Judging by observations made during this period, the result is for participants to have a more realistic and positive self-image before leaving.

The extra days of training have the effect of visibly affirming the company's interest in them and its sincerity in regarding them as its most promising people. Since most of these people have, in fact, been judged promotable by their nominating managers, and many of them will be promoted, the extra developmental session can also be seen as an especially meaningful course in supervisory or management training.

The reactions of participants to developmental programs such as the one described above were measured in the seven-country study noted earlier (Kraut, 1973). The results are shown in Table 13-4. A rather high proportion of the participants—and a majority in every country—felt that the program was useful for their self-development.

Participants were also asked to indicate if they would recommend the program to a good friend. Perhaps this is the most telling question about their participation in the assessment center. The results are shown in the second half of Table 13-4. The projective nature of the question and the highly favorable responses can be seen as a very impressive endorsement.

Table 13-4 Assessees' Opinions: Self-Development and Participation

	n	Of very great value	Great value	Some value	Not very valuable	Not at all
		Question 3: "How do you rate the program's . . . value in giving you additional information . . . for your self-development?"				
Austria	(59)	35%	42%	13%	8%	2%
Brazil	(35)	29[a]	43	14	6	9
Germany I	(60)	36[b]	58	2	4	0
Germany II	(70)	37[b]	57	5	1	0
Japan	(47)	36[c]	55	9	0	0
Netherlands	(24)	33	46	13	8	0
United Kingdom	(11)	18	46	36	0	0
United States	(46)	25	40	31	4	0

	n	Certainly	Probably	Undecided	Probably not	Certainly not
		Question 4: "Would you recommend to a good friend at about your level in the company that he volunteer to participate in an assessment program?"				
Austria	(59)	60%	27%	8%	3%	2%
Brazil	(35)	35	59	6	0	0
Germany I	(60)	53	40	7	0	0
Germany II	(70)	59	37	4	0	0
Japan	(47)	64[d]	32	4	0	—
Netherlands	(24)	55	33	8	4	0
United Kingdom	(11)	82	18	0	0	0
United States	(46)	76	15	7	2	0

[a]Question slightly different: " . . . How do you feel about its usefulness for self-development?" with responses: very useful; useful; moderate; moderate utility; little utility; not useful.

[b]Question same as "A" with responses: very positive; positive; neither-nor; bit negative; very negative.

[c]Question slightly different: " . . . Effectiveness to promote self-development?" Responses: very effective; effective; moderate; ineffective; very ineffective.

[d]Slightly different responses offered: "To all friends; to some friends; not strongly; not at all."

DEVELOPMENT OF OBSERVERS

The potential of the assessment center method for furthering the development of participants is starting to be fully appreciated and exploited. But what about the managers who act as observers, what do they get out of it? Most of the time, quite a bit. In fact, the potential of the assessment center for the development of the observers is even more promising than for the assessees. Based on interviews following assessment centers, the reaction of most managers is that they have gained greatly from taking part in the assessment center.

Managers in some organizations are being sent to assessment centers as observers in lieu of other management development courses, specifically to become more astute in behavioral observation, group dynamics, and problem solving. Increasingly, observer training is being more explicitly geared to helping the managers develop as managers.

COST-BENEFIT ISSUES

Sooner or later, an executive must ask how much the program will cost. The answer can be very straightforward but may vary quite a bit from company to company depending on how it wants to run its program and what costs should be considered. The costs are essentially those of transportation, room and board, materials, consultant's fees, and possibly salaries of staff and assessees. The figures can range from a few dollars for a one-day nonresidential program to many hundreds of dollars for a week-long residential program from many different places. The sum of $500 seems to be close to that quoted by many companies and is about what it costs AT&T, the largest user of assessment centers, for each assessee (including staff salaries).

The basic question of cost is whether the outlay of resources is worth the return. Or, put another way, what is the cost of the information gained relative to the decision for which I am using it? Let's assume, as a rule of thumb, that most organizations consider three candidates for each one who is actually selected for a promotion. If all three went through an assessment center, it means that the cost for information helping to choose among the three would be $1,500 for that one promotion.

An executive, however, has to ask how much a good decision is worth. For example, a promotion which moves a family from one city to another may cost $10,000 for the move itself. If the new job does not work out, the individual may have to be relocated and a replacement brought in, adding perhaps another $20,000. From another point of view, how much does a poor manager cost an organization in terms of bad decisions, customer satisfaction, and employee morale? Executives familiar with the promotion of good salesmen who do not turn out to be good managers lament the fact that they have lost a high-producing salesman and gained a low-producing manager.

The answer for any given organization will vary, but a thoughtful executive can estimate how much a good decision is really worth. What is difficult to put into economic terms is the very real human misery of people put into situations which they cannot handle and the suffering of others who have to work for such misplaced persons.

Still it would be highly desirable to get some hard figures on the amount of savings that might be achieved with the use of this method. One estimate, made for the selection of sales managers for Xerox (Cheek, 1973), indicated that a net benefit of more than $4.9 million could be achieved for a cost of about $340,000. Naturally, the exact cost-benefit ratio would vary with each situation.

A general estimate has been made by Huck (1973b) of the contribution of the assessment approach compared to more traditional methods. By combining a series of independent studies, Huck estimates that the probability of selecting an "above average performer" is 15% if individuals are chosen at random. Using traditional management nomination techniques raises this to 35%. However, if a rating of "acceptable" in the assessment center is combined with management recommendations, the probability increases to 76%. Thus, the probability of selecting a successful performer is doubled.

In general, the cost of an assessment program seems to be just about the same as the cost of a management development program done under similar conditions. When one considers the positive reaction of most managers who have taken part as observers, it makes sense to take some of the funds intended for management development and use them for assessor training and for assessment center operations because they are two of the best types of development for many managers.

Even for assessees, the funds for their participation should be considered as a trade-off with resources that might be devoted to their professional or pre-management training. Overall, these costs might be best considered not merely as expenses, but as investments in the human resources of the organization.

Of course this entire approach of the assessment center is based on the assumption that the organization really values performance abilities and will advance people primarily on that basis. This is not true in some cultures where nonability measures are more highly valued. Thus, seniority, personal connections, and political power may play a relatively large role. Even in such environments, the assessment center technology can be useful as a placement device. Rather than merely moving people upward, the assessment center may provide the information to place them into higher level jobs which are most apt to use their talents and least likely to suffer from their ineptitudes. Even in countries where ability is not the prime determinant of promotion, poor decisions carry an economic cost.

SMALL ORGANIZATIONS

Executives in small organizations frequently have costs uppermost in their minds and are sometimes dismayed to find that so much of the development and use of the assessment method has been done by large companies. They have to be reminded that even in the large companies, most of the programs are run in divisions or subunits that are considerably smaller than the total company. Most small organizations can successfully run assessment centers, although there will be some considerable differences. One experienced consultant (Byham, no date) notes that the programs run by smaller firms tend to be lower in cost because they are run less frequently, and often on company premises using commercially available exercises. They tend to be more flexible and creative in the scheduling and timing of centers and frequently rely on outside consultants. Overall, the issues that bear on the need for an assessment center tend to be the same for both small and large firms.

It is true that smaller firms are likely to be less able to do validity research because of the few people that are assessed and the difficulty in obtaining criterion data that are comparable across people in different functions. However, the assessment center in the small firm can still make a major contribution by providing valid measures of the major dimensions of managerial ability.

CONCLUSIONS

As we can see, there is no shortage of questions which executives might ask about assessment centers and we have covered only the most common ones here. In fact, psychologists involved in assessment centers typically ask themselves the same questions as well (Kraut, 1972). The questioning is a very healthy and productive process. For one thing, raising questions about the technique is a stimulus to refining the method and adapting it as circumstances require. We are already seeing the technique extended to the selection of salesmen, retail store management trainees straight out of the university, and the upgrading of women in industry.

Questions on effectiveness are a useful prod to more meaningful research. Our criteria of success, for example, could be expanded to include peer judgments and the rating of subordinates about the assessee's managerial practices. We also have to look at the broader effects of assessment programs, such as the impact on participant's behavior, self-concepts, and careers. We should examine the programs' effectiveness in training observers to be better managers and stimulating improvement in an organization's personnel management practices.

Perhaps most important, a dialogue is a useful opportunity for educating an interested person about the method. When one considers the evidence, it is a very defensible method. The executive who supports the assessment center with the attention and resources it requires can usually feel quite comfortable putting it into the organization. A meaningful dialogue is critical in achieving this comfort. When enough questions and answers are exchanged between psychologists and executives, the advantages of an assessment center for enhancing the growth and effectiveness of individuals and organizations are likely to be equally obvious to both.

REFERENCES

Anstey, E. The civil service: A follow-up. *Occupational Psychology*, 1966, *40*, 139-151.

Anstey, E. The civil service administrative class: A follow-up of post-war entrants. *Occupational Psychology*, 1971a, *45*, 27-43.

Anstey, E. The civil service administrative class: Extended interview selection procedure. *Occupational Psychology*, 1971b, *45* 199-208.

Byham, W. C. Assessment centers and small organizations. Mimeograph. Development Dimensions, Inc., Mt. Lebanon, Pa. No date.

Carleton, F. O. Relationships between follow-up evaluations and information developed in a management assessment center. Paper presented at the American Psychological Association Convention, Miami Beach, Florida, 1970.

Cheek, L. M. Cost effectiveness comes to the personnel function. *Harvard Business Review*, 1973, *51*(3), 96-105.

Dodd, W. E., & Kraut, A. I. Will management assessment centers insure selection of the same old type? Paper presented at the American Psychological Association Convention, Miami Beach, Florida, 1970.

Hinrichs, J. R. Comparison of "real life" assessments of management potential with situational exercises, paper-and-pencil ability tests, and personality inventories. *Journal of Applied Psychology*, 1969, *53*, 425-432.

Huck, J. R. Assessment centers: A review of the external and internal validities. *Personnel Psychology*, 1973a, *26*, 191-212.

Huck, J. R. The assessment process: Yesterday, today and tomorrow. Paper presented at the First Annual Industrial and Organizational Psychology Conference, Ohio State University, September 1973b.

Huck, J. R., & Bray, D. W. Management assessment center evaluations and subsequent job performance of white and black females. *Personnel Psychology*, 1976, *2*, 13-30.

Kraut, A. I. A hard look at management assessment centers and their future. *Personnel Journal*, 1972, *51*, 317-326.

Kraut, A. I. Management assessment in international organizations. *Industrial Relations: A Journal of Economy and Society*, 1973, *12*, 172-182.

Kraut, A. I., & Scott, G. Validity of an operational management assessment program. *Journal of Applied Psychology*, 1972, *56*, 124-129.

CHAPTER 14
THE RESEARCH BASE *
James R. Huck

INTRODUCTION

This chapter is aptly named. As noted throughout this book, the popularity of assessment centers rests largely on an empirical base of validation. While the chapter appears near the end of the book, it is a most important one as it summarizes much of what has been done in this area.

In many respects, the research conducted on the assessment center method represents a model for much of today's applied validation research. It is not surprising that assessment centers are widely used as a means of identifying talent for affirmative action needs. Due to its focus on behaviors, assessment centers have been examining job relatedness issues long before the term received legal sanction in the courts.

In general, the caliber of criterion measures used and the experimental designs employed by assessment center researchers are superior to those commonly used. Longitudinal studies, before-and-after measures, experimental and control groups have been successfully used.

Dr. Jim Huck of the Wickes Corporation has reviewed the extensive literature in which over 50 studies all show positive findings. These studies, conducted in different organizations by different researchers using different assessment procedures, testify to the strength of this process.

However, a word of caution is in order. As noted in the *Standards and Ethical Considerations for Assessment Center Users*, "The historical

*This chapter appeared in its original form as an article in *Personnel Psychology*, 1973, 26(2), 191-212. Reprinted and revised by permission of Personnel Psychology, Inc.

record of the validity of this process, however, cannot be taken as a guarantee that a given assessment procedure will or will not be valid in a given setting." The need for evaluation is a constant and persistent one.

While validity studies are still needed, there is much additional research which needs to be done. We prefer to distinguish two kinds of assessment research—validity research and process research. We need to know more about the process itself—what exercises are used, the form of its use, how ratings are made, how information is processed, the experience base of the assessor, and the method of ratings employed are but a few. A number of such studies have been conducted, but the potential for further understanding has just been tapped. We can expect to see more laboratory-based studies in the future, which will give us a better understanding of both how and why assessment really works.

* * *

The impact of the assessment center method on organizations throughout the world rates the process as one of the most significant developments in personnel selection in many years. The use of assessment procedures to identify an individual's strengths and development needs has rapidly spread throughout American industry, governmental agencies, educational institutions, and international organizations as well. This is due in large part to the strong, supportive research base which has been established for these techniques.

This method of selection can be defined as one in which:

several different types of assessment techniques are applied to the subjects and the final assessments are made by the combined judgments of several assessors concerning the subjects' predicted behavior outside of the assessment situation. These procedures are 'multiple' in two senses: with respect to the techniques and with respect to the assessors. (Taft, 1959, p. 33)

Multiple assessment procedures were first used on a large scale by the German military psychologists (OSS, 1948). With the belief that orthodox methods of selection took too "atomistic" a view of human nature, they substituted what they called a "holistic" outlook. Their major assumption was that paper-and-pencil test analyses into abilities and traits disrupt the "total personality" of the individual. Therefore, they chose to observe the candidate's behavior in a complex situation to arrive at a "holistic" appraisal of his reactions. No data reporting the success of this assessment procedure were reported by the Germans, nor by the Japanese who made use of similar methods (Eysenck, 1962).

In 1942 the British Army, realizing that their traditional methods of officer selection were producing an alarming proportion of unsuccessful cadets in officer training, formed the British War Office Selection Boards (WOSB). In addition to adopting many of the principles and procedures used by the Germans, the WOSB devised additional assessment techniques for their program, such as the leaderless group discussion, as a basis for judging the social or interpersonal skills of the candidates (OSS, 1948; Taft, 1959).

This selection methodology was in turn used by the American Office of Strategic Services (OSS) in 1943 when it was faced with the task of selecting intelligence agents for service during World War II. The entire OSS assessment technique, including its rationale, model, and operation, has been described in considerable detail (MacKinnon, 1974; OSS, 1948; Wiggins, 1973). A number of studies have been reported using various applications of these procedures since that time (Eysenck, 1962; Stern, Stein, & Bloom, 1956; Taft, 1959). Perhaps the greatest contribution of the multiple assessment approach as used by the military was in the development of "real life" or situational exercises. These situational methods offer the potential for adding to the scope of human behavior that can be observed and evaluated under standardized conditions. The OSS assessment experience highlighted the psychological problems inherent in assessment and won many supporters for the value of combining multiple tests and observations by pooling the judgments of several assessors (Taft, 1959).

Following World War II, the assessment concept moved out of the laboratory, and American industry applied these multiple assessment techniques to assist in the selection of management personnel. The initial step was taken by the American Telephone and Telegraph Company in the Management Progress Study (Bray, 1964; Bray & Grant, 1966; Bray, Campbell, & Grant, 1974). This research-oriented study, which began in 1956, will be discussed later in this chapter. The first nonresearch assessment program in American industry was made operational by Michigan Bell Telephone Company in 1958 (Jaffee, 1965; Michigan Bell Telephone, 1960). This program was designed primarily as an aid to the line organization in the selection of high-potential employees. Focusing on nonmanagement or craft personnel being considered for first-level management, Michigan Bell's Personnel Assessment Program (PAP) has been in continuous operation since 1958. This selection technique rapidly spread to other Bell System Companies, where today over 10,000 employees are evaluated each year at the Bell System Assessment Centers in operation throughout the United States. Since the inception of the program, more than 150,000 candidates have participated.

Likewise, other companies observed the success of the Bell System and have used the assessment technique within their own organizations. In 1970, 12 companies operated assessment centers, while today anywhere from 200 to 1,000 organizations conduct some form of assessment program—depending on what constitutes an assessment center (Huck, 1973b). In addition, an estimated

100 companies are in the process of developing them. Although, the assessment concept has had its major application in the area of managerial selection, assessment programs have also been designed to select salesmen (Bray & Campbell, 1968), engineers (Moses, 1972), college applicants (Kohls, 1970; Moses & Wall, 1975), and blue-collar employees (Thoresen, 1974; Thoresen & Jaffee, 1973). Moreover, assessment is used by different companies for a variety of purposes, including selection, placement, early identification, development, training, and career pathing.

Research using multiple assessment procedures to identify managerial potential has presented two types of evidence which bear on the accuracy of the assessment evaluations (Bray & Grant, 1966). The first kind can be considered "external" or related to the predictive validity of the ratings. It consists of the correlations and other data showing relationships between the evaluations and subsequent "success" in management. The second type of evidence is "internal" to the assessment process. It consists of factorial results and the correlations between the various assessment techniques and the assessment ratings.

The present review focuses on both the "external" and the "internal" validities of the assessment center method in identifying managerial skills.

EXTERNAL VALIDITY OF ASSESSMENT PROCEDURES

The use of multiple assessment procedures in industry is linked to the Management Progress Study, a longitudinal research study undertaken by AT&T in 1956 (Bray, Campbell, & Grant, 1974; Bray & Grant, 1966). The objectives of this study were to develop "career histories" by investigating the factors which determine the career progress of young men entering the management environment. An initial assessment of personal characteristics hypothesized to be of importance to an individual's success in the Bell System was a major aspect of the Management Progress Study. The dimensions assessed were derived from a review of the literature and from discussions with managers in the Bell System Companies.

The sample of the Management Progress Study consisted of 422 men drawn from six Bell System operating companies. Approximately two-thirds of the sample were recruited as management trainees after graduation from college; the remaining third had been employed initially for nonmanagement positions and had advanced into management relatively early in their careers. The technique used was a psychological assessment, which included clinical interviews, projective tests, work samples, paper-and-pencil tests, and participation in group problems and leaderless group discussions. The subjects spent three and one-half days at the assessment center in groups of 12. Immediately following, the assessment staff, consisting primarily of professionally trained persons, discussed each participant extensively and rated him on each of 25 dimensions plus an overall evaluation for potential to advance in management. The candidate's final rating represented the pooled judgments of all assessors. After the evaluation, a narrative summary of each candidate's performance was prepared. The assessment phase of the Management Progress Study extended over a five-year span (1955-1960).

One unique feature of the Management Progress Study is that no information about any candidate's performance has ever been communicated to company officials. All information collected from these 422 subjects during assessment and subsequently has been held for research purposes only. Thus, no contamination of subsequent criterion data by the assessment results has occurred and the judgments of the assessment staff have had no influence on the subjects participating in the study.

Bray and Grant (1966) undertook the most extensive validation of an assessment program in industry, using data from the assessment phase of the

Table 14-1 Relationship Between Assessment Center Predictions and Management Level Achieved

Assessment Prediction		Management Level Achieved (1965)		
College Hires (1957-1960)	N	First-level Management	Second-level Management	Middle Management or Above
Middle management predicted in 10 years	10	2% (1)	48% (30)	50% (31)
Middle management not predicted	63	11% (7)	78% (49)	11% (7)
Non-college Supervisors (1958-1960)				
Middle management predicted in 10 years	41	7% (3)	56% (23)	37% (15)
Middle management not predicted	103	59% (61)	36% (37)	5% (5)

Source: Bray & Grant, 1966.

Management Progress Study. In July of 1965, five of the participating Bell System companies submitted information on the current status of the men assessed as part of the Management Progress Study five to seven years previously. Table 14-1 presents the relationship between assessment judgments and level of management achieved by mid-1965 for both the college hires and the non-college hires. At the time of assessment, half (49.6%) of the college hires were judged as having potential for middle management, and over a quarter (28.4%) of the non-college men were predicted to achieve that level. Dunnette (1971, p. 92) summarizes the actual progress by stating:

> The predictive validities of the assessment staff's global predictions are moderately high; for the college men, 31 (82%) of the 38 men who have made middle management were correctly identified by the assessment staffs; for the non-college men, 15 (75%) of 20 men who have made middle management were correctly identified. In contrast, of the 72 men (both college and non-college) who have not advanced beyond the first level of management, the assessment staff correctly identified 68 (94%).

The combined results of the college and non-college sample show that, at the time of the study, 45% of those who were predicted to make middle management had, in fact, done so; whereas, only 7% of those predicted not to make management had achieved that level. The point biserial correlation between assessment center predictions and level achieved in management was .44 for the college men and .71 for the non-college portion of the sample. The predictive accuracy is particularly impressive considering the original assessment predictions were made for a 10-year period.

Bray, Campbell, and Grant (1974) have provided extensive information on the growth and development of the Management Progress Study college sample during the first eight years of employment in the Bell System. They present data relating to four general areas:

1. the relationship of personal qualities to ultimate managerial performance and progress;
2. changes in personal qualities over the years;
3. the causes and results of such changes; and
4. the effects of business policies and practices on personal growth and progress.

The Management Progress Study will continue to provide valuable research evidence regarding the effectiveness of the assessment center method and the stability of the assessment dimensions over time.

Operational Use of Assessment

Michigan Bell Telephone Company was one of six Bell System Companies which participated in the Management Progress Study. After witnessing the assessment techniques used in the Management Progress Study, some executives at Michigan Bell recognized the potential use of such procedures to assist in evaluating the managerial capabilities of craftsmen. In 1958, Michigan Bell and AT&T modified the research assessment procedures for use on an operating basis in the selection of first-level supervisors from the ranks of nonmanagement employees. Techniques which require professional staff members, such as personality measures and projective tests, were not employed. Michigan Bell's assessment program is the prototype of the assessment centers used in the Bell System today, as well as the model for those used in other companies.

Since the inception of assessment centers in the Bell System, a number of studies have provided information concerning their effectiveness. One study, conducted by Michigan Bell (1962), compared the first 40 men assessed and promoted with the last 40 men promoted before the assessment center program began. The findings show that approximately two-thirds (62.5%) of the assessed group were rated "better than satisfactory" in job performance, as compared to only one-third (35%) of the group not assessed. In addition, results showed that 67% of the assessed group rated had the abilities required for the next level of management, whereas only 35% of the nonassessed group demonstrated this potential. These results suggest that the assessment process is even more predictive of potential to advance to higher levels of management. Later investigations (Campbell & Bray, 1967; Finley, 1970; Huck, 1974; Huck & Bray, 1976; Jaffee, Bender, & Calvert, 1970) have supported this finding.

In 1965 AT&T conducted a study in four associated Bell System Companies which had operated an assessment center for several years (AT&T, 1965). The sample included 506 men, 471 at the first level of management at the time of the study. (No women were included in the sample, as no company had been assessing women long enough at the time for an adequate follow-up.) Five groups were identified in the study:

1. men assessed as "acceptable" at an assessment center and promoted;
2. men assessed as "questionable" at an assessment center and promoted;
3. men assessed as "not acceptable" at an assessment center and promoted;
4. men never assessed but promoted after the assessment program began; and
5. men promoted before the assessment center began.

Individuals in the different groups were compared on several measures of performance at the first level of management and on potential for further advancement. The criterion measures consist of the man's last formal appraisal rating, and a special rating and ranking made by his middle management-level supervisor during a personal interview.

The results clearly show that the assessment center is a valuable technique for identifying management potential. Campbell and Bray (1967, p. 12) draw a number of conclusions* based on their findings:

1. Promotion of those who achieved a good rating at the assessment center led to an improvement in the quality of management at the first level of supervision, particularly in building a pool of men who have the potential to advance to higher levels.

2. The assessment center produced a modest, but significant, improvement in performance at the first level. The difference in the results for performance and potential suggest that the management skills measured at the assessment center are more important in higher levels of supervision.

3. Promotion of a small percentage of the total group of men assessed as neither fully acceptable nor clearly unacceptable, after careful review by the line organization, resulted in generally good selection for management.

4. Promotion of a small, select percentage of the men assessed as clearly unacceptable did not lead to a favorable outcome.

5. Promotion of men who had never been assessed led to satisfactory results in terms of performance at the first level, but only a small percentage of these men had potential to advance to higher levels of management.

6. The payoff seems well worth the time and effort required to operate the assessment program.

More recently, Moses (1971) presented data on 5,943 individuals assessed by Bell System Companies. The criterion used was advancement beyond the first level of management, the level at which the assessment results were used. Since the assessment process was used to identify skills applicable to entry-management positions, progress in management to higher levels would indicate more satisfactory performance as a manager, thus eliminating a certain amount of bias and criterion contamination which may exist in supervisory ratings.

Results showed a highly significant relationship between the assessment rating and the progress in management. Table 14-2 indicates that individuals assessed as "More than acceptable" were twice as likely to be promoted two or

---

*From "Assessment Centers: An Aid in Management Selection," by Richard J. Campbell and Douglas W. Bray, *Personnel Administration*, March-April, 1967. Reprinted by permission of the International Personnel Management Association, 1313 East 60th Street, Chicago, Illinois 60637.

Table 14-2 Relationship Between Assessment Rating and Progress in
Management

Assessment Rating	N	Number Receiving Two or More Promotions	Percent
More than acceptable	410	166	40.5
Acceptable	1,466	321	21.9
Questionable	1,901	220	11.5
Not acceptable	2,157	91	4.2
Total	5,943	798	13.4

Source: Moses, 1971.

more times than individuals assessed as "Acceptable," and almost 10 times more
likely than those rated "Not acceptable." The simple correlation obtained
between the final assessment rating and management progress was .44 (p <
.001). Findings from this study concerning the specific assessment variables will
be discussed later in this review.

AT&T has reported additional studies which further substantiate the
success of the assessment technique in the Bell System (Bray & Campbell, 1968;
Grant & Bray, 1969; Grant, Katkovsky, & Bray, 1967; Huck & Bray, 1976;
Moses & Boehm, 1975; Moses & Wall, 1975). Companies outside the Bell System
have found similar evidence for the validity of operational assessment centers.
IBM has conducted a series of studies of its assessment programs showing
positive relationships between center findings and various criteria of job success
(Dodd, 1971; Hinrichs, 1969; Kraut, 1972). Wollowick and McNamara (1969)
report a study involving 94 lower- and middle-level managers selected to
participate in IBM's assessment program after being "designated as having
above-average potential for advancement." Even with this restriction of range,
they found a correlation of .37 with the global assessment rating and the
criterion of increase in managerial responsibility three years after assessment.

Kraut and Scott (1972) reviewed the career progress of 1,086 nonmanagement candidates who had been observed at an IBM assessment center one to six
years previously. Substantial correlations were reported between assessment
ratings and two major organizational criteria—second-level promotions and
demotions from first-level management. An additional finding, based on
separation rates, was that participation in the assessment program does not
"demotivate" candidates. The proportion of low- and high-rated employees who
left the company did not differ significantly. This is encouraging as candidates

are evaluated at an assessment center only on managerial abilities, not technical skills or current job performance. As Kraut and Scott point out, an undesirable consequence would most certainly be for an assessment program to result in the loss of well-trained, adequately performing individuals.

General Electric (Meyer, 1970, 1972), Sears Roebuck (Bentz, 1967, 1971), Standard Oil (Donaldson, 1969; Hardesty & Jones, 1968; Finkle & Jones, 1970; Finley, 1970; Thomson, 1969), and Wickes (The Wickes Corporation, 1974) have also thoroughly researched and established the validities of their assessment programs. Slivinski and colleagues at the Canadian Public Service Commission have published a series of technical reports on the Career Assignment Program, placing particular emphasis on identifying managerial job functions and participants' reactions to the program. Comparisons across studies from several companies are not always possible where so many differences are operational: assessment dimensions and techniques, samples, criterion measures, target jobs, and level of management. In addition, the variety of uses of assessment programs in different companies further complicates the issue. However, Thornton (1971) reviewed the validity evidence from a number of smaller companies operating some form of assessment center. Although his findings were generally positive, he concludes from his survey that these smaller companies have relied to a large extent on some form of synthetic validation. Their approach has been to analyze the job, identify the major ability dimensions, and select assessment techniques to measure these requirements. "In view of the dearth of empirical evidence available from the companies surveyed for this paper, it would appear that there has been heavy reliance on the evidence gathered in the larger corporations." He identified sampling and criterion problems as the two major stumbling blocks. These issues, especially sampling, are ones every company must face when attempting to validate an assessment program.

Huck (1973b) combined a series of independent studies conducted over a period of years on different assessment programs which provides some useful

Table 14-3 Contribution of Assessment

Selection Method	Chance of Selecting Above-Average Performer
Random (no screen)	15%
Management judgment	35%
And/acceptable in assessment	76%

Source: Huck, 1973b.

information regarding the contribution of the assessment approach when compared to more traditional methods. These data allow us to estimate the probability of success, given various methods of selection. As evidenced in Table 14-3, the probability of selecting an "above-average performer" by choosing an individual at random is 15%. When management nominates an individual for a supervisory position based on whatever factors are available other than assessment results, the probability of selecting an "above-average performer" is 35%. However, if an individual is recommended by management AND rated "acceptable" in the assessment center, the probability increases to 76%. Thus, by utilizing results of the assessment process, the chance rate is substantially increased and the probability of selecting a "winner" more than doubles.

Byham (1970) concludes that the accumulation of research findings from a variety of types of centers lends considerable credibility to the overall validity of the technique. He states:

> In a survey of the 20 companies that operated centers, I uncovered some 22 studies in all that showed assessment *more* effective than other approaches and only one that showed it exactly *as* effective as some other approaches. None showed it *less* effective. As I suggested before, these studies exhibit correlations between center prediction and achievement criteria such as advancement, salary grade, and performance ratings that range as high as .64. (p. 154)

In a recent article, Cohen, Moses, and Byham (1974) reviewed the assessment literature focusing on the predictive accuracy of the overall assessment rating, a global variable common to all assessment programs. Eighteen research studies, conducted from 1964 to mid-1972, consistently showed assessment performance related to several criteria: the predictive accuracy was highest for job potential, followed by progress, then job performance. These assessment programs were conducted in a variety of organizational settings. Kraut (1972) evaluated the assessment center techniques from several perspectives, including validity, acceptability, morality, impact, and development of observers—all aspects produced positive findings.

Even with the substantial amount of positive research evidence on the assessment center method, one interesting observation is noted regarding articles which review the assessment literature (Bray & Moses, 1972; Dunnette, 1971; Howard, 1974). They all conclude on the same theme—the need for still additional research. The present review will be no exception!

The issue of differential validity will be deferred for discussion in a separate section of this chapter.

INTERNAL VALIDITY OF ASSESSMENT PROCEDURES

The validity of multiple assessment procedures to predict subsequent manage-ment success has been established. However, the advantage of using these techniques over traditional and less costly methods, as well as the identification and reliability of the assessment dimensions and procedures, must also be considered. Several investigations have been concerned with this type of "internal" validity.

Glaser, Schwarz, and Flanagan (1958) show that two short, basic ability tests (paper-and-pencil) together yield a correlation of .27 with job proficiency criterion for civilian supervisors employed at military depots. The addition of certain situational and clinical procedures, although nearly doubling the level of predictive variance, produced multiple correlations ranging from only .30 to .33.

Bray and Grant (1966) determined the degree of significant variance which performance in the group exercises added to the overall staff predictions of career success. Partial correlations were computed with ability tests partialed out of the correlation between the staff judgment and the criterion of salary progress. Reliable variance remained after partialing out the test scores, thus indicating that the assessment process does contribute substantially more evidence than was gained by the simple administration of paper-and-pencil ability measures alone. However, their results show that neither the situational techniques nor the paper-and-pencil instruments could have been omitted without the loss of significant information.

Wollowick and McNamara (1969) present results which clearly demon-strate the significant incremental validities of the multiple assessment pro-cedures. The degree of increase in managerial responsibility was the criterion measure used in rating 94 lower and middle-level managers who had been assessed approximately three years previously. The assessment predictors were classified into three composites: tests, exercises, and characteristics. Multiple correlations were then computed for each predictor composite with the following results: .45 for tests alone, .41 for characteristics alone, and .39 for exercises alone. When all three types of measures or predictor composites were included in the regression equation, the resulting multiple correlation was increased substantially to .62 (not cross-validated). Inclusion of techniques unique to the assessment center procedure, essentially the situational exercises, nearly doubled the criterion variance accounted for. They conclude that all three types of predictor composites (tests, exercises, and characteristics) each contribute a substantially unique element to the prediction of managerial success.

One plausible explanation for the predictiveness of the situational simulations is offered by Huck (1974), whose findings are similar for a sample of 126 first-level female managers:

This illustrates the strong emphasis placed on the directly observable behavioral aspects of the assessment techniques, rather than on cognitive test scores. This does not imply that effective intelligence is not required for the management position under study. Rather, it appears that beyond a certain level of effective intelligence, the interpersonal skills and administrative skills are more important determinants of managerial effectiveness. (p. 99)

Concerning the optimum number of variables for multiple assessment procedures, Wollowick and McNamara (1969) report that only seven of the 32 variables contributed significantly to the multiple correlation. They suggest the possibility of eliminating those paper-and-pencil tests that do not contribute to the predictive validity. However, they caution that "eliminating any of the exercises may not give enough opportunity to establish usable characteristic ratings, which are presently based on all the exercises." Since one exercise may provide evidence on a number of assessment characteristics, any reduction in the number of exercises may also reduce the reliability and validity of the significant characteristic ratings. In addition to the increase in predictive power, the characteristic or dimension ratings provide the company and the individual with a reading of specific strengths and weaknesses. Where development is emphasized in an assessment program, an evaluation of a variety of managerial dimensions appears more related to this objective.

Another significant finding emerged from the Wollowick and McNamara study concerning the overall assessment rating (OAR). "The subjectively derived combination of the variables (OAR) correlated .37 with the criterion, while the statistical combination gave a multiple of .62. This suggests that instead of deriving an OAR by subjective means, it might be done more profitably by a statistical procedure." It remains questionable how well this statistical result would hold up under cross-validation.

Data presented by Moses (1971) are not supportive of Wollowick and McNamara's suggestion of the superiority of a statistical combination of assessment scores. He reports a multiple correlation of .463 between all assessment variables and the criterion progress in management beyond the first level. When test scores were not included in the multiple regression, the behavioral assessment variables alone produced a correlation of .461. The uniqueness of paper-and-pencil tests alone was not reported, however, which would have provided a clear basis for method comparison. Nevertheless, the findings concerning the robustness of the final global assessment rating remain quite clear. This judgmental rating by itself correlated .44 with management progress, accounting for nearly as much criterion variance as the statistically refined multiple regression which included all assessment variables.

Huck (1974) demonstrated that trained line managers can integrate diverse sources of behavioral data into a meaningful composite. In fact, he found their success to equal that which can be accomplished by a combination of the dimensions using optimum empirical weights. Multiple regressions were computed between the assessment dimensions and two measures of performance effectiveness, Overall Job Performance (R = .42) and Potential for Advancement (R = .56). Most interesting is the fact that the simple correlations between the subjectively derived Overall Assessment Rating and the criterion measures were equivalent to these multiple regression for both Overall Job Performance (r = .42) and Potential for Advancement (r = .59). He attributes the success of clinical judgments in industrial assessment programs partially to the use of line managers as assessors. These individuals, besides being thoroughly trained in the assessment concept and procedures, are experienced in the criterion situations being predicted. This knowledge of the criterion situations can be taken into account when predictions are made. However, as Dunnette (1971) suggests, the bases for the clinical judgments or the mechanisms used by the evaluators need to be explicated so that others might be trained in the techniques of making successful clinical assessments.

Finally, Hinrichs (1969) shows that ratings of managerial potential based on information already available in the personnel records of 47 IBM managers correlated .46 with the ratings of managerial potential received in their assessment program. Based on this finding, Hinrichs argues that a careful review of company records may produce much of the same information which evolves from an expensive two-day assessment program. This did not hold true for information related to interpersonal behavior which, incidentally, is one of the salient features of a multiple assessment procedure. To this conclusion, Dunnette (1971, p. 106) responds:

> In my opinion, Hinrichs' argument, though reasonable, cannot be sustained on the basis of the single coefficient of .46 he reports in his investigation. Nearly 80 percent of the variance in the assessment program ratings remains unassociated with the ratings based on the personnel records; therefore, it seems highly probable that the "lengthy and expensive" assessment program does contribute independent, valid, and useful diagnostic information about men's abilities and behavioral tendencies that is not contributed by ratings based merely on file information.*

---

*From Dunnette, M. The assessment of managerial talent. In P. McReynolds (Ed.) ADVANCES IN PSYCHOLOGICAL ASSESSMENT, Vol. 2. Palo Alto, California: Science and Behavior Books, 1971.

In addition, the intent of an assessment program is predictive rather than concurrent in design. To this point, Hinrichs maintains that "if the focus is on the early identification of potential where little job history has accrued, then the assessment process is probably a very effective means of synthesizing a rather close approximation of the type of potential prediction which could eventually evolve through on-the-job performance."

Factor Analysis of Assessment Dimensions

A number of factor-analytic studies of assessment variables have been conducted in an effort to explicate the basic elements of assessment performance (Bentz, 1967; Bray & Grant, 1966; Donaldson, 1969; Hinrichs, 1969; Huck, 1974; Huck & Bray, 1976; Thomson, 1969). Bray and Grant (1966) computed correlation matrices for both the college and non-college groups in the Management Progress Study, and factored these separately for the two samples. Although not identical, the factor structures were similar for the two groups, each yielding a higher order factor and several first-order factors. The average commonality for the college sample was .64 and for the non-college sample was .57. Factors which emerged common to both groups are listed below, along with the variables loading most highly on each:

1. General Effectiveness: overall staff prediction, decision making, organizing and planning, creativity, need for advancement, resistance to stress, and human relations skills.
2. Administrative Skills: organizing and planning, and decision making.
3. Interpersonal Skills: human relations skills, behavior flexibility, and personal impact.
4. Control of Feelings: tolerance of uncertainty and resistance to stress.
5. Intellectual Ability: scholastic aptitude and range of interests.
6. Work-Oriented Motivation: primacy of work and inner work standards.
7. Passivity: ability to delay gratification, need for security, and need for advancement (negative).
8. Dependency: need for superior approval, need for peer approval, and goal flexibility.

Huck (1974) factored the intercorrelation matrices among 16 assessment dimensions separately for 241 white females and 238 black females. Both factorial solutions yielded four clearly distinguishable factors, accounting for 63.1% of the total variance in the ratings for whites and 59.5% of the total rating variance for blacks. He found a close correspondence in the loadings of the assessment variables on the factors for the two samples. The four factors were psychologically defined in terms of the assessment variables loading highest on each:

1. Interpersonal Effectiveness: energy, resistance to stress, forcefulness, and leadership.
2. Administrative Skills: organizing and planning, and decision making.
3. Sensitivity: awareness of social environment, self-objectivity, and managerial identification.
4. Effective Intelligence: scholastic aptitude and written communication skills.

Thomson (1969) factor-analyzed the assessment ratings of 119 managers who had participated in Standard Oil's (Ohio) Formal Assessment of Corporate Talent (FACT) program. Five factors emerged from the analysis and accounted for 80% of the total rating variance in 13 scales. Nearly identical factor structures of five factors each were obtained when separate analyses were carried out for psychologist assessors and line-manager assessors (Spearman rho between the two factor loadings was .90). The factors, along with the variables loading on each, are shown below:

1. Group Task Effectiveness: impact, amount of participation, oral communication, quality of participation, overall potential, and self-direction.
2. Need for Structure: orientation to detail, originality, self-direction, and relationship with authority.
3. Interpersonal Effectiveness: personal acceptability and understanding of people.
4. Quality of Independent Thinking: personal breadth, overall potential, quality of participation, originality, self-direction, understanding of people, and relationship with authority.
5. Work-Oriented Motivation.

A direct comparison of these factor studies is not possible due to the differences in variables, variable interpretations, assessment techniques, and objectives of each program. For example, certain factors emerged in the Management Progress Study which did not appear in Huck's research; namely, control of feelings, work-oriented motivation, and passivity. The Management Progress Study's lengthy assessment approach, including projective tests, personality questionnaires, and clinical interviews by staff psychologists would be expected to produce more motivational information than a two-day center conducted by line managers which deliberately avoids personality testing and psychological probing. Likewise, administrative skills did not emerge as a factor in Thomson's investigation since no in-basket was administered. Standard Oil's program concentrates on other aspects of managerial performance, such as interpersonal and group effectiveness skills.

However, consistency is shown in the factor structures underlying the assessment programs mentioned above, as the common elements all reflect behaviorally relevant factors. These results illustrate the strong emphasis on behavior in the assessment process, rather than merely on descriptions of traits. Also apparent is the wide range of behaviors the assessment methods elicit in evaluating performance.

Reliability of Multiple Assessment Procedures

One unique feature of the assessment center procedure is the use of multiple observers or assessors whose judgments regarding the observed performance of candidates are pooled. This raises the question of interrater reliability in the assessment process. Research directed at this issue is rather conclusive in showing that the assessment process is not limited by low reliability. A number of areas concerning interrater reliability are open to investigation, including the assessment dimensions, the assessment exercises, as well as the composition of the assessment staff.

Focusing on the assessment dimensions, Dicken and Black (1965) report a study involving managers from two firms—an insurance company and a manufacturing concern. This sample was selected due to the diversity of jobs between managers of the two companies. High reliabilities (interrater agreement) in the assessment ratings of both samples were achieved. In the insurance sample, reliabilities ranged from .68 to .99, with the median reliability of .89, while in the manufacturing sample, the range was from .85 to .98, with the median of .92. A similarly high level of rater agreement was found by Thomson (1969), who reports a range on 13 dimensions from .74 to .93.

Greenwood and McNamara (1967) determined the degree of interrater reliability of behavior dimensions obtained from the situational exercises used in four IBM divisions operating assessment programs. The mean observer reliabilities for effectiveness ratings on a five-point scale were .66, .70, and .74 for three situational exercises, and the mean reliabilities for the rankings of six participants were .64, .71, and .75. These findings compare favorably with the observer reliabilities reported by Bray and Grant (1966) in the overall ratings (.60 and .75) and rankings (.69 and .75) in two situational exercises. It appears that the observers were rating participants on many of the same aspects of performance.

A study conducted by Michigan Bell (Moses, 1973) provides the most definitive data regarding reliability of the total assessment process. The study was designed to determine the relationship between two multiple assessment programs. A sample of 85 nonmanagement employees (39 men, 46 women, 42 blacks, and 43 whites) who attended Michigan Bell's one-day Early Identification Assessment (EIA) program were later assessed by the Company's more extensive two-day Personnel Assessment Program (PAP). The minimum time between assessments was one month and participants in the study did not receive any feedback on their EIA performance until after completing both programs. Independent assessment staffs were used to evaluate candidates in the two programs, and the PAP staff was not aware of the individual's EIA performance.

The correlation between overall performance in the two programs was quite substantial for the total sample (.73), as well as for each of the subgroups (men, .77; women, .70; blacks, .68; whites, .73). No significant differences were found between the reliabilities obtained for any of these subgroups. This is one of the few studies which deals with the consistency of assessees' performance over time.

All the EIA variable ratings showed significant relationships with their corresponding PAP variable ratings, demonstrating the reliability of the specific assessment dimensions. The highest relationship found was between the overall ratings for EIA and PAP (r = .73).

A correlation of .56 was obtained between the participant ratings in the two competitive group exercises. One would expect the relationship in this study to be somewhat lower than the reliability of the situational exercises reported by Greenwood and McNamara (1967). Several extrinsic factors undoubtedly influenced the reliability of ratings in the group exercises in the Michigan Bell study, such as group variability, characteristics specific to each of the group problems, as well as temporary characteristics of the individuals associated with measurements at different time periods. However, the reliability estimate obtained in this study most likely contains true systematic variance representative of "lasting and general characteristics" of the individuals (Thorndike, 1949).

A few studies have been reported in the literature dealing with the background of managers serving on the assessment staffs. These studies have been aimed at the question of whether or not professional psychologists provide a higher degree of interrater reliability than the trained line managers serving as assessors. The available evidence suggests that they do not.

Thomson (1969) found no significant differences between ratings made by psychologists and by managers with regard to means, standard deviations, and reliabilities of assessment dimensions. No tendency was shown on the part of the psychologist nor the manager to restrict the range of ratings or bias the assessment ratings toward either end of the scale. The factor loadings of the assessment variables as rated by the professional and nonprofessional correlated .90.

Greenwood and McNamara (1967) compared psychologists and managers as evaluators in rating performance in situational tests. As Thomson found with the rating of assessment dimensions, these researchers show that either type of observer can be used interchangeably in evaluating situational exercises. However, they urge caution in interpreting these results:

one should not assume that non-professional personnel, who are without substantial business experience or lack any training in evaluating participants, should be employed in assessing personnel. Furthermore, as in this study, the instructions to the evaluators, whether professional or non-professional, should be explicit as to the specific type of behavior to be evaluated, examples provided as to kinds of behavior that may be expected to be elicited by the specific situational exercises, and standardized rating forms provided for their use.

The marked increase in reliabilities obtained as a result of training observers has been clearly demonstrated by Richards and Jaffee (1972). The mean interrater reliabilities for untrained observers was .46 on a human relations skill dimension and .58 on an administrative technical skill dimension; for the trained observer, these increased to .78 and .90, respectively. Likewise, Thomson (1970) illustrates that simply asking managers to rate subordinates using assessment forms falls far short of the quality of ratings obtained from a trained assessment staff. Prather (1970) has also discussed the effect of training in expanding the variance of performance ratings.

One might view the substantially high reliabilities reported in assessment research as artificially induced due to the methods of training the assessors and the staff's discussion of rating differences, rather than obtaining the reliabilities that would occur by independent judgments. However, common standards and the accurate interpretation of performance data are goals of every performance appraisal system. Unfortunately, many appraisal systems have had only limited effectiveness due to the lack of training provided to the evaluators. Most assessment programs place considerable emphasis on training assessors; based on the findings, these efforts appear to be well-justified.

DIFFERENTIAL VALIDITY OF ASSESSMENT PROCEDURES

The assessment center method, when used as a basis for selection and upgrading, is subject to the same fair employment guidelines (Office of Federal Contract Compliance and Equal Employment Opportunity Commission) as other selection devices, such as aptitude tests. The available evidence suggests that the assessment center method is equally valid in predicting job performance for members of different minority groups.

Huck (1973c, 1974) and Huck and Bray (1976) report the results of an extensive investigation into the determinants of assessment center ratings for white and black females, and the relationship of these dimensions to subsequent performance effectiveness anywhere from one to six years after attending an assessment program. These findings clearly indicate that the assessment procedures result in a high degree of predictive validity for both white and black female supervisors. Only perfunctory differences were exhibited between these two racial groups. A number of specific conclusions are drawn from this research.

1. Each assessment method produces evidence for specific dimensions—the sources of evidence for the assessment dimensions being the same for the two racial groups (Table 14-4).
2. Interpersonal skills (the group exercises) and administrative skills (the in-basket) are most heavily weighed in the Overall Assessment Rating; effective intelligence (the paper-and-pencil tests), the least.
3. The assessors place similar weights on assessment dimensions when deriving Overall Assessment Ratings for whites and blacks (Table 14-5).
4. In terms of the relationship between the assessment dimensions and subsequent job performance, those dimensions predictive for one racial group are also predictive for the other (Table 14-5).
5. Regardless of race, the strongest single predictor of future performance effectiveness is the Overall Assessment Rating.
6. Performance in the assessment program is directly related to performance in a supervisory capacity for both whites and blacks anywhere from one to six years after attending the assessment program. The predictive accuracy is even greater when assessment results are related to potential for advancement (Tables 14-5 and 14-6).
7. Supervisors' knowledge of participation in assessment does not appear to moderate the relationship between assessment ratings and performance effectiveness ratings.

These findings closely parallel the results of the Management Progress Study, which was conducted with college and non-college male employees. In addition to sex and race differences in the samples of these studies, the Management Progress Study predicted success at middle management level; whereas, this research was aimed at first-level supervision. Even with such diverse populations, the results are nearly identical. The available evidence suggests that the assessment process, particularly the behavioral simulations, tends to produce similar validity for males and females, whites and blacks, non-college and college graduates, as well as lower- and middle management positions. However, the findings from these investigations do not necessarily generalize to all assessment programs.

Huck and Bray (1976) conclude that in addition to its strong appeal for general selection purposes, the assessment center method is especially attractive for affirmative action such as the accelerated advancement of minority groups and women. A major attraction is the validity of the method, which substantially increases the likelihood that those advanced will do well on the job,

Table 14-4 Correlation of Assessment Situations and Tests with the Assessment Dimensions

	Interpersonal Effectiveness		Administrative Skills		Sensitivity		Effective Intelligence	
	Whites	Blacks	Whites	Blacks	Whites	Blacks	Whites	Blacks
Situations								
Promotion problem	*69*	*70*	46	48	48	47	20	08
Oral presentation	47	61	45	40	37	23	29	12
Small business	68	62	38	41	43	45	20	29
In-basket	48	31	*83*	*75*	41	30	42	34
Q-sort	41	35	33	07	*54*	*63*	20	33
Paper-and-pencil tests								
SCAT-verbal	29	22	39	18	31	29	*71*	*73*
SCAT-quantitative	36	23	28	17	13	16	*73*	*75*
High school letter	21	03	34	24	32	23	63	51
General information[a]	31	41	43	10	31	14	43	25

[a]Missing data for this variable (Whites = 76, Blacks = 33).

Notes: Decimals omitted; highest correlation between each assessment situation and assessment factors in italics.

Source: Huck, 1974.

Table 14-5 Relationship Between Assessment Dimensions and Global Ratings of Assessment, Performance, and Potential

	Overall Assessment Rating		Overall Job Performance		Potential for Advancement	
	Whites	Blacks	Whites	Blacks	Whites	Blacks
Assessment dimensions						
interpersonal effectiveness	87	87	35	40	51	49
Administrative skills	80	75	37	17	49	34
Sensitivity	68	70	10	27	27	37
Effective intelligence	52	41	26	03	38	25
Multiple R (4 factors)	95	95	45	43	58	51
Overall assessment rating	—	—	41	35	59	54

Note: Decimals omitted. Whites, N = 91; Blacks, N = 35.

Source: Huck and Bray, 1976.

Table 14-6 Relationship Between Overall Assessment Rating and Ratings of Job Performance and Potential for Advancement

	Overall Job Performance			Potential for Advancement		
	Less than Satisfactory	Satisfactory	Better than Satisfactory	Low	Moderate	High
Overall assessment rating						
Whites (N = 91)						
High	2% (1)	23% (11)	75% (36)	4% (2)	33% (16)	63% (30)
Moderate	4% (1)	56% (15)	41% (11)	11% (3)	59% (16)	30% (8)
Low	25% (4)	56% (9)	19% (3)	50% (8)	38% (6)	13% (2)
Blacks (N = 35)						
High	0% (—)	20% (2)	80% (8)	0% (—)	20% (2)	80% (8)
Moderate	31% (4)	39% (5)	31% (4)	31% (4)	46% (6)	23% (3)
Low	25% (3)	58% (7)	17% (2)	42% (5)	42% (5)	17% (2)

Source: Huck, 1974.

thus enhancing further affirmative action. A second attraction is that the assessment center bases judgments on overt behavior paralleling that required on the job and avoids excessive reliance on paper-and-pencil and biographical methods. Subjects in this research, both white and black, who were rated high at assessment showed excellent job performance and high potential for advancement with almost four times the frequency of those rated low.

In a recently published study, Moses and Boehm (1975) compared the assessment center performance of a large sample of women (4,846) to that of men (8,885) assessed in the same assessment program. They found that the distribution of overall assessment performance of women was identical to that of men; that the relationship between assessment center ratings and subsequent progress in management was quite similar for men and women; and that the relationship between the characteristics assessed and progress was quite similar as well. They conclude that assessment centers are both valid and "fair" for identifying management potential of women as well as men. Thus, in view of these studies, the assessment center method appears to be highly useful in providing opportunity to the most capable in an unbiased manner.

PERFORMANCE EFFECTIVENESS MEASURES

The previous discussion has mentioned a number of performance effectiveness measures: salary growth, rate of promotion, increase in managerial responsibility, demotions, managerial level achieved, performance interviews, observations of on-the-job behavior, ratings and rankings of overall performance, ratings of potential for advancement, and personnel record data. A number of problems are, of course, present when these measures are employed as criteria on which to determine the effectiveness of multiple assessment procedures. Inherent in each of these measures are biasing influences beyond the control of the individual. In addition, when assessment information is used as a basis for promotion, contamination of the above criteria and restriction of range often confound the results. Finally, these measures represent an oversimplification of the complexities involved in the "ultimate" criterion. Multiple assessment procedures concentrate primarily on an individual's managerial ability as measured by behavior sampling in simulated exercises. Too often researchers attempt to relate these behavioral observations to some all-inclusive measure of effectiveness and question if the relationship found is sufficiently large to justify the cost. Assessment techniques should be evaluated only on their success in meeting their stated objectives. Future research must determine which aspects of multiple criterion measures are predictable by the assessment procedures and which are not.

Wernimont and Campbell (1968) forcefully argue for the notion of "behavioral consistency," claiming that insistence on the concept that the predictor must be different from the criterion is self-defeating. On the contrary, they emphasize the establishment of consistencies between relevant dimensions of job behaviors and behavior samples obtained from real or simulated situations. "Utilizing the consistency notion confronts the problem directly and forces a consideration of what job behaviors are recurring contributions to effective performance (and therefore predictable)." This requires that research efforts be directed toward samples rather than signs of behavior.

Only a limited number of studies in the literature have emphasized the behavioral demands of a manager's job when evaluating multiple assessment procedures. Thomson (1970) compared assessment ratings on 13 dimensions with supervisors' ratings of current job performance on these same dimensions. On the whole, the level of convergent and discriminant validity obtained in this study compares favorably with the results of other studies on multiple assessment procedures. However, unlike other studies which accept the criterion on faith, Thomson clearly indicated that sources of invalidity were contained in the poor quality of the criterion ratings. Significant differences were found in the quality of the assessment and criterion ratings. The supervisors were unable to differentiate between the criterion dimensions, whereas the assessment raters were able to do so. Apparently, the criterion raters could not arrive at a precise and common understanding of the different scales and had difficulty establishing an adequate frame of reference. The high reliabilities and discriminant validities obtained in the assessment ratings were attributed to the intensive training given the assessors and to the standardized conditions associated with the assessment process.

Considering these criterion restrictions, one approach which shows a great deal of promise as a performance effectiveness measure is the behavior retranslation technique suggested by Smith and Kendall (1963). A number of experimental studies have used this procedure in the development of behavioral scales (e.g., Campbell, Dunnette, Arvey, & Hellervik, 1973; Dunnette, 1970; Folgi, Hulin, & Blood, 1971; Huck, 1974; Landy & Guion, 1970; Maas, 1965; Zedeck & Baker, 1971). This method imposes a common frame of reference on the raters, as managers familiar with the job actually construct the scales. The procedure involves the development of critical job dimensions and specific behavioral incidents related to these defined dimensions. The behaviors are then scaled with respect to their degree of effectiveness. Campbell et al. (1973) contend that a valuable learning experience for the participating managers is an additional outcome of this procedure, as it forces the managers to confront the question of what they really mean by effective performance.

CONCLUSIONS AND FUTURE RESEARCH CONSIDERATION

Research results have been quite impressive in demonstrating both the "external" and "internal" validities of multiple assessment procedures. An equally important finding from this review is that numerous questions regarding the assessment process remain unanswered. Considering the large and increasing numbers of individuals affected by assessment results, a critical need exists for additional research dealing with the assessment center approach. The following conclusions and suggestions for future research can be drawn from this review:

1. Multiple assessment procedures have consistently been related to a number of performance effectiveness measures. Future studies must investigate different aspects of behaviorally relevant multiple criteria to determine which can best be predicted by the assessment process.

2. The overall assessment rating has consistently been shown to be the best single predictor of the various ratings and measures generated from assessment. Trained line managers can integrate diverse sources of behavioral data into a meaningful composite rating. However, the basis for these clinical judgments needs to be explicated so that others might be trained in the techniques of making successful clinical assessments.

3. The available evidence suggests that the assessment center method can be a useful tool to enhance affirmative action, such as the accelerated advancement of minority groups and women. No differential validity was found to exist for these subgroups when assessment results were related to subsequent performance. Additional research must focus on both the assessors and the assessees with regard to sex, race, and job differences.

4. Procedures unique to the assessment center approach, essentially the situational exercises, contribute a substantial element to the prediction of managerial performance, beyond that which is found in paper-and-pencil measures alone. Multiple assessment procedures provide a number of data sources and the contribution of each to the assessment dimensions, the final assessment rating, and multiple criterion measures must be further clarified.

5. The assessment process focuses on the behavioral demands of a manager's job. A wide range of supervisory skills can be observed at an assessment center. Other relevant dimensions of job performance must be identified and defined, and assessment techniques designed to measure them. Likewise, those variables and exercises which can be eliminated from the assessment process without an adverse effect must be identified.

6. The assessment process is not limited by low reliability. This results from the intensive training provided to the assessment staff in evaluating performance and from the standardization incorporated into multiple assessment procedures.

7. Essentially no differences exist between psychologists and *trained* managers in the role of assessor. The psychologists can be most efficiently utilized in the training of assessment staffs and in research associated with the process.

8. Future research must be designed to systematically investigate the effects of the assessment process on:

    a)   the *assessee*—attitude, self-esteem, motivation, career planning

    b)   the *staff observer*—training value of serving on an assessment staff

    c)   the *organization*—identification of training needs, morale, manpower planning, organizational change and development.

REFERENCES

American Telephone and Telegraph, Personnel Research Staff. *Personnel Assessment Program: Follow-up study*. New York: AT&T, 1965.

Bentz, V. J. The Sears' experience in the investigation, description and prediction of executive behavior. In F. R. Wickert & D. E. McFarland (Eds.), *Measuring executive performance*. New York: Appleton-Century-Crofts, 1967. Pp. 147-205.

Bentz, V. J. Validity studies at Sears. Paper presented at the 79th annual meeting of the American Psychological Association, Washington, D.C., 1971.

Bray, D. W. The management progress study. *American Psychologist*, 1964, *19*, 419-420.

Bray, D. W., & Campbell, R. J. Selection of salesmen by means of an assessment center. *Journal of Applied Psychology*, 1968, *52*, 36-41.

Bray, D. W., Campbell, R. J., & Grant, D. L. *Formative years in business: A long-term AT&T study of managerial lives*. New York: Wiley-Interscience, 1974.

Bray, D. W., & Grant, D. L. The assessment center in the measurement of potential for business management. *Psychological Monographs*, 1966, *80* (17, Whole No. 625).

Bray, D. W., & Moses, J. L. Personnel selection. *Annual Review of Psychology*, 1972, *23*, 545-576.

Byham, W. C. Assessment center for spotting future managers. *Harvard Business Review*, 1970, *48*(4), 150-160, plus appendix.

Byham, W. C. The assessment center as an aid in management development. *Training and Development Journal*, 1971, *25*(12), 10-22.

Campbell, J. P., Dunnette, M. D., Arvey, R. D., & Hellervik, L. V. The development and evaluation of behaviorally based rating scales. *Journal of Applied Psychology*, 1974, *57*, 15-22.

Campbell, J. P., Dunnette, M. D., Lawler, E. E., & Weick, K. E. *Managerial behavior, performance, and effectiveness.* New York: McGraw-Hill, 1970.

Campbell, R. J., & Bray, D. W. Assessment center: An aid in management selection. *Personnel Administration*, 1967, *30*(2), 6-13.

Carleton, F. O. Relationships between follow-up evaluations and information developed in a management assessment center. Paper presented at the 78th annual meeting of the American Psychological Association, Miami Beach, Florida, 1970.

Cohen, B. M., Moses, J. L., & Byham, W. C. *The validity of assessment centers: A literature review.* Monograph II. Pittsburgh: Development Dimensions Press, 1974.

Cronbach, L. J. *Essentials of psychological testing.* New York: Harper & Row, 1970.

Dicken, C. F., & Black, J. D. Predictive validity of psychometric evaluations of supervisors. *Journal of Applied Psychology*, 1965, *49*, 34-37.

Dodd, W. E. Validity studies at IBM. Paper presented at the 79th annual meeting of the American Psychological Association, Washington, D.C., 1971.

Donaldson, R. J. Validation of the internal characteristics of an industrial assessment center program using the multitrait-multimethod matrix approach. Unpublished disseration, Case Western Reserve University, 1969.

Dunnette, M. D. A behavioral approach for describing managerial effectiveness. Paper presented at Bowling Green Symposium, December 1970.

Dunnette, M. D. Multiple assessment procedures in identifying and developing managerial talent. In P. McReynolds (Ed.) *Advances in psychological assessment*, Vol. II. Palo Alto: Science & Behavior Books, 1971.

Eysenck, H. J. Assessment of men. *Uses and abuses of psychology.* Baltimore, Md.: Penguin, 1963, 138-159.

Finkle, R. B., & Jones, W. S. *Assessing corporate talent: A key to managerial manpower planning.* New York: Wiley-Interscience, 1970.

Finley, R. M., Jr. Evaluation of behavior predictions from projective tests given in a management assessment center. Paper presented at the 78th annual meeting of the American Psychological Association, Miami Beach, Florida, 1970.

Folgi, L., Hulin, C. L., & Blood, M. R. Development of first-level behavioral job criteria. *Journal of Applied Psychology*, 1971, *55*, 3-8.

Glaser, R., Schwarz, P. A., & Flanagan, J. C. The contribution of the interview and situational performance procedures to the selection of supervisory personnel. *Journal of Applied Psychology*, 1958, *42*, 69-73.

Grant, D. L., & Bray, D. W. Contributions of the interview to assessment of management potential. *Journal of Applied Psychology*, 1969, *53*, 24-35.

Grant, D. L., Katkovsky, W., & Bray, D. W. Contributions of projective techniques to assessment of management potential. *Journal of Applied Psychology*, 1967, *51*, 226-232.

Greenwood, J. M., & McNamara, W. J. Interrater reliability in situational tests. *Journal of Applied Psychology*, 1967, *31*, 101-106.

Hardesty, D. L., & Jones, W. S. Characteristics of judged high potential management personnel—The operations of an industrial assessment center. *Personnel Psychology*, 1968, *21*, 85-98.

Hinrichs, J. R. Comparison of "real life" assessments of management potential with situational exercises, paper-and-pencil ability tests and personality inventories. *Journal of Applied Psychology*, 1969, *53*, 425-432.

Hinrichs, J. R. Two approaches to filling the management gap: Management selection vs. management development. *Personnel Journal*, 1970, *49*(12), 1008-1014.

Howard, Ann. An assessment of assessment centers. *Academy of Management Journal*, 1974, *17*(1), 115-134.

Huck, J. R. Assessment centers: A review of the external and internal validities. *Personnel Psychology*, 1973a, *26*(2), 191-212.

Huck, J. R. The assessment process: Yesterday, today and tomorrow. Paper presented at the First Annual Industrial and Organizational Psychology Conference, Ohio State University, September 1973b.

Huck, J. R. Research finds equality for females and blacks in assessment. *Assessment and Development Newsletter*, Vol. 1, No. 1, Development Dimensions Press, 1973c.

Huck, J. R. Determinants of assessment center ratings for white and black females and the relationship of these dimensions to subsequent performance effectiveness. Unpublished doctoral dissertation, Wayne State University, Detroit, Michigan, 1974.

Huck, J. R., & Bray, D. W. Management assessment center evaluations and subsequent job performance of white and black females. *Personnel Psychology*, 1976, *2*, 13-30.

Jaffee, C. L. Assessment centers help find management potential. *Bell Telephone Magazine*, 1965, *44*(3), 18-25.

Jaffee, C. L., Bender, J., & Calvert, D. The assessment center technique: A validation study. *Management of Personnel Quarterly*, Fall 1970, 9-14.

Kohls, J. W. Evaluation of assessment center approach to the selection of college recruits in the eastern territory. Sears Roebuck, Chicago, 1970.

Kraut, A. I. A hard look at management assessment centers and their future. *Personnel Journal*, 1972, *51*, 317-326.

Kraut, A. I. Management assessment and international organizations. *Industrial Relations*, 1973, *12*, 172-182.

Kraut, A. I. The use of assessment centers. Paper presented at the Midwest Academy of Management, Ann Arbor, Michigan, April 1975.

Kraut, A. I., & Scott, G. J. Validity of an operational management assessment program. *Journal of Applied Psychology*, 1972, *56*, 124-129.

Landy, F. L., & Guion, R. M. Development of scales for the measurement of work motivation. *Organizational Behavior and Human Performance*, 1970, *5*, 93-103.

Maas, J. B. Patterned scale expectation interview: Reliability on a new technique. *Journal of Applied Psychology*, 1965, *49*, 431-433.

MacKinnon, D. W. OSS applications and research. Paper presented at the Second International Congress on the Assessment Center Method, West Point, New York, 1974.

Meyer, H. H. The validity of the in-basket as a measure of managerial performance. *Personnel Psychology*, 1970, *23*, 297-301.

Meyer, H. H. Assessment centers at General Electric. Paper presented at the meeting of Development Dimensions, San Francisco, California, 1972.

Michigan Bell Telephone. *Personnel Assessment Program: A pilot study.* Personnel Relations Department, 1960.

Michigan Bell Telephone. *Personnel Assessment Program: Evaluation study.* Plant Department, 1962.

Moses, J. L. Assessment center performance and management progress. Paper presented at the 79th annual meeting of the American Psychological Association, Washington, D.C., 1971.

Moses, J. L. The engineering selection program. Management Selection and Development Research Department, American Telephone and Telegraph Company, New York, 1972.

Moses, J. L. The development of an assessment center for the early identification of supervisory potential. *Personnel Psychology*, 1974, *26*(4), 569-580.

Moses, J. L., & Bohem, V. R. Relationship of assessment center performance to management progress of women. *Journal of Applied Psychology*, 1975, *60*, 527-529.

Moses, J. L., & Wall, S. J. Pre-hire assessment: A validity study of a new approach for hiring college graduates. *Assessment and Development Newsletter*, Vol. II, No. 2, Development Dimensions Press, 1975.

Office of Strategic Services (OSS) Assessment Staff. *Assessment of men.* New York: Rinehart, 1948.

Prather, R. Training: Key to realistic performance appraisals. *Training and Development Journal*, 1970, *24*, 4-7.

Richards, S. A., & Jaffee, C. L. Blacks supervising whites: A study of interracial difficulties in working together in a simulated organization. *Journal of Applied Psychology*, 1972, *56*, 234-240.

Slivinski, L. W., & Ethier, L. Development of the assessment center for the career assignment program: Descriptive analysis of the senior executive population. Public Service Commission of Canada, Managerial Assessment and Research Division, November 1973.

Smith, P. C., & Kendall, L. M. Retranslation of expectations: An approach to the construction of unambiguous anchors for rating scales. *Journal of Applied Psychology*, 1963, *47*, 149-155.

Stern, G. G., Stein, M. I., & Bloom, B. S. *Methods of personality assessment*. Glencoe, Ill.: Free Press, 1956.

Taft, R. Multiple methods of personality assessment. *Psychological Bulletin*, 1959, *56*, 333-352.

Thomson, H. A. Internal and external validation of an industrial assessment program. Unpublished doctoral dissertation, Case Western Reserve University, 1969.

Thomson, H. A. Comparison of predictor and criterion judgments of managerial performance using the multitrait-multimethod approach. *Journal of Applied Psychology*, 1970, *54*, 496-502.

Thoresen, J. D. Blue collar assessment at Rohm & Haas Company. *Assessment and Development Newsletter*, Vol. II, No. 1, Development Dimensions Press, 1974.

Thoresen, J. D., & Jaffee, C. L. A unique assessment center application with some unexpected by-products. *Human Resources Management*, 1973, *12*(1), 3-7.

Thorndike, R. L. *Personnel selection*. New York: Wiley, 1949.

Thornton, G. C. Varieties of validity of assessment centers in other companies Paper presented at the 79th annual meeting of the American Psychological Association, Washington, D.C., 1971.

Warbois, G. M. Validation of externally developed assessment procedures for identification of supervisory potential. *Personnel Psychology*, 1975, *28*(1), 77-91.

Wernimont, P. F., & Campbell, J. P. Signs, samples, and criteria. *Journal of Applied Psychology*, 1968, *52*, 372-376.

Wickes Corporation. An evaluation of the management indoctrination program. Management Evaluation Department, Saginaw, Michigan, 1974.

Wiggins, J. S. *Personality and prediction: Principles of personality assessment*. Reading, Mass.: Addison-Wesley, 1973.

Wollowick, H. B., & McNamara, W. J. Relationship of the components of an assessment center to management success. *Journal of Applied Psychology*, 1969, *53*, 348-352.

Zedeck, S., & Baker, H. T. Evaluation of behavioral expectation scales. Paper presented at the Midwestern Psychological Association Convention, Detroit, May 1971.

CHAPTER 15

CURRENT TRENDS AND FUTURE POSSIBILITIES

Douglas W. Bray

INTRODUCTION

It is most fitting that the closing chapter in this book was written by Doug Bray. He, more than any other single individual, is responsible for the widespread application of this method here and abroad. As the principal investigator in the Management Progress Study, Dr. Bray set standards for assessment center research that greatly aided the acceptance of this process by management.

In this chapter, Dr. Bray examines the current trends in assessment—at both the predictor and criterion end of the selection equation, as well as its application to many unique settings in the professional realm. As importantly, he raises a number of research issues still unresolved. Finally, he helps us examine some possible futuristic applications as assessment applications continue to emerge.

* * *

In the mid-1930s Henry A. Murray and his associates at the Harvard Psychological Clinic conducted an historic research study of 51 young men (Murray, 1938). The research, which extended over a two-and-one-half year period, was unique in that many investigators using a variety of techniques not only studied the same subjects but adopted a common set of concepts and pooled their observations to arrive at an overall view of each person studied. Murray, in his preface to *Explorations in Personality*, the volume in which the research is reported, states:

The planned procedure for achieving unity was this: to have all experimenters study the same series of individuals with the same concepts actively in mind, and then in assembly—a meeting being devoted to each case—to report their findings and collaborate in accomplishing a common purpose: the formulation of the personality of every subject.

It is in this approach and in this study that the roots of the assessment center method lie.

Assessment center methods did not come generally to the attention of psychologists, however, until 10 years later with the publication of *Assessment of Men*, a report of the use of the method in the Office of Strategic Services during World War II (OSS, 1948). Murray was once again a key figure along with his associates, particularly Donald W. MacKinnon, who had participated in the Harvard studies and who was later to direct the Institute for Personality Assessment Research at the University of California at Berkeley.

Even the wider publicity given to assessment centers as a result of the OSS application of the method did not produce a lasting trend toward wide usage of the approach. Some noteworthy studies made prominent use of the methodology, such as those dealing with the selection of clinical psychologists for the Veterans Administration and of psychiatric interns at the Menninger Clinic, but by the early 1950s interest in assessment centers was essentially moribund.

The Bell System's adoption in 1956 of the assessment center as a tool in an ambitious longitudinal study (Bray, 1964) led to a reawakened interest in the method. Although individual assessment results in this Management Progress Study (Bray, Campbell, & Grant, 1974) were not used operationally, the research quickly led to the trial of an assessment center as an aid in selecting first-level managers. The pilot program, conducted in the Michigan Bell Telephone Company, was highly successful and the assessment center movement was underway.

A novel feature of the Michigan Bell center was its staff, which was made up entirely of laymen. Previous assessment center applications had relied exclusively, or at least heavily, on psychologists and related professionals. Had that remained the case, no great expansion of the use of assessment would have been possible. The demonstration that trained nonprofessionals could use the method effectively opened the way for organizations to adopt assessment procedures on a scale that would otherwise have been out of the question.

Until recently, most Bell System assessment centers were devoted to evaluating the promotability of candidates selected by management as likely candidates for advancement. The great majority of centers processed non-management employees who were candidates for first-level management positions; the remainder assessed those already in management at lower and middle levels. Assessment findings were reported back to local management for use in making final promotion decisions as well as to the candidate. Assessment centers thus functioned as a kind of final hurdle to be cleared before advancement in supervisory management.

RECENT BELL SYSTEM DEVELOPMENTS

Although such assessment centers are still flourishing and continuing to show great organizational usefulness, new Bell System directions for assessment are emerging which appear to presage a shift in emphasis. One development is the use of assessment to evaluate the potential of recent nonmanagement employees for first-level management jobs in an assessment application known as the Early Identification Program. This approach contrasts with the original use of management assessment centers. That, as noted earlier, was a final check just prior to promotion. The fact that some candidates lacked sufficient ability to warrant advancement was not discovered until almost the last moment. Early identification seeks to locate those with high potential well before promotion is imminent. Access to appropriate career paths and other developmental opportunities can then be provided. Although promotion to some jobs takes place soon, in other cases several years may be required. Not all who are promising at assessment will eventually reach the target job. Good job performance in the post-assessment period is obviously a requisite.

The Early Identification Program encompasses an assessment center for identifying those with potential for first-level management work and a career development phase to facilitate their acquiring the experience and training needed to bring them to first-level jobs. The first early identification application was concerned with potential for supervisory positions and thus the procedures parallel those in the original Bell System assessment centers. They include, for example, an in-basket and a leaderless group discussion. The number and length of the techniques have been reduced, however, so that assessment can be completed in a single day. Post-assessment career development has been described in Chapter 11.

Another AT&T trend is the growing application of assessment center methodology to nonsupervisory positions. A second early identification program has been developed for three entry-level management positions in engineering. These jobs, which include about 60% of starting engineering assignments, are those concerned with central office equipment, private branch exchanges, and outside plant. The assessment segment of the program is unique in that it includes no group exercises. Instead, due to the nature of the jobs for which the candidates are being considered, emphasis is on logical reasoning and decision making from data and other written material. A trained assessment staff, dimensions to be rated, and an overall assessment judgment are still, however, essentials of the process. As in early identification assessment for supervisory positions, assessment is accomplished in one day.

Although supervision and the engineering positions just discussed account for the majority of first-level management jobs in Bell System telephone companies, there are many others. The Early Identification Program is expected to be broadened, therefore, to include other types of work. Examples are data processing, secretarial assignments, various staff assistant positions, and sales. (Sales assessment centers have been used in the Bell System for some time but have not yet been formally tied into the Early Identification Program.) Such a far-reaching management entry program is needed not only to provide employees an opportunity to show their potential and advance to a management position suited to their abilities, but there is, in addition, a very important placement function to be performed. Movement from one department to another or even from one job family to another is difficult once a career in management is begun. It is crucial, therefore, that people be assigned to the management job most suited to them at the outset.

A management entry system has an important use in addition to that of finding promising nonmanagement employees for accelerated advancement. Not all jobs which fall technically within the first-level of management are equal in pay. For this and other reasons (such as type of work), some current incumbents in first-level positions would welcome an opportunity for lateral transfer. Candidates for such transfer could readily be considered through the same assessment process used in early identification.

The Early Identification Program has an analogue in the Bell System's Management Assessment Program. Although this program had been operative in one telephone company (New York) for a number of years, it was given much greater and wider impetus by its inclusion as part of the consent agreement between the EEOC and other governmental agencies and AT&T. As part of that agreement, three regional assessment centers were set up which evaluated approximately 1,700 college graduate women, most of whom were at the first level of management. The purpose was to determine which of these women had potential for at least the third level of management. One of these regional centers was continued for other management employees not covered by the consent agreement. This program is concerned with "early identification" since most of the candidates are at first level and the third level of management is often several years away. The post-assessment program for recommended candidates has been described in Chapter 11.

DEVELOPMENTS ELSEWHERE

New applications of assessment outside of the Bell System include several important innovations in various educational contexts. One of these, developed jointly by the Educational Research Corporation and Development Dimensions, Inc., is the Educational Leadership Appraisal Program. Its purpose is to evaluate and diagnose the management abilities of school administrators. The uniqueness of the program lies in its attack on the problem of assessing candidates who are widely dispersed geographically precluding the usual requirement of a full assessment staff to observe the performance of each assessee directly. (This problem is often solved by transporting candidates to the assessment center. In other instances such as this one, however, travel costs would have made the program unfeasible.) In the new program a trained assessor goes to each assessment location and administers and videotapes the assessment exercises (which include group techniques). These, along with the written material collected during assessment, are later presented to a trained staff, which uses them to rate dimensions and judge overall ability and potential in the usual way.

A more radical application of assessment, also in an educational setting, has emerged at Milwaukee's Alverno College. Here assessment methods are being used in a new program called Competence Based Learning, which has abolished the usual academic grades. Assessment techniques serve to evaluate achievement in each competence learning unit. With respect to contemporary affairs, for example, students (in a group of five) discuss what they have read in newspapers or magazines or seen on TV. Local, national, and international events are included. The discussion is evaluated by a four-member assessment team made up of a professional or business representative, a faculty member, an Alverno alumna, and an upper classman. Among the dimensions rated in this and other exercises are some which have not appeared in managerial assessment. They include the making of distinctions and drawing of relationships, value clarification, the assessment of the impact of people and events, and emotional responsiveness to ideas, people, and art.

The developments at Alverno are exciting and significant. For generations, the complaint has been raised that colleges impart vast amounts of intellectual information but do not go beyond that in the direction of helping their students to use that information effectively in later life. Nor, it is said, do colleges provide training in the less intellectual aspects of effective functioning. Assessment methods can not only determine the degree to which students have such competence but will eventually improve the learning experience itself. The imposition of better measurement of educational outcomes has often resulted in constructive changes in the educational process.

A pilot program being developed under the auspices of the American Board of Professional Psychology has perhaps even more far-reaching implications. The Board has as its primary function the examination and diplomating of professional psychologists as possessing a high degree of professional competence. In pursuit of this objective the Board has used various examining techniques, including on-the-job observation of performance, work samples, written tests, and group interviews. It has been felt by many, including Board members themselves, however, that there is room for improvement in the examining procedures. This need was manifest also, and far beyond just the area of professional diplomating, at the recent Vail Conference on professional psychology. One of the resolutions called for a vigorous effort to develop a direct measure of professional competence which could be applied during and at the conclusion of professional training as well as at various times throughout the career, as appropriate.

Since there are many specialties within professional psychology, the Board has selected the area in which the diplomate exam is most often requested, that of individual psychotherapy, as the first area for experimentation. The determination and definition of dimensions, the necessary first step in developing an assessment process, has been completed. These dimensions depart widely from those in any assessment procedure to date. They include such variables as genuineness, conceptualization, circumspection, interpretation or clinical inference, intervention skill, and dealing with manipulation. Although it is too early to say whether the application of assessment methodology to such a difficult field will be successful, success would have enormous implications. These implications could extend to the licensing of psychologists, resolution of the MA versus PhD controversy, and the certification of professional training programs.

A related development, although not as ambitious as the above, is still highly significant. This is the use of assessment procedures as a criterion for determining the efficacy of training. The field of management development has long been plagued by an absence of convincing evidence that managers do in fact profit by undergoing various training experiences. Assessment has proven to be an effective method of evaluating management abilities which training often attempts to develop, such as planning and organizing, decision making, leadership, and behavior as a team member. Assessment techniques focusing on the dimensions a particular course seeks to improve could easily be developed.

The Bell System has recently made such use of assessment methodology to test the effects of a new course for lower level managers called Supervisory Relationships Training. This program, based on behavior modeling principles, is intended to train supervisors to handle problem interactions with subordinates more effectively. Assessment designed to evaluate changes resulting from training consisted of three role-play situations designed to elicit behavior supposedly learned in the course. Managers who had completed the training were assessed several weeks later, as was a control group. Behavior in the role plays was observed and rated by experienced assessors. The results demonstrated that the training was highly effective. Assessment methods offer the promise of breaking the long impasse in the evaluation of management training efforts.

APPEAL OF THE ASSESSMENT CENTER METHOD

The well-publicized uses of assessment centers in the 1940s produced no immediate rush to use the method, but its widespread adoption in the last few years has been little short of phenomenal. The method is attractive for several reasons. It accomplishes its basic purpose—the prediction of job performance— very satisfactorily and is even more highly related to potential for further advancement. The method, furthermore, is highly credible. Assessment exercises impress observers as convincing analogs to the jobs themselves and assessment staffs are usually managers drawn from the organization using the center. Their judgments are expected to be not only responsible but attuned to the needs of the organization.

A more subtle appeal of the method is that the assessment center may be viewed as an extended achievement test. Assessors judge the extent to which candidates exhibit behavior required in certain levels and types of jobs. This emphasis on behavior is a far cry from other selection methods which rely on biographical facts, self-reports of motivation, or cognitive aptitude items. Even though such devices, particularly aptitude tests, may show significant correlations with performance or advancement, they do so on an indirect basis and they allow the "failing" candidate little recourse; you can hardly escape from your biodata. Educational credentials and job experience are forms of such data. Rejection for employment or advancement is often based on deficiences in one or both of these kinds of credentials. Yet the applicant may reasonably object that although on the average such background experiences are needed, in his or her particular case this does not happen to be true. Since an actual trial on the job is often expensive and impractical, the possibility that the person can do the job is never tested. The assessment center offers a way to test probable performance more directly and provides an escape from the tyranny of credentialism.

FUTURE POSSIBILITIES

Since the accelerating interest in assessment centers shows no signs of abating, it is reasonable to expect that the method will be applied to an increasing number of occupations. Occupations which may be candidates for assessment applications can be expected to be those which have many incumbents. Development of unique assessment programs might not otherwise be economically feasible. Another characteristic of attractive targets for new assessment approaches will usually be the importance in the job of interpersonal skills. Although assessment methods are now being used for other than such jobs, the fact remains that the evaluation of interpersonal skills is the area in which assessment has such a striking advantage over other methods.

One type of job which certainly meets the above criteria is that which includes the trainer, the instructor, and the teacher. When all the individuals involved in training in business and the government are added to the nation's school teachers, the occupation is certainly populous. The task of instruction also appears to be highly susceptible to simulation. Oral presentation, questioning, rapport building, and preparation of written tests are, for example, aspects of the task which would be easily assessable. In addition, it is important that the skill of teachers be accurately evaluated. Complaints about the quality of classroom teaching are heard continually, but attempts to measure teaching proficiency have not been very successful. The assessment approach would appear to have a valuable contribution to make.

Another family of occupations that involves a large number of persons and in which interpersonal skills are critical are those in the broad area of social work, including public welfare workers, probation officers, family counselors, etc. Assessment dimensions which come quickly to mind are oral fact finding, persuasiveness, and resistance to manipulation. Nor need assessment be limited to public contact jobs requiring a college or professional degree. The army of airline reservation personnel, bank employees, service representatives for public utilities, insurance adjustors, and clerks at motor vehicle bureaus—to name only a few possibilities—offers wide opportunity for assessment applications and a reduction in the level of public irritation.

Although more appropriate selection for such jobs is in order, that need not be, of course, the only purpose of assessment. Using assessment to review the proficiency of present incumbents can identify training needs and lead to improved performance even for many of those who are not ideally suited to their work.

Assessment center applications have to date focused more on the needs of organizations than on those of individuals. Yet assessment does have the potential to help people make better decisions about their educational and career options. Those who have been assessed commonly report that the assessment process and the frank feedback of assessment results to them have been very meaningful in their own process of self-evaluation. It is often the only time in their lives that they have heard an objective and unbiased statement of their assets and liabilities. Paper-and-pencil tests have been eagerly taken for years by those seeking to learn more about themselves. Such tests are, however, not particularly useful in evaluating behavioral characteristics of importance in day-to-day and occupational life. Assessment may have a future as a tool in self-development. Might the weekend assessment session come to replace or supplement the weekend encounter group?

NEEDED RESEARCH

Although the predictive power of the assessment center method has been well researched, there are other areas in which considerable work remains to be done. These include the nature of and definition of the dimensions to be rated, the assessment techniques themselves, methods of observation used by the assessors, the characteristics and training of the assessors, methods of combining judgments from the multiple techniques, and methods and effects of feedback of assessment center findings. The following are examples of some of the research possibilities.

Do assessment dimensions defined in terms of expected future behavior differ in their reliability of validity from those defined simply in terms of behavior observed at the assessment center?

Do assessment dimensions concerned with motivational characteristics differ in reliability or validity from ability and skill dimensions?

What is the optimal amount of redundancy among techniques at a particular assessment center in terms of the dimensions to be rated?

To what extent does pre-knowledge by the assessees of the dimensions to be rated in a technique influence assessee behavior?

Should assessors share observations before rating and reporting on an assessment center technique?

What effect on assessee understanding, acceptance, and retention of assessment center findings do different methods of feedback have? Examples are written versus oral, private or with a supervisor present, quantitative or descriptive, with or without an overall rating, etc.

What are the effects of the feedback of assessment center results to the assessee on job motivation, self-esteem, and self-development efforts?

Since the whole focus of the assessment center method is the behavior of the assessee, the most important research questions have to do with the potency of assessment techniques in eliciting behavior relevant to the dimensions to be rated. If relevant behavior is not observed, there is always the possibility that the behavior was in the individual's repertoire but that the particular assessment exercise did not bring it forth. Comparability between apparently similar exercises is a related question. There are, for example, a variety of short business games played at assessment centers. Some of these use tinker toys, others digits, some geometrical shapes, and others miniature stock exchanges. Do such differences in the type of material used make significant differences in the amount of leadership manifested by different individuals within the assessment group? Similar questions could, of course, be raised about the subject matter of leaderless group discussions and in-baskets. Although assessment research leaves little doubt that assessment techniques currently in use do often elicit behavior relevant to the dimensions, we still do not know enough about the conditions for evoking the particular behavior in which we are interested. A whole new area for scientific research may be presenting itself.

As one looks back over the 35 or so years since the assessment center method first came to the attention of psychologists generally, the method has come a long way. It has moved from the status of a special technique applied to special problems to the status of a general methodology—a methodology ideally suited to a wide variety of selection, placement, development, and self-evaluation applications. The time has passed when we can be content with attempting to predict complex future behavior only from responses to paper-and-pencil test items or verbalizations during an interview. Although such methods may be part of a complete appraisal of the individual, they are no longer enough. Credentials, too, have become an insufficient standard. When we need to know whether people can and will perform effectively, what could be a more obvious solution than observing whether they can and do perform?

REFERENCES

Bray, D. W. The management progress study. *American Psychologist*, 1964, *19*, 419-420.

Bray, D. W., Campbell, R. J., & Grant, D. L. *Formative years in business: A long-term AT&T study of managerial lives.* New York: Wiley-Interscience, 1974.

Murray, H. A. *Explorations in personality.* New York: Oxford University Press, 1938.

Office of Strategic Services (OSS) Assessment Staff. *Assessment of men.* New York: Rinehart, 1948.

APPENDIX

STANDARDS FOR ETHICAL CONSIDERATIONS FOR ASSESSMENT CENTER OPERATIONS

Task Force on Development of Assessment Center Standards
Joseph L. Moses, PhD, Chairman

Albert Alon
Douglas W. Bray, PhD
William C. Byham, PhD
Lois A. Crooks
Donald L. Grant, PhD
Lowell W. Hellervik, PhD
James R. Huck, PhD

Cabot L. Jaffee, PhD
Alan I. Kraut, PhD
John H. McConnell
Leonard W. Slivinski
Thomas E. Standing, PhD
Edwin Yager

Endorsed by Third International Congress
on the Assessment Center Method
Quebec, Canada
May 1975

1. *Rationale for Assessment Center Standards*

   The rapid growth in the use of the assessment center method in recent years has resulted in a proliferation of applications in a variety of organizational, educational, and governmental settings. Serious concerns have been raised by many interested parties which reflect a need for a set of minimal professional standards for users of this technique. These standards should:

   - define what is meant by an assessment center
   - describe minimal acceptable practices concerning:
     - organizational support for assessment operations
     - assessor training
     - informed consent on the part of participants
     - use of assessment center data
     - validation issues

   These standards are not designed to prescribe specific practices. Neither do these standards in any way endorse a specific assessment center format or specific assessment techniques. Rather we have attempted to provide general principles which can be adapted to meet existing and future applications. The reader should keep in mind the spirit by which these standards were written: as an aid to the assessment center user, rather than as a set of restrictive prohibitions.

2. *Assessment Center Defined*

   To be considered as an assessment center, the following minimal requirements must be met:

   - Multiple assessment techniques must be used. At least one of these techniques must be a simulation.

     A simulation is an exercise or technique designed to elicit behaviors related to dimensions of performance on the job by requiring the participant to respond behaviorally to situational stimuli. The stimuli present in a simulation parallel or resemble stimuli in the work situation. Examples of simulations include group exercises, in-basket exercises, and fact-finding exercises.

   - Multiple assessors must be used. These assessors must receive training prior to participating in a center.

   - Judgments resulting in an outcome (i.e., recommendation for promotion, specific training or development) must be based on pooling information from assessors and techniques.

   - An overall evaluation of behavior must be made by the assessors at a separate time from observation of behavior.

   - Simulation exercises are used. These exercises are developed to tap a variety of predetermined behaviors and have been pre-tested prior to use to insure that the techniques provide reliable, objective, and relevant behavioral information for the organization in question.

—The dimensions, attributes, characteristics, or qualities evaluated by the assessment center are determined by an analysis of relevant job behaviors.

—The techniques used in the assessment center are designed to provide information which is used in evaluating the dimensions, attributes, or qualities previously determined.

In summary, an assessment center consists of a standardized evaluation of behavior based on multiple inputs. Multiple trained observers and techniques are used. Judgments about behavior are made, in part, from specially developed assessment simulations.

These judgments are pooled by the assessors at an evaluation meeting during which all relevant assessment data are reported and discussed, and the assessors agree on the evaluation of the dimensions and any overall evaluation that is made.

The following kinds of activities *do not* constitute an assessment center:

—panel interviews or a series of sequential interviews as the sole technique

—reliance on a specific technique (regardless of whether a simulation or not) as the sole basis for evaluation

—using only a test battery composed of a number of pencil-and-paper measures, regardless of whether the judgments are made by a statistical or judgmental pooling of scores

—single assessor assessment (often referred to as individual assessment)—measurement by one individual using a variety of techniques such as pencil-and-paper tests, interviews, personality measures, or simulations

—the use of several simulations with more than one assessor where there is no pooling of data—i.e., each assessor prepares a report on performance in an exercise, and the individual reports (unintegrated) are used as the final product of the center

—a physical location labeled as an "assessment center" which does not conform to the requirements noted above

3. *Organizational Support for Assessment Center Operations*
The assessment center should be administered in a professional manner with concern for the treatment of individuals, accuracy of results, and overall quality of the operation. Assessment centers should be incorporated as part of a total system rather than as a process that operates in a

vacuum. Considerable care and planning should precede the introduction of an assessment center. Policy statements concerning assessment operations should be formally developed and agreed upon by the organization. Minimal considerations in developing this policy should include:

—the population to be assessed

—the purpose of assessment

—the kinds of people who will serve as assessors

—the type of training they receive and who is to provide it

—the responsibility for administration of the center

—specific restrictions concerning who is to see the assessment data, and how they are to be used

—procedures for collection of data for research and program evaluation

—feedback procedure to participants and management

—expected "life" of assessment center data—i.e., the length of time assessment center data will be kept in the files and used for decision-making purposes

—the professional qualifications (including relevant training) of the individual or individuals initially responsible for developing the center

4.   *Assessor Training*

Assessors should receive sufficient training to enable them to evaluate intelligently the behaviors measured in the center. "Sufficient training" will vary from organization to organization and is a function of many factors including:

—the length of time an individual serves as an assessor

—the frequency of individual participation as an assessor

—the amount of time devoted to assessor training

—the qualification and expertise of the assessment center trainer

—the assessment experience of other members of the assessment staff

—the use of professionals (i.e., licensed or certified psychologists) as assessors

The above list is illustrative of the many issues related to assessor training. There is more variability in this area than in any other section of the standards.

While we do not wish to establish minimal standards concerning the number of hours of assessor training needed, it is difficult to imagine assessors functioning effectively with only a one- or two-hour orientation prior to serving as an assessor. However, whatever the approach to assessor training, the essential goal is attaining accurate assessor judgments. A variety of training approaches can be used, as long as it can be demonstrated that accurate assessor judgments are obtained. The following minimum training is required:

- —knowledge of the assessment techniques used. This could include, for example, the kinds of behaviors elicited by each technique, relevant dimensions to be observed, expected or typical behaviors, examples or samples of actual behaviors, etc.
- —knowledge of the assessment dimensions. This could include, for example, definitions of dimensions, relationship to other dimensions, relationship to job performance, examples of effective and ineffective performance, etc.
- —knowledge of behavior observation and recording including the forms used by the center
- —knowledge of evaluation and rating procedures including how data are integrated by the assessment center staff
- —knowledge of assessment policies and practices of the organization, including restrictions on how assessment data are to be used
- —knowledge of feedback procedures where appropriate

In addition, some measurement is needed indicating that the individual being trained has the capability of functioning as an assessor. The actual measurement of assessor performance may vary and could, for example, include data in terms of rating performance, critiques of assessor reports, observation as an evaluator, etc. What is important is that assessor performance is evaluated to insure that individuals are sufficiently trained to function as assessors, prior to their actual duties, and that such performance is periodically monitored to insure that skills learned in training are applied.

5. *Informed Consent on the Part of Participants*

Informed consent is a fundamental concern in conducting an assessment center program. This means that the participant is given sufficient information *prior* to assessment to evaluate intelligently the nature of the program and the consequences of attending or not attending a center. While organizations have the right to require participation in an assessment program as a condition of employment or advancement, individuals should not simply be "sent" to a center with little awareness of why they are going. Rather, they should be provided with sufficient information to decide whether or not they should attend.

While the actual information provided will vary from organization to organization, the following basic information should be given to all prospective participants:

- —the purpose of the center and the objectives of the program

—how individuals are selected to participate in the center

—general information about the assessors—the composition of the staff and their training

—general information concerning the assessment process itself. This should include a description of the techniques and how the results will be used, the kind of feedback given

—reassessment policy

It is recognized that many assessment center programs have descriptive names or titles which are often neutral or purposefully general. This is an acceptable practice. However, it would be inappropriate to suggest to participants that the assessment center is for personal development or training when the clear intent is for selection or management staffing.

6. *Use of Assessment Center Data*

One characteristic of an assessment center is the volume of data produced. There are many different forms of assessment data, ranging, for example, from observer notes, to reports on performance in the assessment techniques, to assessor ratings, and reports prepared for management. The preceding is not exhaustive and could also include participant and peer reports and observations, biographical and test data, etc.

The specific purpose of the reports and data obtained by the assessment center should be clearly established. This will include a statement concerning individuals who will have access to assessment data, the kind of information they will receive, and the format that will be provided.

The recipient of assessment data will be given sufficient information or training so that the data provided can be clearly interpreted. This will include an estimate of the relevance of current assessment data for the use in the future.

The individual assessed should be informed of how the assessment data are to be used. This will include:

—who has access to assessment reports

—whether participants will normally receive feedback concerning assessment performance. If not, provisions must be made to provide such information upon specific request

—how long assessment information will be retained for operational use (as opposed to research use)

7. *Validation Issues*

A major factor in the widespread acceptance and use of assessment centers is directly related to an emphasis on sound validation research. Numerous studies have been conducted and reported in the professional literature demonstrating the validity of the assessment center process in a variety of organizational settings.

The historical record of the validity of this process, however, cannot be taken as a guarantee that a given assessment program will or will not be valid in a given setting. Because of this, each user must ascertain the validity of the program as applied in one's organization. The technical standards and principles for validation are well documented and appear in "Principles for the Validation and Use of Personnel Selection Procedures" prepared by the Division of Industrial and Organizational Psychology," American Psychological Association, 1975, and "Standards for Educational and Psychological Tests and Manuals" prepared by the American Psychological Association, 1974.

In addition to the above standards, which include provisions related to demonstrating fairness and validity, some specific guidelines are provided for assessment center programs. These include:

—the ability to document the selection of dimensions, attributes, or qualities evaluated in the center

—the ability to document the relationship of assessment center techniques to specific dimensions, attributes, or qualities evaluated

—the ability to document the demographic composition of the assessment staff as representative of the group of individuals assessed

8. *Concluding Statement*

It became obvious in developing these standards that the standards should serve as guidelines rather than doctrine. Rather than create a set of standards that become ends in themselves, the authors attempted to provide a series of general principles which can apply to both managers and professionals using this technique. These standards should enable the assessment center professional to create, implement, and maintain assessment center programs that protect the rights of individuals while meeting organizational needs at the same time.

Current Membership—Assessment Center
Research Group

Alverno College
American Telephone & Telegraph Company
Atlantic Richfield Company
Caterpillar Tractor Company
Consulting Psychologists, Inc.
Development Dimensions, Inc.
Educational Testing Service
Ford Motor Company
General Electric Company
General Motors Company (Chevrolet)
International Business Machines
Minnesota Mining and Manufacturing Company
Ontario Hydro
Public Service Commission of Canada
Sears, Roebuck and Company
Standard Oil Company (Ohio)
Steinberg's Limited
The Wickes Corporation